Praise for *Brilliant Graduate Career Handbook*

'Cracked it! This is the must-have companion for every graduate worrying about how to get that all important first job.'

Nick Newman, Founder of National Careers Week

'This is a well-researched, reader-friendly, practical and positive guide to the challenges and opportunities presented by the twenty-first century graduate job market. It is full of useful nuggets of information, and wise tips for success.'

Paul Gaunt, Head of Careers and Employability, University of Liverpool

'If you recommend just one book to your graduating students, let it be this one. Simply brilliant.'

Jane Artess, Principal Research Fellow, International Centre for Guidance Studies, University of Derby

brilliant

Graduate Career Handbook

third edition

Judith Done and Rachel Mulvey

PEARSON

Harlow, England • London • New York • Boston • San Francisco • Toronto • Sydney • Auckland • Singapore • Hong Kong
Tokyo • Seoul • Taipei • New Delhi • Cape Town • São Paulo • Mexico City • Madrid • Amsterdam • Munich • Paris • Milan

PEARSON EDUCATION LIMITED
Edinburgh Gate
Harlow CM20 2JE
United Kingdom
Tel: +44 (0)1279 623623
Web: www.pearson.com/uk

First published 2011 (print and electronic)
Second edition published 2014 (print and electronic)
Third edition published 2016 (print and electronic)

ISBN: 978-1-292-15887-7 (print)
        978-1-292-15888-4 (PDF)
        978-1-292-15889-1 (ePub)

British Library Cataloguing-in-Publication Data
A catalogue record for the print edition is available from the British Library

Library of Congress Cataloging-in-Publication Data
A catalog record for the print edition is available from the Library of Congress

10 9 8 7 6 5 4 3 2 1
20 19 18 17 16

Print edition typeset in Plantin MT Pro 10.5/14.5 pts by SPi Global
Print edition printed and bound by Ashford Colour Press Ltd, Gosport

NOTE THAT ANY PAGE CROSS REFERENCES REFER TO THE PRINT EDITION

To WD and PG

Contents

About the authors

Dr Judith Done is a visiting research fellow at the University of Chester, where she was formerly Director of Careers and Employability. She is a fellow of the Institute of Career Guidance (ICG) and an associate fellow of the British Psychological Society.

Her working life has been spent in career guidance as a practitioner, trainer and manager. Her research interests are in career guidance, personal development and interpersonal communication.

Judith is a volunteer advice worker, school governor and occasional freelance trainer.

Professor Rachel Mulvey holds a chair in career guidance at the University of East London (UEL), where she is Dean of Psychology. At the University of Warwick, she is an associate fellow of the Institute for Employment Research. She is a fellow and past president of the Institute of Career Guidance, associate fellow of the British Psychological Society and principal fellow of the Higher Education Academy. She is a national teaching fellow.

For many years, Rachel worked as a careers adviser in schools and colleges, before moving into the management and training of career professionals. Her recent research seeks to enhance teaching employability and enterprise, and explores how people take learning and skills from one context to another. She is the author of *Brilliant Passing Psychometric Tests* (Pearson, 2015).

Acknowledgements

We are very grateful to colleagues and friends in career guidance and higher education for the many and varied contributions they have made to the development of this handbook, and to our families for their unwavering encouragement and support. We would like to acknowledge the generosity of all the people we refer to in our brilliant examples, and quote in our brilliant quotes. Our thanks also to the warden and staff of Gladstone's Library, who have no idea how helpful they were in providing the perfect writers' retreat. Also to emeritus professor Philip Gammage who continues to inspire.

Particular thanks are due to Charlie Ball for permission for us to draw freely on the Higher Education Careers Services Unit (HECSU) publication *What do graduates do?*, to Helen Webster of the University of Chester and Vanessa Contreras Negretti at UEL. Finally, our heartfelt thanks to Steve Temblett and his colleagues at Pearson for their expertise and enthusiasm.

How to use this handbook

If you are a student or recent graduate

If you are an undergraduate or recent graduate, this handbook is primarily for you. (If you are an academic tutor, careers advisor or parent, please skip down to your heading below.) We hope that you will use it frequently, dipping in to whichever topics are relevant to you at the time. Like other careers handbooks we will give you pointers for applying for jobs. However, unlike other careers handbooks, we will help you to understand the graduate labour market, as we believe that this is fundamental to planning for and achieving your brilliant graduate career. Since writing the first edition of this handbook, the graduate labour market has recovered well and there are more jobs than ever on offer for graduates. That said, competition remains tough and with entry standards high you will have to work at securing a job of your choice. We would advise you to start on developing yourself from day one of your degree. Throughout the book we illustrate and reinforce our key messages with brilliant features – tips, dos and don'ts, quotes, case studies and recaps – and we hope you find them useful.

What do you hope to do after university?

The obvious answer to this question is: to get a job that recognises your talents, offers you the chance to shine, allows you to do interesting things and ideally to earn enough money to have a good lifestyle and to repay your student loans. You could call that the *Brilliant Careers* answer.

However, in the real world, the answer could be very different. Your first step might be to get a job, any job, just to pay the bills. This may be a service sector job in a supermarket, bar or fast-food outlet, perhaps a job you did part-time while at university – which might make you wonder why you bothered to go to university in the first place. If that's where you are at the moment, or where you think you might be in the future, read on. We'll help you to see how any job can help you, even in a small way, work towards your brilliant career. The key is to be positive and assume that there will be a good outcome eventually – though perhaps not straight away.

Your options

Your first step after graduation is usually one of the following choices:

- A graduate entry job: by this we mean a job that demands a degree, and we include graduate training schemes.

- A direct entry job: you don't need a degree for the job but having a degree will speed your progression and may help with promotion, e.g. police or retail management. A direct entry job can be a key step in your career plan; it can be your active choice.

- A direct entry job by default: likely to be your fall-back plan, perhaps because of stiff competition in your chosen field. You can definitely use this for extending your professional repertoire to gain leverage in the graduate job market.

- Time out by choice, e.g. for travel, perhaps to work abroad, or just for taking stock.

- Postgraduate study: either to qualify for a particular job or for love of the subject (vocational/professional or academic).

- Self-employment – starting your own business.

More than one option

Of course, you could follow more than one of these options in sequence. For example, you could have a year of working abroad then take up postgraduate study or get a job. Or you might need a year of postgraduate, vocational study before you can enter a graduate-entry job like teaching or law. Taking a longer view, you might decide, some years after leaving university, that you are ready to take on more study, either part-time or full-time.

One handbook, in two halves

What's out there, or part one

Deciding what to do after university is very personal; not just what you decide, but when you decide, is different for everyone. Even if you have come to university with a very clear career choice in mind, you may choose, in the light of experience, to change your career plan, or even to change your university course; and, even if you yourself don't waver from your original career thinking, the graduate labour market may have changed around you. So, in the first part of this book we will help you to get to know and understand the graduate labour market so that you will be well prepared. We will set out the popular options for graduates – travel and how to get the most from it, postgraduate study, and graduate training schemes – and flag up those where forward planning is needed. Finding out more about your options is a good first step – it doesn't commit you but it starts to equip you. We will help you to avoid putting your head in your hands and wailing: 'If only I'd known sooner – why did nobody tell me?'.

How to make the most of what's out there, or part two

In the second part of this handbook we will focus on what you can do to influence your graduate career. Unlimited choice sounds great in theory, but in practice it can be overwhelming. If someone offers you the chance to travel to anywhere in the world, that can be a surprisingly difficult choice, and the prospect of what to do after university might feel a bit like that. A good career plan involves a narrowing down of options under serious consideration as you progress through university – but with some flexibility built in for when setbacks occur. We will help you first with some strategies for making connections between what's out there and you as an individual, with your unique package of strengths, interests and circumstances. Then we will give you some good tips and tactics for getting into the labour market, in particular, how to seek out and make the most of experiences and opportunities. We believe that, regardless of the state of the job market, a positive, proactive approach is vital; and we hope that this book will help you to adopt our view.

Notes for academic or personal tutors

How this book can work for you

We were able to write this book because career guidance is our specialism. Between us we have a span of experience including practice, management, practitioner training, research and broadcasting. We feel confident we know what we're talking about, and we think we can help students to manage their career well. We also believe we can help fellow academics.

Delivering graduate employability is no longer an optional extra

Concerns about graduate employability are expressed very simply: 'Will I get a job at the end of my degree?' and 'Is a degree worth the debt?' are questions frequently asked at open days. If admissions tutors cannot reassure applicants that as undergraduates they will be supported in this aim and that the cost is indeed worth it, applicants will go elsewhere, taking their tuition fees with them. Ensuring that your undergraduate programme tackles career development alongside the subject discipline has never been more important.

Research in the field of employability points very clearly to the importance of integrating career awareness and career development in the curriculum (Knight & Yorke, 2004, Cole & Tibby, 2013). This message has been taken up by the Confederation of British Industry and by the National Union of Students (CBI & NUS, 2011, NUS 2014), who together urge undergraduates to work on their employability from day one of their course, and was most recently endorsed by the Association of Graduate Recruiters (AGR, 2015).

Employability is long established as a key metric in annual university league tables but government policy is now relentless in its emphasis on graduate employability, defined as 'teaching students the transferable work readiness skills that businesses need, including collaborative teamwork and . . . a positive work ethic' (BIS, 2015). Career development and employability preparation, alongside entrepreneurial awareness, will be increasingly expected of a degree course.

Use this book to structure tutorials or for employability teaching

If you are a personal tutor, the employability coordinator in your department, or you feel at a loss when students come to you for help and advice on careers, this book is for you.

It can help you personally because it has everything you need in one place. You can also use it to structure input to scheduled tutorials or the employability element of the curriculum.

Unlike other careers handbooks, we explain how the graduate labour market operates, and have included a lot of labour market information. This is in addition to the practical know-how about career planning and job applications that all students need at some stage, and many students told us they wanted. Although written for students and graduates, there are exercises and tasks that you could build into taught sessions and workshops. For example, Chapter 2 'The graduate labour market' and Chapter 3 'Labour market information: analysis of what graduates do' both offer a theoretical and knowledge base for your teaching on skills and employability modules. You could also use Chapter 10 'Dates and deadlines: your timeline for action' and Chapter 11 'Making applications: getting past the first post' to structure your tutorial input. Most chapters end with a call for action, inviting the student reader to take a practical step in developing their career thinking. You could use these as formative assessments. We hope you find this book works alongside your input, and enhances both the teaching and learning experience.

Notes for Parents Plus

We know that behind every successful graduate, there are people rooting for them, willing them on, wanting them to achieve their potential. We use the term parents plus to include anyone who is 'behind' a graduate. If you are one of those people (you may be a grandparent, friend, or partner) whatever your relationship, this is a good book for you – and for your graduate. (Of course, we think it would make a brilliant present!)

Look beyond the headlines on graduate employment

You might be concerned about your graduate: you might think they should be doing something about getting a job, even though all their time is taken up with the course and perhaps some paid work. You might even be wondering what was the point of them working so hard for their degree, given the uncertainty about graduate employment. However, if you look beyond the headlines, you will find that there are jobs, although securing a brilliant job might take time and effort. This book shows your graduate how to navigate the graduate labour market, and how to keep going when it gets tough.

The 21st-century graduate faces a different job market

We also have a message for you, which is this. If you are basing your advice on your own experience of getting your first job, *particularly* if you are a graduate, your advice is out of date. The graduate labour market has changed: although jobs are readily available, entry standards are high and competition can be tough. Employers now expect graduates to have developed a good set of transferable skills and understanding *before* they start graduate-level work. To do this, your graduate might have to take on unpaid work, take up an internship, take a fixed-term contract or start with a non-graduate job. None of these reflects badly on your graduate: this is simply how the graduate labour market works in the 21st century.

Keep an open mind and challenge your graduate to do so too

In this book, we support your graduate, but we also challenge them. We go so far as to tell them that any job is better than no job, and that even the most lowly task can help them build up the know-how that applies to any job. We know you are behind your graduate, so don't worry: keep an open mind, and support them as they carve out their own path towards their brilliant career.

Notes for careers advisers

Extensive use of labour market information

This book differs from other career handbooks aimed at students and graduates in the extent to which we have included labour market information (LMI), and have given clear advice to readers on how to access and make use of LMI. We recognise that you know your students and their courses and the employment patterns of your graduates, and you know your local and regional labour market. We hope that this handbook, with its broader LMI perspective, will be a useful addition to your practice and a helpful reference for your students.

Working with academic colleagues to share expertise

Strong partnerships with academic colleagues, based on mutual understanding, lead to provision for students which builds on careers advisers' expertise and tutors' specialist subject knowledge. Please have a look at our 'Notes for academic or personal tutors' for our thoughts about how this handbook might support your academic colleagues – and indeed you yourselves – in the planning and delivery of workshops, seminars and taught modules.

We hope to enhance your existing offer to students

We hope you will find that this handbook enhances the work you do with students and graduates – it certainly isn't designed to replace it. You will see that we frequently signpost students and graduates to their university careers service. We hope that you will welcome this. While we know that there are differences in style, provision and resources in different universities, we hope you will be able to respond if readers come your way.

Notes on our brilliant examples and brilliant quotes

Brilliant examples

In this book you will see brilliant examples in most chapters. These quotes are by real students and graduates, drawn from a range of universities and subject disciplines. We also approached people working in small to medium-sized enterprises (SMEs) because that is an important employment sector. All were kind enough to let us quote their stories and we have used their own words, with their permission. We are very grateful to them for their willingness to share their experiences in this book. We've chosen these brilliant examples because they bring to life some of the key messages in this handbook. We also hope that these brilliant examples will inspire and encourage you.

Brilliant quotes

We know that whatever we say, as career guidance professionals, it's good too for you to hear direct from employers. So we approached two people, with different perspectives, and asked them to tell us what key messages they want graduates to hear. We are very grateful to both of them for their willingness to be included in this way. You'll see them quoted in most of the chapters in the book, so let us introduce them to you.

Carl Gilleard was for many years the Chief Executive of the Association of Graduate Recruiters (AGR). AGR is dedicated to supporting and representing employers in all aspects of graduate recruitment and development. It represents over 800 organisations that, between them, offer a high proportion of graduate opportunities in the UK.

Julian Radley is Financial Director of Evotel Holdings, which supplies televisions to electrical retailers, and operates across the UK, Europe and the Far East. Nearly 60 per cent of private sector employment in the UK is located in small to medium-sized enterprises. Evotel, his highly successful company, is a brilliant example of the kind of SME that is vital to the economy.

PART 1

What's out there

CHAPTER 1

Accessing job opportunities

Headlines will always be negative: look beyond them. The market is tough – but there are always vacancies.

Carl Gilleard, Chief Executive, Association of Graduate Recruiters

This chapter looks at how employers get their vacancies into the marketplace, which means we show you where the job opportunities are, and how you can find them. It is important to remember that employers are looking for the right person to fill their job with just as much commitment and concern as you show when you are looking for your brilliant job.

Supply and demand: it takes two

The basic principle of the graduate labour market is that two equally important elements must be in place for the market to work, namely: supply and demand (for an in-depth exploration of the graduate labour market, have a look at Chapter 2). In the graduate labour market you as the jobseeker are the supply, and the employer offering the job is the demand. Clearly, for the job market to function at all, both supply and demand each need to know of the other's existence, which means that you (supply) have to make your presence in the marketplace known, and the employers (demand) equally have to make it known that they have a job that they want to fill.

definitions

> You, the jobseeker, are the supply side of the graduate labour market; the
> employers are the demand side.

The employer's perspective

For an employer, taking on a new person is a big deal. It is going to increase
their payroll, it is probably going to cost them money just to get their vacancy
publicised and, when they do find someone, they are going to have to allocate
time (which is a valuable resource) to integrate the new employee into the
workplace quickly, so that they can function well and be a valued addition to
the organisation. Employers care a great deal about getting the right person
for the job. They don't want a huge range of applicants: what they want is to
choose from a range of suitable candidates so that they recruit the right one
for their job, which is why employers are keen to get their job out there where
people can see it. They can use a range of media to do this: print, online and
networking (sometimes called word of mouth) and also social media including both Twitter and LinkedIn. Instead of responding to job vacancies that
are advertised, you can take the initiative and approach an employer to see if
there is a possible vacancy; this is called a speculative application. You can also
choose to work for yourself, rather than work for someone else, namely self-
employment (more on this in Chapter 6). So let's look at each of these in turn.

How employers get their jobs out there

Vacancies in print

 tip

> Check the national quality newspapers to see what kind of job vacancies are
> advertised. This is particularly useful once you've got graduate work experience
> and want to change jobs.

Regional and local papers

You have plenty of choice when it comes to local and regional papers: over 1,000 titles are listed in the UK. Some publish daily, such as: the *Manchester Evening News;* the *Evening Standard* (London); the *Belfast Telegraph* and the *Glasgow Evening Times.* Others come out weekly, such as the *Whitby Gazette,* and many of them are freely accessible online. These newspapers will include the whole range of jobs on offer in the locality, not just graduate-only jobs. You'll have to comb through all the ads to check for graduate or direct-entry jobs, but this will give you a good overview of the labour market conditions in that area. If you are keen to live in a particular location, this actually could work to your advantage, because it will make you look at non-graduate jobs as well, and tell you about jobs in that area. So you could always apply for that kind of job to get you to the place you want to be and, once there, start looking for the perfect job for you.

brilliant tip

Quality newspapers offer very good student discounts; just go online and subscribe to daily downloads. Not only will you get regular access to job ads, you'll also develop a good habit of serious reading.

Vacancy bulletins and directories

Periodically, vacancies are publicised together, typically in a bulletin or directory. There may be some hard copies of these available in your university careers centre but they are now pretty much only accessible online. The *Prospects Student Career Guide* has really great careers advice plus extensive vacancy information (**www.prospects.ac.uk/prospects_publications. htm**).

Specialist bulletins and directories

As well as these general publications, there are also specialist ones such as *Prospects Law,* which lists training contracts and law course vacancies for both law and non-law students. It is freely available online on the Prospects website (see above). Other sector guides include: *Prospects Accountancy, Banking* and Finance; *Prospects Business, Consulting & Marketing; Prospects Engineering & Manufacturing;* and *Prospects Information Technology.* All of the guides here are packed with useful information about working in that sector, complete with all the options for working or further study. Again, these are freely accessible online at the Prospects website.

Postgraduate bulletins and directories

There are several specialist directories for postgraduate opportunities, including the *Prospects Postgraduate Directory,* which includes everything you could want to know about postgraduate courses and opportunities. This is a digital-only publication that is updated every year in September and is freely accessible online. The *Postgrad Magazine* covers the same ground, but is published three times a year, in autumn, spring and summer. Again, this is freely accessible, digital only. The *Prospects MBA Guide,* another digital publication, restricts itself to Master in Business Administration programmes; and finally, the *Prospects Postgraduate Funding Guide* (published annually in September, digital only) is definitely one you'll need if you intend to continue your studies to postgraduate level.

Work experience and internships for non-finalists

No need to feel left out if you're not yet in your final year. You can find lots of useful information on work experience and internships you can explore from the start of your degree in the 'Employability' section of the *Prospects Student Career Guide,* which is freely accessible as a digital-only publication online at **www.prospects.ac.uk/prospects_publications.htm**.

 brilliant tip

You can freely access all these digital editions online at **www.prospects.ac.uk**.

Vacancies online

Posting job vacancies online is pretty much standard practice now. To find them, you simply need to go online and start looking. You'll find plenty of employers advertising direct to online jobsites. Or perhaps their newspaper advert is made accessible online by the newspaper in question. The official government jobsite (**www.jobseekers.direct.gov.uk**) is searchable by region, industry or company. There are also employment agencies that work on behalf of a range of employers, which means that they might be comprehensive (e.g. **www.monster.co.uk**) or specialised by: occupational sector, such as healthcare and medical jobs (e.g. **www.healthcare.jobs.com**); jobs in the financial sector (e.g. **www.roberthalf.co.uk**); by restricted entry (e.g. **www.thegraduate.co.uk**); or by geography. Certainly, if you are looking for a job outside the UK, online searches are probably the easiest way to access vacancies. Some big employers may have their own vacancy web pages such as the NHS (**www.jobs.nhs.uk**). Graduate Prospects is the best-known graduate careers website and is pretty comprehensive (**www.prospects. ac.uk**), but there are other websites that specialise in graduate recruitment, including **www.milkround.com** and **www.graduate-jobs.com**.

brilliant tip

Include social media such as LinkedIn, Facebook and Twitter in your jobsearch. Recruiters make use of any medium that is cost effective, so don't rule any out.

Print vacancies accessible online

The distinction between print and online is increasingly blurred; most newspapers run their advertised vacancies online, and actually make this a selling point when persuading employers to advertise with them. As a jobseeker, this is useful if you forget to check a specific newspaper on a particular day or if you overlooked a specific vacancy.

Many of the *Prospects* publications listed earlier in this chapter (see 'Vacancies in print' (p. 6)) are also available online and are, in some cases, free to download.

Choose a handful of online sites and limit yourself to those for a couple of weeks. You can always change your choice of sites if you're not getting the leads you want from the sites you have chosen.

Online vacancies: is more necessarily better?

There is no doubt that by advertising a vacancy online an employer can reach a far greater pool of potential applicants. What is more doubtful is whether the greater pool will necessarily have greater talent. The same goes for you as the jobseeker. By browsing online, you can easily access thousands of job vacancies. In one way, this is great, but you will need to narrow this choice down so you find the kind of job you want, and the kind of job you are a suitable candidate for. Without some kind of filtering mechanism, you could waste a lot of time looking at irrelevant jobs, and you could waste even more time applying for jobs without really thinking. You might even find that you are overwhelmed by the sheer volume of vacancies advertised online and that you become stuck, not knowing how to deal with them all. You do need to have a look at these websites and get a feel for what they offer and how they work. Then you need to make them work for you by being selective.

 timesaver

Actively manage your online jobsearch: set filters and review your website choices regularly. Allocate a specific, limited time for checking vacancies online.

Registering with a recruitment agency

Recruitment agencies work to an employer's brief, taking on the task of finding a suitable person for a particular vacancy. It can often happen that they handle a vacancy that is not advertised anywhere else, so they are a really important part of your job search.

Agencies do a lot of the selection work, so will sift through application forms and CVs, and often run selection interviews either in person or at a distance, either on the phone or by video. They pride themselves on building up contacts so they can draw on a pool of applicants they know when putting forward candidates for the vacancy in question.

Agencies have a huge amount of up-to-the-minute insider information on their particular industry or sector specialism. So they can give you valuable insight on what an employer is looking for – and what you might need to develop in order to be successful.

 brilliant **timesaver**

Register with a recruitment agency for your chosen jobsearch area. They put jobseekeers in touch with employers and have valuable insight into their industries.

Networking or word of mouth

Why network?

You'll hear a lot about networking within the context of jobsearch in particular and business in general. There is no doubt that networking is important and, in some occupational sectors, e.g. photography, creative arts, it is invaluable.

 example

'During my internship, I was invited to an event with the then Shadow Home Secretary (Chris Grayling). Quivering like a nervous wreck, I shook his hand, and could barely speak . . . I felt so inferior and out of my depth. I plucked up the courage to ask a question . . . but could literally barely speak I was that nervous. Six months on, we visited a local homeless charity. Chris Grayling arrived . . . he recalled my question from six months back. I realised afterwards the huge difference in my demeanour from our previous encounter.'

Kevin, BSc (Hons) Politics

Networking in principle

In essence, when you network you take a conscious decision to make the most of every new contact you make, and you treat every single encounter as a possible job lead. You aren't asking them directly for a job, you are simply making them aware that you exist, and that you are the kind of person anyone would want to have working with them. So, no matter how unlikely it may seem, or how remote the chances are of getting a job opening from a random encounter, you work on the principle that every lead could be the one that takes you further towards your brilliant career. Unfortunately, there is no set formula that determines how many contacts equal a job lead. You simply have to be on the alert and be ready to present yourself as a possible employee at any time.

 tip

When you network, you aren't asking directly for a job, you are simply making people aware that you exist, and are the kind of person anyone would like to work with. Just by introducing yourself you show that you are confident, so – go and say hello!

Networking in practice

Graduate job fairs

You may be invited to network in a formal, organised way: graduate job fairs, for example. A graduate fair brings together graduate recruiters, employment professionals and graduate jobseekers. A fair may be generalist (covering all aspects of graduate employment) or specialist (by region or occupational area). It gives you the chance to meet people, and for people to meet you. It makes sense to treat a job fair as a possible recruitment opportunity, so think about how you want to appear. For example, in thinking about what to wear, you might choose something that is more formal than informal. So, without going all out for the power suit, perhaps wear trousers rather than jeans, shirt rather than T-shirt, and go for something clean and ironed rather than something grubby and creased. You might also like to think about taking some copies of your CV, just in case the opportunity to give it to an employer arises. You may also want to take note of contact details; a notebook is fine for this, but if you do take notes on your phone, make sure you've turned the sound off and do not be tempted to make personal calls when you're on display.

brilliant tip

Make sure your mobile is switched off when you are at a job fair. Potential employers are interested in you, not your ringtone.

Alumni or invited speaker events

There may be alumni events at your university, to which you as a student may be invited. Alumni means people who have already graduated from your university. Sometimes the alumni events are social, but sometimes they are set up for students to make contacts. The big advantage of talking to alumni is that you already have something in common: your university! And, although they may not have a job opening right now, they may at some point in the future have a vacancy they need to fill, and they may remember meeting you. It may be hard for you to believe it when you meet them, but they too were once a student, just like you, so take the plunge and introduce yourself. Invited speaker events usually involve representatives of particular job areas. They may be in a position to recruit themselves, they may have their own story to share and to inspire you, or they may offer some useful advice. You'll only know what you can get out of it by going to hear them.

brilliant example

'I'm currently working for BBC Arabic in Cairo. I didn't apply through formal means, I used the lesson I learnt when applying for my year abroad. I asked. I met someone who told me you don't have to be a native speaker of Arabic to apply to BBC Arabic. So at a film screening of a documentary, when I saw that the Cairo Bureau Chief of BBC Arabic was there, I asked her if there were any jobs for native English speakers. ▶

She gave me her card, I emailed her a cover letter-style message and she said if I could start soon, she'd give me a month's trial in Cairo. I rushed through my Master's final project and now, following that month's trial, I'm planning to stay for up to a year.'

Claire, BA (Hons) Modern Languages (Arabic and Spanish),
MA International Journalism

Networking online

The Internet offers unprecedented possibilities of making yourself known to a very wide audience; and these possibilities can work for you or against you. It is possible to find job opportunities and useful leads through your online presence. However, once you have an online presence, it can be readily accessed by your employer or potential employer – who could think the less of you for having seen uncensored comments or images on your page.

You can establish a presence online by: creating a website or a blog; opening a Twitter account; or joining a social network such as LinkedIn. You may be asking yourself whether you need to go online to network but, before we address that question, let's run through the online options.

Websites and blogs

Setting up your own web page allows you to showcase who you are and what you can do. In some sectors it is a very good idea to have a web page. The creative industries, for example: if you are looking for a job in design, it is really important that an employer can view your work. This applies as much to a web designer as to a jewellery designer. The web page then functions as a sort of portfolio that can be accessed by anyone at any time.

A blog (the term is a contracted form of web log) is also a type of web page, but with the explicit intention of charting what has been happening. It allows you to update easily, and should really be updated regularly as an out-of-date blog creates a bad impression. Again, a blog can show what you are capable of, and what you have been doing.

tip

If you have an online presence, keep it up to date. Perhaps not daily but certainly on a regular basis and at least every week.

Forums

A forum may be set up on a website or blog so that the online readers can share responses and ideas on a particular theme. They allow you to express your opinions without necessarily committing to regular input. They also allow you to see what other people are thinking, which might help you to work through a particular issue or challenge. You yourself can use a forum to pose a question and this can be a good way to get into a challenge or problem when you feel really stuck and don't have any clear idea of the way forward. Examples might include: what's a telephone interview like? or, what should I wear to the evening meal at an assessment centre? In this way, you are learning from the collective experience and wisdom of others.

Social networks

Social networks are, at heart, online communities. Just like a real community, you join as a newcomer, make friends and then make friends with your friends' friends. You can then chat, share photos, set up meetings, seek advice and do all the things you would do in real time, but online. There is, however, a clear distinction between different types of social network, what they are used for, and how they are viewed.

Drawing the line between personal and business networks

Broadly speaking, the distinction is between social networking for personal reasons (having fun, gossiping, showing off even) and social networking for professional reasons (getting a job, making business contacts, showing off even). The trick is never to confuse the two. This distinction shows up in the way different social networking sites have developed. Facebook, for example, is definitely for having fun and is therefore a personal space. LinkedIn, on the other hand, is a social network that is clearly aimed at the professional and business side. Keep this distinction clear by making LinkedIn your professional presence and keeping Facebook strictly for friends – double-check your privacy settings to ensure this.

 tip

Facebook is for fun, LinkedIn is for business. Keep personal and professional quite separate.

Looking at your personal pages from the employer perspective

While your friends might find it funny and endearing to hear about you embarrassing yourself at a party, your employer (or potential employer) may take a very different view. There are more and more cases of employers seeing material that their workers have posted and, as a consequence, taking disciplinary action including dismissal; and this is where the material has been posted in a personal capacity. If you are on Facebook, go through your pages and take down anything that would put you in a bad light if seen by an employer. And before you post anything from now on, ask yourself if you would be happy to put the post in your window, where it could be seen by passersby, friends of the family or people who know you but aren't necessarily your friends. Then check your privacy settings to keep Facebook private. Make sure that you have a LinkedIn profile because employers do use this for recruiting. Look at other profiles in your chosen sector to ensure you set the right tone for your own profile.

 tip

Review any social network presence you have set up. Ask yourself this: is my online behaviour how I would behave if a potential employer was in the same room?

Twitter

Twitter is also another online social network, but it has the unique selling point of microblogging. As with a blog (or indeed the status aspect of a social network page), people post an update on their page to show what they are doing, what they are thinking, what is happening in their life right now. On Twitter, however, these posts are restricted to a maximum of 140 characters: this makes for microblogs or tweets.

Using Twitter for job opportunities

Twitter can be useful for following people who lead the way in particular industries as you can see what their thinking is and in what direction they, and by extension their work domain, are heading. Twitter can also be a practical source of job vacancies, and employment agencies do post tweets about new vacancies even before the adverts are posted online. Of course, you'll only get a very brief sense of what the vacancy is (because of the restricted length of the tweet) but that might be enough for you to decide whether to follow it up or leave it alone.

brilliant tip

If you don't want to commit to a permanent online presence, just contribute to a one-off forum or follow someone on Twitter. Come out of your comfort zone and show you can take on a new challenge.

Do I really need an online presence?

We know that not all undergraduates are the same; many will be familiar and happy with virtual communities in an online world, others might feel less comfortable, confident or convinced. There is no clear-cut answer about the need to have an online presence. In some industries, it is vital. In others, it is of little consequence. The important thing to know is that you are always in control of what you post. You can choose to have only a professional presence online and you can closely monitor what you post. You could perhaps limit your commitment, by joining a specific forum to add your voice to a particular debate, or using Twitter just to follow a particular person in a field that interests you. It is probably wise to use online networking, even to a limited extent, and for a limited time, because it does show that you are willing to embrace the new and maybe even to come out of your comfort zone.

 Networking dos and don'ts

Do

✔ treat every encounter as a possible lead;

✔ be polite and pleasant to everyone at all times;

✔ be prepared to ask questions as much as answering them;

✔ follow up any leads promptly: send a message or email the next day at the very latest.

Don't

✘ be intimidated: even if it is a disaster the first time, you'll get better with practice;

✘ be casual: don't chew gum, swear or make phone calls;

✘ get disheartened: if you have nothing concrete to show for an hour of networking, at the very least you have made an effort;

✘ monopolise a contact: let other people get access too.

Speculative applications

Speculative applications (sometimes called applying on spec.) are where you take the initiative and approach an employer to see if there is a possible vacancy, rather than responding to a vacancy once it is advertised. You can of course make speculative applications in a range of media: in person; by email; online; by post. You can waste a lot of time (both yours and also the employer's time) in sending off speculative applications that have no chance of success. And you can feel a lot of rejection if the speculative applications you send out get you nowhere, not even a response. But speculative applications do work, especially in very niche areas. Take a look at our brilliant example, in which Oliver's first job as a junior engineer pays very little, but gives him valuable experience which he uses to secure a better job not once but twice in a row: a brilliant example of leverage in the labour market, as well as speculative applications.

brilliant example

'When a new Formula One team was starting up for the following season, I saw an opportunity and speculatively applied for a position. Luckily they saw potential in me, and recognised my experience and qualifications. I spent two-and-a-half years at this Formula One team as a systems engineer on the race team, until they had to withdraw from racing due to financial reasons . . . due to contacts I had gained in the industry, I quickly secured employment with a motorsports electronics company, providing hardware and services to the governing body of motorsport.'

Oliver, MEng (Civil), MSc Motorsport Engineering and Management

Focusing your speculative approach

It is important to invest time before you send a speculative application. You'll need to know the market, be clear who are the relevant employers, and have a very good understanding of what their business needs. With a speculative application, you are basically offering your blend of skills and know-how as the solution to a staffing problem the employer hasn't really worked out yet. Online research can really help you here: to look at the individual employer and to put that employer in the overall context of the current market. Networking also plays a strong part, as you identify who to approach, and you approach people who may have some idea of who you are either from a previous encounter or by recommendation.

brilliant example

'I started off looking for a job on the Mediterranean coast because I'd got the chance of accommodation there. So basically I got a load of CVs and went round pretty much every restaurant, because that was where I had most experience . . . it was horrible, really scary because I didn't really know what I was saying (in French). One place phoned back, invited me for an interview, and gave me a job as a runner.'

Hannah, (undergraduate) Economics and Politics with International Studies

Self-employment

You might like to consider creating your own job vacancy by working for yourself. Self-employment is quite common in some sectors, notably the creative industries. However, it can also work in less obvious occupational areas: for example, counselling or computer programming. It will involve a lot of hard work, but it can be very rewarding to shape your own destiny, and to make your first million. Have a look at Chapter 6 for more about self-employment.

brilliant tip

Make the most of help on offer for a business start-up. This includes help targeted at graduates. Banks can offer useful information, as can jobcentres.

Dimensions: of time, of geography, of chance

The time dimension: watch out for closing dates

A daily newspaper will carry vacancies for which the closing date is likely to be a couple of weeks later; in a magazine published less frequently, the vacancies will be around for longer; and in the annual directories, the publication of the directory may happen some months before the closing date. Don't be lulled into a false sense of security here: although there may well be a rolling programme of recruitment, it is nearly always better to apply sooner rather than later.

The geographical dimension: working where *you* want to work

The geographical reach of jobsearch can also vary from local through regional and national to European or global. This applies equally to both sides of the market: you might be looking very widely, and the employer may also be putting a vacancy out into the marketplace at different levels. At the most local level, they can simply put up a notice in the workplace. Typically, this would be in a shop window, just saying something like: VACANCY – ENQUIRE WITHIN. A wider local search would be through local newspapers, the weekly paid or freesheets. Regional search would use daily regional newspapers or local radio. There could even be a regional website advertising, for example, jobs in the North West of England, or a job fair that also covers a regional area. A nationwide approach would use national daily or weekend papers, or websites: these could also be used for global search.

brilliant tip

If you are keen to work in a particular location, try looking at a local paper or vacancy publication in that area. You could even walk around the area and see what kind of employers there are, and then send speculative applications to them.

The chance dimension (sometimes called serendipity)

Sometimes it looks like some people just get lucky: everything comes together and they are in the right place, at the right time, with the right skills for the right job. It can happen like that and, without making any great effort, somebody gets lucky and a job falls into their lap. If you see that happen for someone else, you might be tempted to wait around in the hope that the job fairy will come to your rescue. Or you can start to create your own luck. Because often, much, much more often, things come together after a lot of hard work.

tip

If you aren't making progress in your jobsearch, try another approach. Think laterally, be resourceful and use the full range of possibilities presented in this chapter.

Creating your own luck

So what can you do to get everything in place? Well, you need to ensure that you have developed the necessary skills and know-how. 'The graduate labour market' (Chapter 2) takes you through the skills employers are looking for, and 'Work experience; making it purposeful' (Chapter 9) shows you how to develop your range of desirable skills through purposeful work experience. You also need to ensure that you are ready to respond quickly to a job possibility, by having your CV up to date, perhaps having a completed job application form you can adapt to a new vacancy. 'Making applications: getting past the first post' (Chapter 11) takes you through all these processes and more. Fundamentally, to get a job you have to be in the job market, and employers have to know that you are in the market for their job. It goes right back to the opening of this chapter: for the market to work, supply (you) and demand (employers) have to know about each other.

 recap

- Look at vacancies from the employer's perspective.

- Use printed media: directories, newspapers, magazines.

- Use online media: online newspapers and websites.

- Look widely to check what's out there, then narrow your search so you aren't wasting your (or the employer's) time with unfocused applications.

- Use timesaving devices: filters, alerts, Twitter.

- Get networking: job fairs, alumni events, contacts – treat every encounter as a possible step forward towards your job.

- Use social networks, but review your online presence to ensure you present online at all times as a serious contender for a job opening.

- Consider the option of self-employment: take up any help on offer.

- Give the Job Fairy a helping hand by doing everything you can to create your own luck.

What to do next

Check out the demand side of the labour market

If you are thinking about what to do next, you could take one step towards checking out what is in demand in the job market by checking out a quality newspaper (*Guardian, Independent, Daily Telegraph, The Times*) to look at the job vacancies advertised there. Go online, visit a few of the job websites we have included in this chapter.

Make your presence known in the supply side of the labour market

You could take one step towards making your presence (as a jobseeker) known in the job market, by checking if your university is running a job fair – and, if they are, go along to it. Tell people that you are actively seeking work. Think about posting your CV online on one of the job websites. Ideally, you should cover both sides of the job market: checking out the demand side, and making your presence known on the supply side.

CHAPTER 2

The graduate labour market

Increasingly, employers will look for some more interesting skills; things like cultural sensitivity and what makes a global graduate. Sometimes you have to go sideways to get to where you want to be.

Carl Gilleard, Chief Executive, Association of Graduate Recruiters

This chapter will help you to make sense of the graduate labour market. You are going to need to understand how the labour market works if you are to find your way around it – which you need to do as you work towards securing your brilliant career. You need to know that the labour market is both complex and dynamic. This is the chapter you are most likely to turn to when riffling through this book, and it is probably the most difficult chapter to write. Difficult to write, firstly, because we want to present some fairly complex concepts in a very accessible way. Difficult, secondly, because any labour market is not only complex, but also dynamic: it doesn't stand still but constantly shifts and changes in response to a range of factors which shape the supply of and demand for workers. That dynamism means that you may want to consult some online sources of up-to-the-minute data if you want a real-time assessment of what's going on in the graduate labour market when you actually read this.

So this chapter is going to take you through some key concepts in employment, then it will look at why employers want graduates and what graduates have to offer in terms of knowledge, skills and abilities. We will also look at small to medium-sized enterprises (SMEs) as these play a significant role in graduate recruitment, but can be overlooked by graduate jobseekers. We then have a brief overview of what kind of employment sectors graduates have gone into in recent years and the kind of wages they start out with.

 tip

The labour market is constantly changing but you can easily get the most up-to-date information online.

Fundamentals of the labour market: supply and demand

There are two sides to any market, and that includes the labour market

You'll hear talk of 'the labour market' when issues of employment, unemployment, job vacancies and employability are discussed. 'Labour' here means simply to do with work. The term 'labour market' is used to describe the interactions between employers who need labour (or workers, to put it another way) and employees (those who can supply that labour or undertake that work). The study of the labour market is of interest to economists, and can be seen as a discipline in itself. Understanding how the labour market works and keeping up to date with what's happening with job vacancies and demands is important for careers advisers too.

Picture a market in your mind's eye

The idea of a 'market' helps us to envisage what is going on. So just take a moment to think of a market (or supermarket or shop) from your own experience. It might be a bustling, chaotic place with people shouting out what they are hoping to sell – or it might be extremely organised into tidy aisles stacked full of goods with special offer stickers pointing out the best buys.

You are the 'supply' in the graduate labour market

Whatever the setting, there are always two sides in play. On the one hand, there are people offering goods for sale (goods such as a pair of trainers or a bunch of grapes); on the other, people who are looking to buy what's on offer. And that's the first key point: for the market to work, you have to have supply (stuff being offered) and demand (stuff being wanted). Don't be insulted if we now compare you to a pair of trainers or a bunch of grapes, but you are the supply in the labour market. You are available, on show, ready to be snapped up by someone with money to secure you – and a discerning eye to know a quality product (be it trainers, grapes or graduates) when it's up for grabs.

 brilliant definitions

The term **supply** refers to all the people who are actively seeking work – which of course includes you.

The term **demand** refers to all the jobs that are looking to be filled – which is, of course, what you want.

The relationship between supply and demand is critical in your jobsearch

It is clear that 'supply' and 'demand' are the two fundamental forces driving the labour market. So the relationship between supply and demand is critical. As you are part of the supply side, it is important that you think about the market from the other perspective and get a sense of how employers work and what kind of supply they are looking for (demanding). This allows you to tailor your offer (of yourself for hire) to their demand. That could be a relatively simple task: presenting your skills, knowledge and understanding in a way that makes it easy for an employer to understand exactly what you have to offer and how that fits with what they need in their workforce. Have a look at Chapter 11 for advice on making sure that your application gets past the first post. It could, however, require a complex, more lengthy task which might be that you seek to expand your skills, knowledge and understanding (that is, working on expanding your professional repertoire) by undertaking voluntary work or work shadowing, or accepting a job that you don't really want to do now in order to get the job you want in the future: your brilliant career.

 tip

When you are looking for a job, so that you present what you have to offer in a way that the employer will easily recognise, try to think from the employer's perspective. Look at what they want and why they want it. Then make sure that you've got what they want and you showcase that in your application.

What's distinctive about the graduate labour market?

Graduate labour as a distinct sector within the labour market

You may be wondering why graduates are treated as a distinct subgroup within the labour market. Defining sectors is just a way of examining the labour market in more detail, and is helpful in getting a hold on labour market information which could otherwise be unwieldy and overwhelming. Market analysts often drill into data so that they can get the low-down on a particular sector. A sector can be defined by occupation (e.g. Engineering or Business or Creative Arts) or by geography (the South East or Greater Merseyside) or by shared characteristics of the workforce (graduates). We'll look at occupational sectors in more detail in Chapter 3 'Labour market information: analysis of what graduates do', but for now we'll look at the graduate labour market: which simply means that the demand is for graduate-level jobs, for which the jobseeker (the supply) must have an undergraduate degree (at least).

The labour market can be subdivided into **sectors,** which makes it easier to focus. These **sectors** can be defined by occupational grouping, by geographical territory, or by shared characteristics of the workforce, such as being a graduate.

What work do graduates actually do?

Every year the Higher Education Statistics Agency (HESA) asks graduates to report what they have gone on to do after they finished their degree. A questionnaire goes out to all those finishing an undergraduate degree, which includes Foundation degrees. It only goes to people who are resident in the United Kingdom or the European Union, so does not include postgraduates or overseas students who are not UK residents. It only asks about their 'first' destination: that is, what they were doing six months after completing their degree. Destinations include: work (paid employment); further study (perhaps at postgraduate level); looking for work; and not available for work (e.g. travelling). Chapter 3 'Labour market information: analysis of what graduates do' goes into some detail about what graduates from different degrees go on to do. This makes it easy for you to check where people who did the same degree as you ended up. The results are presented by broad subject area (e.g. Social Sciences) then broken down into its particular disciplines (for Social Sciences this would include Economics and Sociology).

Graduate earnings

One noticeable characteristic of the graduate labour market is that wages are higher. Of course, it is perfectly possible to earn higher than average earnings without a degree, where your skills and talents are in demand. This is particularly true where the supply of skill is very limited, so employers are competing with each other to secure the services of a limited pool of talent. These highly sought-after skills come at a premium, which means the employers have to pay more. A classic example here would be a footballer: the employer's primary concern is ability as a footballer, not the level of formal education achieved.

However, if you look at graduates in the labour market as a whole and compare their lifetime earnings, graduates on average earn more than non-graduates. This is often referred to as the 'graduate premium'. In 2001, the average lifetime earnings of a graduate, when compared to the average earnings of someone with two A levels, amounted to £400,000 or 41%. In the decade from 2001 to 2011, the number of graduates increased hugely, by 41%. This meant that the supply of graduates increased and subsequent research, published in 2007, revised the graduate premium down to £160,000 which still amounts to 20–25% more than someone with two A levels. These are only averages, and the actual earnings of any individual graduate can vary considerably from this average figure. The degree subject you take, the job you go into, the kind of employer you work for and the location of your employment will all have a bearing on your earnings over your lifetime.

Is the graduate premium guaranteed?

What happens to the graduate premium in the future is largely a question of supply and demand. Even when the supply has increased, although the premium has diminished, it still represents an additional 25% in lifetime earnings. The Office for National Statistics (ONS, 2012) reported average graduate pay at £15.18 per hour, in contrast to £8.92 per hour paid on average to non-graduates in the same age range. There are, of course, big variations in the hourly pay of graduates with medicine and dentistry paying at the top of the range and arts subjects towards the bottom.

Although the recession has certainly affected graduate recruitment, economic forecasts expect the demand for graduates will rise in the coming years, and the graduate premium may have diminished, but it is still there. So there are clear economic benefits to having a degree. This may not ring true if you are battling through difficult economic times when graduate jobs are hard fought and hard won. It may be difficult to think about this now, or to believe that it's important, but when you get towards retirement age you will look back and see what a difference having a degree has made in the long run.

brilliant definition

The **graduate premium,** in labour market terms, is the difference in earnings potential for graduates as a sector of the market compared with other groups of workers. The graduate premium requires employers to pay higher wages to secure a graduate to fill their vacancy. The graduate premium means that graduate earnings over a lifetime are likely to be higher than for non-graduates.

How graduates differ from other occupational sectors

There are a couple of other significant differences when you compare graduates in the labour market with other groups of workers.

They are more mobile in the labour market, which means that they are more likely to move to another part of the country to take up work and may even work outside their country of origin. Employers are also more likely to move their graduate workers about, though will often offer incentives and rewards for doing so.

Another curious characteristic is that graduates are more likely to be given further training. This can often be in-house or on-the-job training, but can also mean sending graduate workers on specialist and/or postgraduate courses at universities.

 Most graduates now are expected to do regular evaluations of where they are at and where they are going . . . developing the individual to the point where they can take control of their life, their learning and their career.

Carl Gilleard, Chief Executive, Association of Graduate Recruiters

It may seem odd that employers want their skilled people to get even more skilled – but they know that graduates can learn (see below) and a more highly skilled worker is more highly prized because they can do more. The flip side of being offered this kind of opportunity is that employers expect their graduate workers to progress in their careers and invest in their own professional development. Of course, expanding your professional repertoire in this way benefits you because it gives you more leverage in the labour market.

Not all graduates are the same

 example

'My last job was a stop-gap really: it wasn't the job I wanted and it wasn't the money I wanted. But I wanted to learn, I was interested and, gradually, it built. The longer I was there, the more things were handed over. So then when it came to the pay review I could say: "I'm doing this now, and I want to be paid for it." I'd proved myself. After five years, I was earning nearly three times the salary I started on.'

Sophie, employee in small to medium-sized enterprise

brilliant example

'I was a (very) mature student, already in my chosen career as a mental health recovery and rehabilitation worker. I decided to study Psychology for several reasons: I enjoyed it at A level, I never had the chance to go to university when I left school and wondered if I could do it, and the subject is closely linked to my work . . . I have much more confidence in decision making and suggestions I make at work now. I feel the knowledge I now have of theories and empirical evidence . . . enhances the experience I already had.'

Linda, BSc (Hons) Psychology

We have been talking of a graduate labour market as if all graduates are the same, but that's clearly nonsense. Graduates are different, one from the other, because people are different. Two students may be studying on the same programme, even in the same tutor group, and yet hold very different values and so will be looking for jobs in distinctly different ways. One may be highly motivated by money; the other by job satisfaction and a work–life balance. One may be happy to relocate from one place of work to another within an organisation, or even to move from one country to another if their employer demands it or if a good job offer comes up. For other graduates, family responsibilities, emotional ties or just a strong sense of belonging may keep them in one place, and so they may restrict their jobsearch to a particular geographical area. Some graduates are changing career direction completely and have retrained in order to step out in a completely new career direction. Others will be starting out and their first graduate job may well be their first job. Some graduates will hold out for the job that matches their specification of a dream job. For others, any job will do: they just need to earn money to live. So, even though this chapter treats graduates as a set of workers sharing graduate-level qualifications, there are huge differences for individuals, who will make their own decisions and carve their own path to what is a brilliant career, for them.

 recap

- As a group, graduates earn more over the course of their working life than non-graduates.

- Graduate workers tend to move location and/or employer more than non-graduates.

- Graduates undertake more training and personal development than other workers.

- Employers will pay a premium for highly skilled workers, especially if supply is limited.

- All graduates are individuals who will carve out their own brilliant career.

What's distinctive about graduates as a labour supply?

Why would employers pay more for a graduate?

So why are employers prepared to pay more for workers who have a degree? Graduate employees tend to bring innovation and creativity to their work, which solves business problems and can increase productivity. That's not to say that other groups of workers don't do that but graduates, as a workforce and on the whole, have a proven track record for doing so. Broadly speaking, graduates are paid to think, so they add value to their work, which in turn adds value to the organisation they work for, which in turn repays the 'graduate premium'.

How do employers know what graduates are capable of?

You might think that employers are just taking it on trust that graduates can think, and will be able to apply intellectual and cognitive abilities. Well, yes and no. Employers can take it on trust, because there are clear standards of achievement that are expected before a student can be awarded a degree. Although individual universities award their own degrees, all degrees in England, Wales and Northern Ireland work to the framework for higher education qualifications published by the Quality Assurance Agency for Higher Education. The framework sets the benchmark for what graduates should achieve in their degree, whether Foundation, Honours or Masters.

 tip

As a graduate, you are trained to think: to think critically, to think creatively, to think things through. You need to show an employer how your training in thinking can benefit their organisation or add value to their enterprise.

What graduates should be able to do

For example, on successful completion of their programme, an Honours graduate should be able to:

- understand key aspects of their field of study (including coherent and detailed knowledge);
- conduct analysis and enquiry; devise and sustain arguments, and/or solve problems;
- appreciate uncertainty and ambiguity; and
- manage their own learning.

What graduates are able to do from the employer's perspective

All of these competencies would relate primarily to the subject or discipline you are studying, whether that is Fine Art, Computer Science or Medicine. From an employer's point of view, that ability to think transfers into the workplace as:

- the exercise of initiative and personal responsibility;

- decision making in complex and unpredictable contexts;

- effective communication of information, ideas, problems and solutions to specialist and non-specialist audiences; and

- the learning ability needed to undertake appropriate further training of a professional or equivalent nature.

So, when an employer specifically advertises a graduate job, and demands that their employee has a first degree, they expect graduate employees to work at this level of sophistication in their workplace.

How employers view subject discipline

Between 60 and 70 per cent of graduate jobs advertised don't specify the degree discipline – which means you can apply no matter what subject you studied. This statistic has remained fairly constant for a long time, so we can assume that it will hold good for some time to come. What it tells us is that it is your thinking power that employers want, not necessarily the specialist knowledge of your discipline. You might have to help the employer recognise that, despite you studying a very different subject from them, you have got what they are looking for. (Of course, where an employer wants a specialist, such as a doctor, lawyer, dentist or graphic designer, then they will advertise specifically for those roles and qualifications. This accounts for about half the graduate jobs advertised.) The important thing here is to remember to look at things from the employer's perspective. You might well have a degree in a subject about which the employer knows nothing at all. This could be anything, from Classical Civilisation to Sports and Exercise Studies. The employer may even have preconceptions about your degree, thinking, for example, that Arts and Design graduates don't have any commercial understanding, or not realising that Psychology requires a good understanding of statistics. So you may well have to scrutinise your skills and experience and present what you know in a way that the employer can't fail to grasp. What you can know for sure is that, if you have achieved an undergraduate degree, you have proven thinking power – and that is in demand.

 tip

More than half of the graduate vacancies on offer do not specify a particular degree discipline. So you can broaden your jobsearch beyond your field of study.

Not all employers are big organisations

 example

'I've worked in SMEs for several years now. It's actually far more challenging working for a smaller company than it is working for a larger company. You have more opportunity to shine, in fact, and to move up quickly.'

Sophie, Evotel Holdings employee

Why are small to medium-sized enterprises important?

SMEs play a huge part in the economy: in the EU, 99 per cent of all enterprises are SMEs. In the UK, annual data published by the Department of Business and Skills (BIS, 2015) shows that SMEs accounted for 99.9 per cent of all private sector businesses and 59 per cent of private-sector employment. That means a lot of people are actually working in SMEs (14.1 million at the last count) and that includes graduates. Now do you see why they are so important?

brilliant example

Evotel Holdings supplies televisions to electrical retailers in the United Kingdom. They import televisions and they import components which are assembled in the UK and in the European Union. They are in a network of repair agents, working for manufacturers, insurers and retailers. Their market is characterised by high volume and low margin, which means very little tolerance if they are to make a profit. They must deliver on quality, on quantity and on time. A successful small to medium-sized enterprise, Evotel has to stay smart to keep ahead of its competitors.

What is an SME?

SMEs are vital to the economy, both in the United Kingdom and throughout Europe. But what exactly is an SME? The letters simply stand for small to medium-sized enterprise, but we need to define these terms too in order to understand what an SME is.

What is an enterprise?

There is no one definition, but in economic terms, an enterprise is an organisation created for business venture. So an organisation intends to do business and preferably to do business that makes a profit.

Small, medium-sized – or micro?

The size of an enterprise can be determined either by the number of people or the amount of money involved. The technical terms here are headcount or turnover/balance sheet total. From an employment perspective it is probably easier to think in terms of how many people are involved in the business: the headcount. In a headcount, no distinction is made between full-time and part-time workers: so if an SME has five full-time and five part-time, that makes ten workers. In the EU, the headcount includes employees and self-employed people working in the enterprise. Whereas in the UK, the headcount applies only to employees (BIS, 2015). But both the EU and the UK agree the headcount categories for SMEs, which are as follows:

micro = headcount up to 9

small = headcount of at least 10 and up to 49

medium-sized = headcount of at least 50, up to 249.

Although we often think of SMEs as small, they can actually be very small indeed, or quite sizeable. They can often be overlooked because the individual enterprises aren't household names. However, the opportunities in SMEs are statistically significant, and certainly worth investigating.

brilliant tip

Include SMEs in your jobsearch. You may not have heard their name, but they are a powerful force in the labour market. They are less likely to spend much money on advertising, so do your research and consider making a speculative application to a targeted SME. They really don't have any time to waste, so make sure you focus your application.

What to do next

There is every chance that you know someone who works for an SME – why not ask them about their work and their workplace? It would be interesting to see if they felt they had had any particular opportunities because of the small scale of their employment – or if they perceived any disadvantage.

Graduates need employability skills

What employers want: skillset and mindset

Having said that graduates are in demand in the labour market because of their proven ability to think, and having shown that employers pay a 'graduate premium', graduates are expected to offer more than their intellect: all graduates need good employability skills. This message comes through loud and clear from employers surveyed by the Confederation of British Industry (CBI, 2011) and Universities UK. Now, there is no one agreed definitive list of employability skills – there isn't even one agreed term. Sometimes these skills are called 'soft skills' or 'transferable skills' as well as 'employability skills'.

It is interesting to look at these terms in turn because they give an insight into what is in demand in the labour market, which allows you to pinpoint what you, as the supply, can offer or may need to develop. There is growing evidence that employers also value mindset. This refers to a set of attitudes and behaviours that allow workers to add value to their employing organisation. Some of these attitudes benefit the employee just as much as the employer: taking pride in your work and giving your best makes for greater satisfaction and self-esteem – both key in positive psychology.

The graduates we employ are over-qualified for work in the warehouse or the call centre. But we employ graduates because they're more attentive, more willing to do a proper day's work. You have to assume they've got the ability to do the job, but if they haven't got it 100 per cent, it's not going to take us long to train them.

Julian Radley, Director, Evotel Holdings

Hard skills refer to such abilities as numeracy and literacy, managing a project or working in a team. It is relatively easy for an employer to check that you have them (have a look at Chapter 12 for more on what kind of selection tests are used and how best to succeed in them). In contrast, soft skills are less easy to test for with any scientific reliability, but they can be observed and demonstrated. So 'soft' here doesn't mean that they are easier skills to acquire, but that they are more difficult to pin down for assessment. Transferable skills mean simply that the skills can be developed in one job and taken with you to another job. A good example here would be customer care.

Customer care means dealing with customers: it involves the ability to listen, to question, to understand the issue, to convey that understanding to a customer (without losing your temper!) and to work towards resolving the issue in hand to the satisfaction of both parties. Customer care is important in a wide variety of contexts: looking after patients in a hospital; dealing with complaints from corporate clients; handling irate customers in a queue or on a shop floor. What the customers/clients/patients are concerned about doesn't matter: your skills and abilities can be used effectively no matter what the context. The transferability of these skills also means that you can develop skills in one aspect of your life that may not necessarily be paid work, and can then use them in your employment. An example of this would be the negotiation skills you have to develop as a parent (particularly of toddlers), which stand you in good stead when negotiating in a work environment.

 definition

Employers value a range of behaviours and aptitudes, which can be used in a range of employment contexts. They might be called **transferable, soft** or **employability** skills. Their name doesn't matter, but the skills do.

Employability skillset and mindset

Here is our list of employability skills, drawn from a range of sources including the Confederation of British Industries and the National Union of Students (CBI/NUS, 2011). As they represent employers, this is very much from the demand perspective. They aren't presented in any particular order, because each of these skills is important in its own right, and different employers will place different emphasis on different skills at different times in the lifecycle of their own business. Although we can't give a precise indicator of demand for each of the skills, in an employer survey (CBI, 2011) 36% were not satisfied with foreign language fluency, and 44% of employers were not satisfied with graduate levels of business and customer awareness.

 It doesn't matter what the business is, there are some fundamental principles: cash flow is king; you've got to make sure there's a bottom line for the profit; and you've got to look at risk. Graduates need to ask where they fit into the critical path within the business process.

Julian Radley, Director, Evotel Holdings

Self-management

Broadly speaking, self-management is the ability to take responsibility for a role or a given task. If you accept responsibility, then a number of attitudes and behaviours will follow from that. You will probably be prepared to be flexible and you may need to be assertive as and when appropriate. You'll need to be a self-starter, getting on with things and not waiting to be asked or to be directed. You'll also have to be aware of the need to manage your time. A key aspect of self-management is that you are prepared to improve your own performance with every task, role or job that you do. This improvement will come from two complementary perspectives. Firstly, your own reflective practice, where you think about what you've done, what went well and what could be done better next time round. Secondly, feedback from others, which is likely to be a mixture of positive and negative feedback. You will learn, and take the lessons you learn with you, no matter where you go next.

brilliant example

'Aside from academic development, personal skills gained through my time at university are arguably as valuable. I've always been fairly confident, and university life allowed me to understand myself better: my strengths, weaknesses and life goals. Within two months of leaving university (in a very tough economic environment) I had secured a great job. I believe my time at university equipped me with the creative problem-solving skills that I need to excel within my industry – online brand reputation management.'

Alex, BA (Hons) Graphic Design

Resilience

Resilience is what sustains you to keep going with a task or responsibility even when the going gets tough and you might be tempted to give up. Resilience requires your commitment to stay involved, some degree of control or influence and a sense of personal challenge to develop. Optimism plays an important part, but it has to be realistic, not hoping for some magic wand you can wave. Knowing what you're feeling and why is also important here, as is the ability to slow down and consider alternatives when you seem to hit a blank wall.

 example

'I was working in France as a runner in a big American-themed sports bar. Although it was an American place, everybody spoke French all the time. I didn't think I was going to take it: it was really busy and I didn't know anyone, not a single person . . . at first it was overwhelming: everyone was older; everyone was French; there was so much to learn, the menu and the ordering, but eventually I made friends and in the end I was sorry to leave.'

Hannah, (undergraduate) Economics and Politics with International Studies

Team-working

This is obviously about working well with others. However, in order to do that you have to be aware that your individual contribution (and success) can be separated out from that of others in your team: you have to be aware of this interdependence and have to be able to manage yourself as a team-worker, not just as an individual. The behaviours that support effective team-working are sharing ideas with others by contributing to discussions and planning, and what follows from that is the need to cooperate with others and to respect them. Negotiating and persuading skills are key here.

 example

'A lot of the course I studied was teamwork-based, which enabled me to increase my confidence in working within a team. We also had to give a lot of presentations, which I found really nerve-racking, but it really did boost my confidence. I actually realised I did have a special talent for talking to groups and this encouraged me to consider teaching as a career.'

Katie, BSc (Hons) Animal Behaviour and Welfare

Business and customer awareness

Although this really is a soft skill, in that you can't necessarily train or test people in it, you can see very clearly when people don't have it. Some employers of graduates say that this is the employability skill most often missing in applicants and new entrants. Although you would expect it to be very much in demand in the retail and business sector, it is actually very important in service and public service sectors too. It means understanding what drives a successful business or service, but that doesn't necessarily mean at the high strategic level. It is very much the bottom-up approach: keeping customers satisfied, understanding why you need to build customer loyalty, understanding how innovation can drive a business forward – and how the lack of innovation can mean a business grinding to a halt. It also includes an appreciation of the need to take calculated risks: not reckless, but bold nonetheless.

Initiative is an important thing in an employee; but they've got to be aware of what that opportunity is, and when the opportunity comes, and then how to deal with it. We needed some marketing expertise – someone remembered marketing was on Seb's CV, so he got the chance to step up to it.

Julian Radley, Director, Evotel Holdings

Problem solving

Another skill that is pretty obvious, really. It will involve you analysing facts or data, and weighing up the context or situations. You'll need to work creatively, perhaps coming at problems from different angles and looking for a variety of approaches; and in order to solve the problem, you'll need to come up with appropriate solutions. A lot of your undergraduate work gets you to do this kind of thing, even if it isn't immediately obvious: linguists translating unfamiliar phrases need to puzzle things out, not simply reach for the nearest dictionary.

What happens is: we need to do something quickly and the only way to get someone quickly is to use someone that's here. Suddenly we realise someone's got more ability than we realised. Spotting talent is mostly by luck, which I think is wrong; we should be a bit more observant.

Julian Radley, Director, Evotel Holdings

Project management

This skill is increasingly sought after. As a graduate employee, you may be asked to manage projects – and you need to be clear that you will probably be asked to manage more than one project at time. Effective project management calls on many of the skills listed here: communication and literacy; team-working; problem solving and resilience. You probably will have had direct experience of managing a project on your degree – just think about your final year dissertation or project or end of year show – and you had to do that while managing other 'projects' – your brilliant career included.

Communication and literacy

This means the ability to read, write and to get your message across, which may seem really obvious. You should be able to write clearly and be able to structure your written work so that it makes sense. You should also be able to modulate the tone of your work to reach your intended readership. You should have good communication skills (sometimes called oral literacy), which means the ability to listen carefully, check your understanding and question appropriately. Poor communication is one of the greatest sources of frustration and irritation to employers; yet you can improve on this every single day, no matter what context you are operating in.

brilliant example

'I completed a foundation degree in animal management. As well as the huge variety of academic knowledge I gained, I also made a lot of personal developments which have really helped boost my confidence. What was particularly useful was the greater understanding of general writing skills I gained, including grammar and written communication. I feel that my academic writing improved over my time at university and, not only did these skills give me further confidence when completing assignments, but these are skills that I can use in any job environment, whatever the sector.'

Jessica, FdSc Animal Management

Numeracy

You do need to get your head around what is understood by numeracy. It does not mean advanced mathematical tasks, but fairly general awareness of the importance of maths as a tool in practical day-to-day work. The confidence to tackle mathematical problems in the workplace is in demand by employers. To dismiss this because you think you can't do maths is like saying you can't read and write. If you haven't got a formal qualification in maths (such as Maths GCSE grade A*–C or equivalent), you really should think about doing some basic maths programme so that you aren't cut off from a lot of jobs that need you to have confidence with numbers on a fairly basic level.

Application of Information Technology

This includes a range of Information Technology skills such as: word processing; using spreadsheets; setting up and managing files; using email and Internet search engines appropriately and using social media for corporate communication. As IT applications develop, it is important to keep up: not just in terms of playing with the latest games or applications, but also in terms of how these new ways of working and communicating and problem solving translate into everyday work.

Foreign language skills

This is quite a tricky one to get to the bottom of, but an easy one to dismiss if you think that, if you speak English, you don't need to worry about language competence. Languages are in demand in addition to the skill set outlined above: there are few jobs where language ability on its own is the key demand. The level of language skill can vary: in some cases technical mastery and fluency is called for, but everyday conversational ability can be useful, as can a general awareness of cultural differences. Even having a few key phrases in another language can really pave the way for effective relationships, which are at the heart of any business or dealings.

 example

'What's difficult about working abroad? I want to say the language, but it's not that. It's the way of doing things, getting your head around things.'

Hannah, (undergraduate) Economics and Politics with International Studies

Developing employability skills, even when you're not employed

Employers demand that graduates can demonstrate a range of transferable skills which have been shown to enhance their performance in the workplace. This is on top of your degree. The more you develop these employability skills the more attractive you become to an employer, so the greater your chances of success in your jobsearch. It is important to understand that you don't need to be in paid employment to develop all of these skills. For example, if you don't have a job, you can still develop your fluency in a foreign language just by listening to the radio or podcasts in that language, reading an online newspaper or novel, or even watching a film or TV programme. You can develop your customer awareness and business sense just by being aware of what is going on around you: think about how businesses advertise for and treat their customers. What promises do they make about customer service and how do they deliver on that promise?

Observing and analysing behaviours that you come across every day just as a possible customer (not even a consumer) will enhance your understanding. And, of course, if you are struggling to secure a job in a difficult labour market, you are continually practising resilience and self-management; and the real beauty is that, having developed these skills, whether through paid employment, volunteer work or simply on your own, they stick with you and you can use them to move around and progress in the labour market.

✶ brilliant tip

Seek out opportunities to develop employability skills. You can do this in any job at any level. You can also do it through volunteering and even in unpaid work. Keep a record of your skills development to use when applying for jobs.

What do graduates earn?

It is perfectly reasonable for jobseekers to ask what graduates earn, but it is a surprisingly difficult question to answer. You will find plenty of answers if you search online, with the figure usually expressed in whole numbers or to the nearest £500. In the same year, three different sources published three different figures for the average graduate salary; ranging from £20,000 to £29,000. The challenge is to look more closely to see what these figures are actually telling us about what graduates earn.

Average graduate starting salary

Analysis published annually by the Higher Education Statistical Agency (HESA) uses information on what graduates are doing six months after completion of their degree (known as their first destination) to calculate their average salary. In 2014, HESA reported the mean salary as £20,000 and the median graduate salary as £21,000. The difference between these two figures is due to the way in which averages are calculated. The *mean* is the sum total of all the salaries added together then divided by the number of people in the survey. It can be skewed by a relatively small number of extremely high salaries at the top end, or equally by a relatively small number of extremely low salaries at the bottom end. As the *median* salary is the value in the middle of the whole range of salaries, it is less affected by these two extremes. It is reasonable therefore to work with the median salary which happens to be the higher figure of £21,000.

It is important to remember that this is the average of the first destinations of all new graduates, which means that it covers every region of the UK, every single subject discipline and includes every graduate who has found employment, including those who have taken casual or non-graduate jobs which often pay less. The Association of Graduate Recruiters (AGR) also publishes an annual calculation of what their employers are paying graduates as a starting salary. Their most recent figure, published in 2015, also the median, was £28,000. The AGR reported figure is significantly higher than the HESA figure. A number of factors can explain this variation. The AGR report concentrates on graduate recruitment and graduates are, historically, paid more than other employees. Whilst AGR members are located all over the UK, many of them are recruiting in London, where salaries tend to be higher. Finally, AGR members tend to be larger organisations, which again tend to pay more.

Variations within average ranges

An average salary sits somewhere in the middle of the range; so some actual starting salaries will be higher and some will be lower (a point that is often overlooked by jobseeking graduates when considering advertised jobs). A survey of graduate employers published in 2015 reported median graduate salary at £30,000 and the highest salary (£42,000) offered by supermarket chain Aldi.

It is important to remember all the factors which can, and do, affect starting salaries. We've already seen regional variation, with the example of London generally commanding higher pay than elsewhere in the UK. There are also significant variations by occupational sector: oil and energy, investment banking and law have often appeared at the top end of the scale; while hospitality, retail, the public and voluntary sectors are often to be found towards the bottom end of the scale.

 The work has changed. When I was a kid you wanted to be a bus driver! You learn there are certain job markets and there needs to be a reality check, to learn what job markets pay.

Julian Radley, Director, Evotel Holdings

Starting, not finishing salaries

It can be disheartening to read news headlines about fabulous starting salaries which seem to be very far from what is actually on offer in your own jobsearch. You can easily find out (from the HESA survey) what the average starting salary was for students from your university, which can be useful in giving you a realistic benchmark of what to expect. Having a better understanding of how these headlines come about leads to a grounded perspective of what is actually happening in the labour market you find yourself in, which in turn helps you to make sense of what is happening to you.

Points of entry and points of leverage

Points of entry

It is important here to remember that these are the average starting salaries; that is, the kind of salary you can expect when you are starting out in a designated graduate job. That starting position is your 'point of entry'. In a survey of 16,000 undergraduates in their final year (they were due to graduate in 2010) a third were prepared to accept any (graduate) job they were offered, and a fifth admitted that they had applied to employers they weren't really interested in simply because they felt they didn't have much choice, given how tough the labour market was looking at that time. The key thing for them was to secure a point of entry into the labour market.

'You can't expect to have it immediately – you might do a few jobs and then, suddenly, you know: oh, *this* is what I want to do. For me, it's important to keep your brain going. To keep learning something is always going to be better than doing nothing. And if you can't get the job you want, do any job. Earning some money is better than earning no money.'

Sophie, employee, Evotel Holdings

We've looked at transferable skills and how the skills, knowledge and understanding that you develop in one job stay with you. This means that you can evolve as a graduate worker, increasing your know-how and thereby increasing your value to an employer. It is also crucial to recognise that you can start your evolution from day one of an entry-level job. You'll then arrive at a point where you are ready to move on, to look for a greater challenge and a better-paid job. This is what we call leverage in the job market.

Points of leverage

A longitudinal study tracked graduates not only into their first job on graduation (their point of entry – what is called the first destination in the national data collection), but also as they moved through the graduate labour market for several years further on. The researchers discovered that, three-and-a-half years after graduation, 81 per cent were in graduate occupations (that is, jobs for which a degree is required) and 87 per cent were 'fairly satisfied' or 'very satisfied' with their job. Leverage got them where they wanted to be. So, even if your point of entry is less than brilliant, you will find points of leverage towards your brilliant career.

brilliant recap

- Graduates have proven thinking skills.

- They have shown that they are prepared to learn.

- They want to progress in their career and to develop their range of competencies (their professional repertoire).

- They can bring flexibility and innovation to an organisation.

- They bring skills, attitudes and behaviours which can enhance a company's productivity.

- Over half of the graduate jobs advertised don't specify the degree discipline: you can apply no matter what subject you study.

- Include small to medium-sized enterprises in your jobsearch.

- Develop transferable skills in everything you do: paid employment, voluntary work, daily life.

What to do next

A very simple next step would be to locate your own degree in Chapter 3 and read through what graduates have done overall, and what kind of occupational sectors they have gone for.

You could make a note of what interests you, and then follow it up by getting more information from your university careers service, or by using some of the other chapters in the first part of this handbook to move you on.

You could also look at the list of transferable skills and see if you can identify examples from your own experience which demonstrate you have that skill. This is as much a help for you yourself as it is for a potential employer. If there is an employability module on offer, have another look at it and see if it could help you – or if it did help you and you didn't realise it at the time.

CHAPTER 3

Labour market information: analysis of what graduates do

This chapter is in two sections. The first section takes you through labour market information, labour market intelligence and labour market experience. It explains what each of the terms mean, and how all of them can work together to support you in focusing your jobsearch.

The second section is much longer, because it takes you through what real graduates actually went on to do in the first six months after completing their first degree. You won't work through the whole of this section, just focus in on your own subject discipline to see what people who did the same degree as you went on to do in their careers.

SECTION ONE

What is labour market information (LMI)?

Confusingly enough, LMI can stand for two things, both of them important for any jobseeker which includes, of course, the graduate jobseeker. LMI can refer either to labour market information, or to labour market intelligence. Labour here means simply to do with work, and Market here describes the interactions between employers who need labour (or workers, to put it another way) and employees (those who can supply that labour or undertake that work). For graduates, LMI is collected by subject discipline. So you can look at what graduates from a particular discipline actually went on to do once they had graduated. This chapter works through the arguments for making use of LMI, and then looks in turn at what graduates from 27 different degree disciplines went on to do.

 definition

Labour market information means everything to do with employers and workers. This includes statistical information on vacancies, redundancies, people moving in and out of unemployment and people moving in and out of employment.

Why do you need to know about LMI?

This may all seem rather technical and you may well be wondering why you need to know anything at all about LMI when all you want to do is get started on your brilliant career. Well, the reason you need to know about LMI is because you live in a world that responds to the inevitable flux and changes within the labour market and particularly within the graduate labour market. If you are blissfully unaware that demand is changing you may well be trying to chase a kind of job that simply no longer exists. You might then start to think that this is all your fault, that you'll never find your way through the labour market. However, if you know that the market is changing, you know that you need to adapt to the new reality. Also, if you can be clear about what exactly the demand is for, you can tailor your jobsearch to the jobs that are actually on offer right now, rather than chasing jobs that exist only in your dreams or in the memories of others who haven't kept up with how the job market has changed since their day – which could mean only a few years rather than decades ago.

 tip

If you understand what is happening in the graduate labour market, you can be smarter in your jobsearch.

Points of entry and points of leverage in the labour market

The two concepts of knowing where jobs are and knowing when to move in or out of a job or sector are also key elements of moving into and through the job market. Moving in being the 'point of entry' and moving on being the 'point of leverage'. Knowing that you have amassed skills that are in demand and that therefore the time is right either to take any job now or to move on from that entry-level job is also important. Thus, understanding the labour market means that you are making informed decisions and that you have some sense of direction in the real world.

 brilliant definitions

Point of **entry** means the first job you do to get into a particular area of the labour market. This could mean the graduate labour market, or the arts profession labour market or the labour market in Merseyside.

Point of **leverage** means that you have skills, knowledge, experience and know-how, which are in demand in the labour market, so you can use them to move from one job to another, or one occupational sector to another, normally to secure what you consider to be a better job.

Broaden your jobsearch horizons

Understanding the labour market can also help you to broaden your horizons: you will come across occupational sectors and jobs that you may not even have heard of, and you will see that people with a degree like yours have gone on to do a whole range of graduate jobs that you may never have considered. Thus, knowing what is happening in the job market will give you the courage to expand the range of jobs you are prepared to consider. It allows you to envisage yourself working in an occupational sector quite different from the one your original, limited outlook pointed you to. By keeping more options open, you increase your chances of securing graduate employment – even when more people are chasing fewer jobs. So now let's look at what you need to know to make sense of the labour market.

How LMI is collected

Quantitative and qualitative data

Labour market information simply means data collected on work; and includes data on job vacancies, employment, unemployment and employees. Labour market information can be either qualitative or quantitative.

Quantitative LMI is statistical and is often gathered by conducting a survey or taking a sample which is representative and can, therefore, reliably be generalised to offer conclusions. Quantitative LMI is often referred to as 'hard' data. It can be presented in spreadsheets or tables, or can be depicted as charts, graphs or maps.

Qualitative data are often gathered using research techniques such as focus groups or interviews, which can be in person or (in the case of interviews) done by phone. Qualitative data can be presented as case study or illustration. Filmed interviews of people talking about their experience of work can give you a powerful insight and real sense of immediacy (have a look at **www. careersbox.co.uk**). These approaches yield rich data, which can enhance our understanding of what the statistics seem to be telling us.

Geographical and sectoral territories

LMI is normally collected by territory. Territory can mean a geographical area, so LMI can be collected at a local, regional, national, European or even global level. Territory can also be defined by the kind of work that is done or by the kind of worker that does it, so we can collect statistical data by occupational sector, or by what kind of employers or by what kind of job. For these last two, there are agreed classifications so that comparisons can be easily made. The Employer classification is called the Standard Industrial Classification (SIC) and the Job classification is the Standard Occupational Classification (SOC).

Interrogating the data

Although it is tempting to take this kind of LMI at face value and trust it implicitly, the quality of the data can't be taken for granted and you need to be an intelligent consumer – more of which later. It can also be presented in reports that might be specialist by authorship (e.g. written by economists), specialist by readership (e.g. aimed at graduate jobseekers) or generalist (e.g. written by journalists and published in a newspaper for general readership).

Labour market intelligence

Labour market intelligence refers to the outcome of analysing labour market information, so it simply means taking the data (whether statistical, anecdotal or a combination of the two) and critically analysing them. Sometimes the data or the facts can simply 'speak for themselves' and there is no need to do anything more than present them, preferably in an accessible way. Other times it is helpful to look for what these data could be telling us: and so the analyst (or writer or presenter) tries to look for meaning in them. Obviously, meaning can be very subjective: the analysis might seek to present the data in the best possible light perhaps to encourage a slow job market, or to downplay emerging problems. We should also remember that statistics themselves are subjective: what is collected, from what sample population, at what time and for what purpose are just some of the parameters that are not given automatically but set for each individual survey or report. In fact, all labour market information and all labour market intelligence will have in it somewhere some element of subjectivity; so long as you are aware of this, you can approach LMI as an intelligent consumer, making your own mind up about what is presented to you, and deciding for yourself whether it is illuminating or helpful to you in your particular circumstances.

 brilliant definition

Labour market intelligence consists of either quantitative or qualitative data, or a combination of the two. It is often presented as statistics, tables or graphs. It may also include some written analysis or commentary which explains what the data show.

Labour market experience

Sometimes, labour market information can be anecdotal, where one person recounts a particular experience (their own or that of someone else). This can also be referred to as labour market experience. Anecdotal information can be very helpful in giving us a way into the statistical data, or offering a picture of lived experience. Getting a sense of what a particular job feels like to someone who has done it can really enhance the statistical data, and give us a much fuller understanding of what the data tell us, which is why we have used case studies throughout the book and why we suggest you have a look at some online films where people talk about their own experience of jobs within occupational sectors. However, there is a danger in generalising from anecdotal information: of assuming that because one person had a bad experience of a job then everybody will have an equally bad experience of that job. To generalise from anecdotal information is inappropriate: we can generalise only from data that are robust enough to sustain that process.

 brilliant definition

Labour market experience draws on the individual story. It offers powerful insight into what it feels like to do a given job, but can't be used for generalisation.

How to be an intelligent consumer of LMI

Part of your training as a graduate is to challenge what is taken for granted, to inquire and to reach your own conclusions. This applies equally to how you should approach LMI. There are a few key tests that you should run through when you come across labour market information in whatever form it is presented to you. Whether that's information from an employer, a newspaper report on what's happening to graduates in the job market, or what someone you know says about unemployment, job opportunities or transferable skills. The three key tests are for: currency, validity and fitness for purpose.

Currency: how up to date is the information?

If written or published, even if the article is pretty fresh, is there a date given for the data set that has been used as the base for the article? If someone is talking about an experience, how far back does it go? And how old do you think things have to be before they are questionable in their relevance to the here and now? Have things in the sector you are looking at changed much over the last few years or stayed pretty stable? Do you have a feel for the currency of the data: is it past its sell-by date or still fit for consumption? Although you need to go back several years (even decades) to identify a trend and, although there is, inevitably, a time lag between data collection and its publication, we wouldn't expect information to be much more than a couple of years old.

Validity: how reliable is the information?

Is the source reliable – and do you actually know what the source of the information is? If it is in print, does the article quote or refer to the source of the original data? If online, can you identify who either the author or the source is? Could there be any advantage for them in presenting a particular perspective – perhaps to back up a point they want to make or to present something in a good light? Could there be any 'spin' on this? Look at any footnotes – check if they explain any rounding up of figures or acknowledge that things have been left out. Omissions can be perfectly legitimate and even necessary (for example, when a sample size is too small to be of statistical significance), but this should be made clear. Is there any sense of presenting competing perspectives or alternative interpretations, or is the commentary rather fixed in its views?

Is the LMI fit for purpose?

Does the information or article tell you something you need to know? Is it helpful to you in getting you to think afresh? Perhaps it has helped you to examine what you yourself have taken for granted or assumed to be the case without really knowing what the basis for your assumptions is and therefore your own take on the issue. Look at the sample size and the composition of the sample: does it make sense to you? Ultimately, the question here is whether the LMI is relevant to you and what you are trying to do in the labour market. It may not seem immediately relevant; you may have to run these quick tests to work out if it helps you, or not.

 tip

Intelligent consumers check labour market information by asking these questions before taking action.

- **Currency**   Is this information sufficiently up to date?

- **Validity**   Is it reliable: is the source noted somewhere?

- **Relevance**   Is it telling me anything new or something I need to know?

It doesn't matter in what order you apply the tests and, to some extent, it doesn't even matter how rigorously you apply them. What matters is that you consider the LMI in front of you, you do your best to make sense of it, you interrogate your superficial impressions and you make an informed decision whether or not to take this particular nugget of LMI into account as you navigate your way into or around the graduate labour market.

How do we know what graduates actually do on completion of their degree?

Destinations of Leavers from Higher Education Institutions (DLHE)

One source of LMI passes all three of the key tests outlined here and we are going to make extensive use of it in this chapter. It is the annual *DLHE* report or, to give it its full title, *Destinations of Leavers from Higher Education Institutions*. The Higher Education Statistics Agency (HESA) collects information on what graduates are doing six months after completion of an undergraduate or foundation degree. First destinations cover: employment; training; further study, or a combination of these. They also include:

working overseas; not being available for employment; being unemployed or presumed to be unemployed.

Who is included in the data collection?

Data are collected from students who are domiciled in the UK and the EU: they don't include overseas students who are not normally resident in the UK. Students are invited to respond, via questionnaire, in the winter following the summer in which they graduated, which means that someone who graduated in Summer 2014 responds in December 2014. The destination data are published the following summer; so the responses of the class of 2014 are published as raw data in July 2015. The Higher Education Careers Services Unit (HECSU) and the Education Liaison Task Group of the Association of Graduate Careers Advisory Services (AGCAS) then work together with Prospects to write *What do graduates do? (WDGD)*. This is published annually in November. The most recent edition of *WDGD*, which uses data from those who graduated in the summer of 2014, was published in November 2015: this is the edition we have used.

What kind of jobs do graduates do?

Where students report that they are in employment, they are asked to give some more detail on the kind of job they are doing and the kind of employer they are working for. This allows the data to be classified for easy comparison across occupation and across sector. The *DLHE* data and the *WDGD* report give us a pretty accurate snapshot of what graduates go into as their first destination.

---

brilliant tip

Look at what other graduates with your degree have gone on to do and note where they have moved into an occupational sector that might seem far removed from the subject area you are studying. Remember that you are developing thinking, competence and transferable skills, so you can move around the labour market. Widening your jobsearch increases the number of jobs you can consider, thus increasing your chance of securing graduate employment.

Increase the sample size by completing your own DLHE data request

It is worth adding here that, the more respondents there are, the more comprehensive the sample set is. So if you are reading this as a final-year undergraduate, please respond to the questionnaire when you receive it a few months after your own graduation.

Not every degree subject is included in WDGD

WDGD is certainly pretty comprehensive in its coverage of undergraduate degrees. Some degree titles are grouped into a broader discipline category, for example Women's Studies is included in Sociology, and War Studies is included in History. For HND Foundation degrees, there is no distinction by discipline; rather the analysis is of the whole cohort of students who completed their Foundation degree or HND in that year, irrespective of the subject they studied. Data for biomedical degrees (Medicine, Nursing, Anatomy, Physiology and Pathology, Pharmacology, Toxicology and Pharmacy, Occupational Therapy, Physiotherapy and Teaching degrees) are published separately and can be accessed on the Graduate Prospects website (**www.prospects.ac.uk**).

Limitations of the DLHE survey

Although the destination data are very useful, the first destination survey does have its limitations. For example, we don't know *why* graduates choose these particular paths or went into these particular jobs. Nor do we know how long they are going to stay in their first destination. A graduate can be working in a bar every night, whilst making applications and going for job interviews all day, every day. Overnight, their employment status changes category: from 'Retail, catering, waiting and bar staff' to 'Legal, social and welfare professionals', but their first destination on graduating will, forever, be bar work. Also, in a sense, the report is backward looking: it tells us what has happened, but can't forecast how things might be in the future. Obviously, we can identify changes and, if those changes are consistent over a few years, we can even identify trends, which helps us make sense of what has happened, and can alert us to things changing in the future. But the *DLHE* survey doesn't pretend to be anything more than a clear snapshot of the first destination of UK domiciled students six months after they graduate.

Ensure you access current data

Although general trends are not likely to change significantly year on year, it is nevertheless important to check for currency. As there is inevitably a time lag between data collection and their analysis, publications can become dated and are regularly superseded. Online sources are more easily updated than printed versions, so do follow the leads below if you want to be sure you are up to the minute.

Graduate Prospects

This is the best point of reference for graduates, because that is what it specialises in and is set up to do. It addresses final-year undergraduates in particular, so don't just bookmark it – consult it.

UK Commission for Employment and Skills

Signposts expert and up-to-date articles on sector changes and general trends including, but not limited to, graduate entry.

Office for National Statistics (ONS)

Publishes a wide range of official statistics for the United Kingdom, including reports on the labour market in general, not just the graduate labour market. It also produces a regular bulletin called *Intelligence*. This includes analytical comment including, but not restricted to, the labour market. You can sign up for alerts when the latest edition is published.

Annual Survey of Hours and Earnings (ASHE)

This is also published by ONS. It gives overall population and trend data, which is helpful when you want to put graduate information in context against the wider, more general, labour market.

recap

- LMI can mean labour market information, i.e. data.

- LMI can mean labour market intelligence, i.e. data plus analysis.

- Labour market experience reflects lived experience of a particular job, and it can illuminate what the data tell us.

- Use your critical faculties when you come across LMI.

- Look at your own degree subject as well as some others.

- Point of entry means your first graduate job.

- Point of leverage is job changing once you have competencies.

SECTION 2

What do graduates do?

The next part follows the sequence used by *WDGD*, which comprises six broad categories of undergraduate study, plus all Foundation degree subjects. The groupings are as follows:

1   Science (Biology; Chemistry; Physical and Geographical Sciences; Physics; and Sports Science).

2   Mathematics, Computer Science and IT.

3   Engineering and Building Management (Architecture and Building; Civil Engineering; Electrical and Electronic Engineering; and Mechanical Engineering).

4   Social Sciences (Economics; Geography; Law; Politics; Psychology; and Sociology).

5   Arts, Creative Arts and Humanities (Fine Arts; Design; English; History; Media Studies; Languages; and Performing Arts).

6   Business and Administrative Studies (Finance and Accountancy; Business and Management; Hospitality, Leisure, Tourism and Transport; and Marketing).

7   HND Foundation degrees (all subjects studied at this level).

These broad categories are then broken down into degree subject. For example, Science comprises: Biology; Chemistry; Environmental; Physical Geographical & Terrestrial Sciences; Physics; and finally Sports Science. These headings in turn embrace quite a range of specialisms in congruent areas of study. Chemistry, for example, lists Inorganic Chemistry, Petrochemical Chemistry and Crystallography, to name but 3 of the 21 titles included.

For every degree subject, we start by setting out the *Range* of degree courses included. For some, the range of degrees is relatively limited, e.g. Accountancy. For others, the range is considerable, e.g. Performing Arts. For most subjects, it is really interesting to see the multiple perspectives that are possible within an over-arching subject area.

We then go on to report on the *Response rate and destination percentages*, so you can see how many students actually responded and, of these, what percentages went into employment, combined work and study, or went on to study in the UK or overseas. The categories also include the percentage of graduates unemployed at that point in time. The category 'other' covers those taking time out from the labour market, e.g. to travel. We always present these in the same order for ease of comparison. Graduates who combine working with studying are counted in both 'employment' and 'study' percentages, because they legitimately belong in each category. Therefore, the percentages do not necessarily add up to one hundred.

Finally, we look at *What occupational sectors did they go for?* where we drill into what kind of employment respondents from that discipline went on to do. This gives you a sense of what jobs were taken up, and what employers were recruiting. There are only a handful of examples for a response size of thousands, but it does help to illustrate the statistical data. Please note that, where necessary, we have followed the convention of rounding percentages up or down to one decimal point, because it makes the numbers a little easier to read. This means that sometimes the totals (for example, of the destination percentages) are slightly more or less than 100 per cent. Obviously, this doesn't alter the overall picture of what graduates do.

In a handful of cases, the total number of respondents is greater than the sum of female and male respondents. This can happen where someone sends a response, but doesn't specify their gender. Obviously, it is important to include such responses in the sample, although that does throw up this anomaly.

How to use this section

You can use this section to see what other people, doing the same kind of degree as you, have gone on to do. This can reassure you that you are not on your own in your chosen field. Or it can challenge and inspire you to think more widely in your jobsearch. It can also help you to counteract some of the uninformed advice (no doubt well-intentioned) that may be putting you off track. The most important benefit of this section is that you will end up better informed about labour market information in relation to your current field of study.

 dos and don'ts

Do

- ✔ check out what people on your degree course have actually gone on to do;
- ✔ think about broadening your jobsearch to include jobs you haven't thought about or maybe hadn't heard of before;
- ✔ think about points of entry and then points of leverage.

Don't

- ✗ rely on what other people remember from their day: things change, particularly in labour markets;
- ✗ worry that your job isn't a graduate or professional job; you can learn a great deal and use that for leverage;
- ✗ despair at gloomy headlines: graduates are still in demand and are still being employed, even if it takes time and effort.

1 Science

Five subject areas are included within Science, namely: Biology; Chemistry; Physical and Geographical Sciences; Physics; and Sports Science. Biology has more female than male students with Physics the reverse: here males out-number females by around 3:1. Sports Science is by far the biggest by student numbers. Physics, by contrast, is the smallest by student number. Sports Science also has the highest proportion of students going into employment, and Physics the highest proportion of students going on to higher degrees.

brilliant example

'I completed my undergraduate degree in Sport and Exercise Sciences. The department put a strong emphasis on how the theory we are taught can be and currently is being used within applied settings, by actively encouraging students to get their "hands dirty" and get out into the applied setting to get as much applied experience as possible. Several internships and placements were on offer for willing students to get involved in. I'm now employed as a performance analyst at a county cricket club and am enjoying working within one of my favoured sports, and learning how performance analysis is perceived and used within cricket. I think that my placements at Warrington, Liverpool FC and Stoke City FC and the skills and experience I have gained made my CV stand out. I would advise students to follow the advice I was given and get their "hands dirty" in as much applied experience as possible.'

Stuart, BSc (Hons) Sport and Exercise Sciences

1.1 Biology

Range

Biology degrees include specialisms within the discipline, such as Cell, Reproductive, Population Biology and Biometry. There are specialisms by context such as Freshwater, Marine Biology and Parasitology. Applied Biology, of course, and also Applied Cell Biology. Biodiversity and Ecology are also here.

Response rate and destination percentages

A total of 4,550 graduates responded, 80.8% of graduates in these disciplines. There were 2,650 female and 1,900 male respondents. Of these graduates, 53.2% were in UK employment, with a further 1.8% in overseas employment. 5.8% were combining work with studying. Added together, that makes 55% in employment. A total of 25.2% went on to study for a higher degree, which included PhD Biological Sciences, MSc Clinical Science and MRes Physiology and 11.7% progressed to a Postgraduate Qualification in Education, with another 8.6% taking on other further study. The total percentage of students studying was 25.2%, which is rather higher than the average across all degree disciplines. A further 6.0% came into the 'other' category, leaving 8.0% reporting unemployed.

What occupational sectors did they go for?

Of the employed graduates, 7.3% secured work as science professionals, including jobs such as a scientific officer with a banknote printer. Of course, many scientific research jobs will demand a higher degree, which is, in part, why a higher proportion of Biology students progress to higher education compared with all graduates. A further 16.3% went into other professional jobs, including business analyst with an energy company. Health professional jobs account for 1.9% of these graduates, and education professionals for another 4.3%, jobs here including Science teachers. Business and finance professionals absorbed 8.5% and included assistant tax adviser. Another 9.1% went into clerical and secretarial occupations, and 10.5% into other occupations. Retail, catering, waiting and bar staff took 20.2% of employed graduates.

1.2 Chemistry

Range

The range of Chemistry degrees reflects orientation within the discipline, including: Analytical; Biomolecular; Polymer; Structural; and Organic Chemistry. Degree title can also reflect application and/or sector, such as: Pharmaceutical; Petrochemical; Medicinal; Industrial and Colour Chemistry.

Response rate and destination percentages

A total of 3,005 graduates responded, 84.8% of graduates in these disciplines. There were 1,255 female and 1,750 male respondents. Of these graduates, 51.3% were in UK employment, with a further 1.4% in overseas employment. A total of 4.3% were combining work with studying. Added together, that makes 52.7% in employment. 31.1% went on to further study, which included MPhil/PhD Detection of Biological Warfare Agents, and 13% progressed to a Postgraduate Qualification in Education, with 4.5% taking on other further study. A further 4.5% came into the 'other' category, leaving 7.4% reporting unemployed.

What occupational sectors did they go for?

Roughly equal percentages of these Chemistry graduates went into two professional domains: 18.4% are classified as scientific, research, analysis and development professionals, and 19.0% as other professional and technical. The scientific professional jobs included pharmaceutical analyst in a laboratory. Then follows a tail of professional destinations: business and finance professionals claimed 14.6%, education professionals 5.3%, marketing, sales and administration took 6.1%, engineering professionals 2.7%, health and associate professionals 1.1%. 9.1% went into retail, catering, waiting and bar staff, with jobs here including visual merchandiser with Debenhams. Management jobs in commercial and public services accounted for 3.1%. Other occupations absorb 6.8%.

1.3 Physical and Geographical Sciences

Range

This section encompasses an interesting range of related scientific disciplines including: Physical and Maritime Geography, Geomorphology, Cartography and Geographical Information Systems, Meteorology, Climatology and Pollution Control.

Response rate and destination percentages

A total of 3,050 graduates responded, 81.6% of graduates in these disciplines. There were 1,440 female and 1,610 male respondents. Of these graduates, 58.1% were in UK employment, with a further 2.7% in overseas employment. A total of 5.9% were combining work with studying. Added together, that makes 60.8% in employment. 19.8% went on to further study, which included MSc Environmental Business Management and MBA

Construction and Real Estate. A surprising 25% of those opting for further study progressed to postgraduate qualifications in education. A further 7.4% came into the 'other' category, leaving 6.1% reporting unemployed.

What occupational sectors did they go for?

The biggest single destination was retail, catering, waiting and bar staff with 18.6% of all employed graduates from these disciplines. Other occupations accounted for a further 10.8% and other clerical occupations for 10.4%. The professional destinations did show the relevance of the discipline, as 12.6% went into other professions. Scientific professionals absorbed only 1.4% but included catastrophe analyst with an insurance company. Engineering professionals was of greater significance with 4.4% and 15.2% secured professional jobs in business and finance, including financial assistant for a County Council.

1.4 Physics

Range

With very few exceptions (Acoustics, Electromagnetism and Quantum Mechanics) the degrees included here have Physics firmly in the title: Maths and Theoretical Physics, Quantum and Computational Physics. The descriptor may well relate to the orientation by sector: Engineering, Chemical, Medical, Optical and Environmental Physics, for example.

Response rate and destination percentages

A total of 2,295 graduates responded, 84.3% of graduates in these disciplines. There were 495 female and 1,800 male respondents, putting the gender balance firmly with male students. Of these graduates, 44.9% were in UK employment, with a further 1.1% in overseas employment. Another 5.8% were combining work with studying. Added together, that makes 46% in employment. Overall, a lower proportion of students went on to study: 34.7% in all. Of these an impressive 80% progressed to higher degrees including PhD Astrophysics and MSc Physics. Of those in further study, 11.1% were taking teaching qualifications. A further 5.3% came into the 'other' category, leaving 8.2% believed to be unemployed.

What occupational sectors did they go for?

In terms of professional destinations, business and finance takes the greatest percentage, with 18.9%. Jobs here include tax professional with HMRC and analyst for Accenture. Scientific and engineering professions absorb 6.0% and 9.1% respectively, and include RAF officer and development engineer with Rolls Royce. Information technology and education professions take 18.9% and 7.4% respectively. Marketing, sales and advertising professionals account for 4.8% and arts, design, and media professionals a further 1.9%. Commercial and public service managers claimed 3.1%. Retail, catering, waiting and bar staff absorbed 7.5%.

1.5 Sports Science

Range

The range in Sports Science is not wide. It includes Exercise Science, Science in Health, Exercise and Sport and then a cluster of titles which indicate the application in practice: Conditioning, Development, Therapy and Rehabilitation.

Response rate and destination percentages

This is the biggest student body within the Science division, with a total of 8,630 graduates responding, 79.1% of graduates in these disciplines. There were 2,925 female and 5,705 male respondents. A high proportion, 67.6% of these graduates, were in UK employment, with a further 1.8% in overseas employment. A total of 7.6% were combining work with studying. Added together, that makes an impressive 69.4% in employment. A figure of 13.9% went on to further study, which included higher degrees in MSc Sports Performance and MSc Biomechanics. Of these, 39.3% progressed to teaching qualifications. A total of 4.7% came into the 'other' category, leaving only 4.3% reporting unemployed – an impressively low proportion.

What occupational sectors did they go for?

Sports jobs are dispersed across several occupational categories: 22.5% in other professions; 11.5% in childcare, health and education occupations; and 11.1% in other occupations. 8.5% went into education professions. There then follows a flurry of small percentages: 4.8% to health professions,

5.5% to business and finance professions, 4.8% to marketing, PR and sales professions. Although still modest, 4.5% went into commercial and public service management. Finally, 15.5% went into retail, catering, waiting and bar work, including customer assistant with Debenhams.

2 Mathematics, IT and Computing

There are two subject areas included in this short section. Mathematics stands alone, followed by Computer Science and IT. Both disciplines have more male than female students. In Maths the male to female ratio is not that much, certainly less than 2:1. But in Computer Science and IT the difference is very noticeable, nearer 5:1. For Maths students, the percentage going on to higher study is well above average. It is noticeable for Computing graduates that the vast majority of graduates secure professional jobs in IT.

---

brilliant example

'Maths is my passion: I really enjoyed my course, which taught me so much. I was also able to develop many other useful skills during my studies including communication, time management and organisation. As part of my course I got involved in a recycling project at a housing trust. I gained a lot of experience about the environment and associated issues. It also gave me an insight into full-time working and the pressures that go with it. I successfully gained a job working as a research assistant for an innovations company, which I really enjoy.'

Jo, BSc (Hons) Mathematics

2.1 Mathematics

Range

The range of degrees included is narrow. It includes Pure, Applied, Engineering and Industrial Mathematics, Mathematical Modelling, Numerical Method and Numerical Analysis.

Response rate and destination percentages

A total of 5,195 graduates responded, 82.9% of graduates in these disciplines. There were 2,100 female and 3,095 male respondents. Of these graduates, 54.4% were in UK employment, with a further 1.4% in overseas employment. 8.2% were combining work with studying. Added together, that makes 55.8% in employment. A total of 23.3% went on to further study, which included PhD Climate and Atmosphere Science and MSc Financial Mathematics. Of those in further study, 33.2% progressed to teaching qualifications. 5.0% came into the 'other' category, leaving 7.7% reporting unemployed.

What occupational sectors did they go for?

The majority destination, with 40.4%, is business, HR and financial professionals, where the numeracy of the degree discipline is directly relevant. Jobs here included financial risk analyst and trainee chartered accountant. Other professional destinations follow behind: 8.9% into education professions, including trainee Maths teacher and 10.8% into IT professional jobs, including software developer. Marketing, PR and sales professionals took 4.0%, with smaller percentages going into engineering and scientific professions: 1.8% and 0.8% respectively. In total, nearly 72% of jobs were in professional categories. In addition, 3.1% went into commercial or public service management. Retail, catering, waiting and bar staff absorbed 8.7% and included jobs such as jewellery assistant in a pawnbrokers. A total of 9% went into clerical, secretarial and numerical clerks, and 4.6% into the other occupations category.

2.2 Computer Science and IT

Range

A wide range of degree titles is included in the broad category of Computer Science and IT. It includes Computer Science, Computer Vision and Computer Architecture. There is a cluster around programming including Procedural and Declarative Programming. Systems Analysis is here, along with Systems Design and Systems Auditing. The final sub-set would include Artificial Intelligence, Speech and Language Processing, and Neural Computing.

Response rate and destination percentages

A total of 10,045 graduates responded, 79.2% of graduates in the discipline. There were 1,620 female and 8,425 male respondents, making these male-dominated subjects. Of these graduates, 74.6% were in UK employment, with a further 1.3% in overseas employment. 2.6% were combining work with studying. Added together, that makes 75.9% in employment. Only 6.7% went on to study: a low proportion explained perhaps by high employment. Degrees included MSc Computer Science and MSc Geospatial Analysis. A total of 15.1% progressed to teaching qualifications and 3.4% came into the 'other' category, leaving 11.4% reporting unemployed.

What occupational sectors did they go for?

Most of the graduates who secured employment got jobs as information technology professionals: a very pleasing 58.8%. The job titles reflect the degree titles mentioned earlier, and include: data analyst, BAE Systems and innovation coordinator in a hospital. There then follows quite a long tail of other professional sectors: 3.4% into arts, design and media professionals; 6.0% into business, HR and finance. Education professionals account for 1.5%, marketing, PR and sales professionals for another 2.9%, engineering professionals for 1.4%, commercial and public service management for 2.3%. A higher percentage, 5.9%, went into other occupations and 3.8% went into clerical and secretarial work. A significant percentage, some 10.2%, went into retail, catering, waiting and bar staff, including marketing assistant in a retail store. This should not obscure the fact that 76.8% of these graduates went into professional jobs.

3 Engineering and Building Management

There are four subject areas included here: Architecture and Building, Civil Engineering, Electrical and Electronic Engineering and Mechanical Engineering. Men outnumber women across the board, although the ratio varies, from more than 2:1 in Architecture and Building, through 6:1 in Civil Engineering to 10:1 in Mechanical Engineering. Employment rates in each of the disciplines is higher than the average across all graduates from all subjects. It is highest in Architecture and Building. Closer scrutiny of the destination data shows high proportions of graduates secure work as professionals in their field. This may be only to be expected, but should nonetheless be celebrated.

brilliant example

'From around my GSCEs onwards, I thought that I would enjoy a career in Civil Engineering. It seemed suited to my skills in Maths and Physics, particularly Mechanics, and Physical Geography. During my second year studying Civil Engineering I started to realise I had doubts about whether Civil Engineering would be right for me. I wondered if it might be possible to transfer . . . to another part of the engineering industry, one that had interested me for a long time: motorsport. I realised I would need a more relevant degree to appeal to potential employers (in motorsport). I also thought it crucial to finish my Masters in Civil Engineering . . . in case I needed to fall back on it, as this is a well-respected degree throughout the engineering sector. I'm now a systems engineer on a Formula One team.'

Oliver, MEng Civil Engineering, MSc Motorsport Engineering and Management

3.1 Architecture and Building

Range

Architecture degrees are here, of course: Architectural Design Theory and Architectural Technology. Building degrees too: Construction Management, Building Technology and Conservation of Buildings. Closely related is Surveying, with both Building and Quantity Surveying. Landscape is evident in Landscape Architecture, Studies and Design and a wider perspective brings in Planning, ranging from Regional, Rural and Urban to Housing and Transport Planning.

Response rate and destination percentages

A total of 5,830 graduates responded, 82.4% of graduates in these disciplines. There were 1,660 female and 4,170 male respondents. Of these graduates, 77.9% were in UK employment, with a further 1.8% in overseas employment. 6.2% were combining work with studying. Added together, that makes 79.7% in employment. A total of 5.4% went on to further study, which included MSc Real Estate. Of these, 2.1% progressed to teaching qualifications and 3.5% came into the 'other' category, leaving 5.3% reporting unemployed.

What occupational sectors did they go for?

The highest proportion, 44.7%, went into engineering and building professions, with 22.9% going into the category of 'other professionals', which includes architectural assistant, architectural technician, landscape architect and building surveyor. It makes absolute sense that the vast majority of employment is secured here. Employers include private architectural firms and public service providers. Commercial and public service managers accounted for a further 7.8% with jobs such as operational support manager for British Gas. There follows a long tail of small percentages going into a range of sectors, with only 4.9% into business and finance, and 4.8% into retail, catering, waiting and bar staff.

3.2 Civil Engineering

Range

Civil Engineering covers a wider range of degrees than might be expected. Civil and Structural Engineering degrees, of course, plus Surveying degrees including Engineering Surveying and Surveying Science. Transport Engineering, Urban Studies and Permanent Way Engineering are joined by Environmental Engineering, Energy Resources, Environmental Impact and Coastal Decay.

Response rate and destination percentages

A total of 2,540 graduates responded, 83.4% of graduates in these disciplines. There were 370 female and 2,170 male respondents. Of these graduates, 74.6% were in UK employment, with a further 2.0% in overseas employment. 5.0% were combining work with studying. Added together, that makes 76.6% in employment. A total of 8.7% went on to further study, which included MSc Transport Planning and Engineering. Of these, 4.1% progressed to teaching qualifications and 4.4% came into the 'other' category, leaving 5.3% reporting unemployed.

What occupational sectors did they go for?

An impressive 73.5% of graduates employed went into engineering and building professions with job titles including civil, structural and field engineer. Employers included Thames Water and Atkins. There was a long tail of named professional sectors (e.g. health, education), but in total nearly 86.5% of graduates from civil engineering went into professional destinations. That leaves a few smaller destinations: 4.4% into retail, catering, waiting and bar staff and 3.9% into 'other occupations'.

3.3 Electrical and Electronic Engineering

Range

The range is not very broad, including Electrical, Electrical Power, Electrical Power Generation and Electrical Power Distribution. Another cluster is degrees in Satellite, Telecommunications, Broadcast and Communications Engineering. Cybernetics, Robotics and Virtual Reality complete the list here.

Response rate and destination percentages

A total of 2,410 graduates responded, 80.1% of graduates in these disciplines. There were 230 female and 2,180 male respondents. Of these graduates, 72.2% were in UK employment, with a further 1.3% in overseas employment. 3.6% were combining work with studying. Added together, that makes 73.5% in employment. A total of 10.4% went on to further study for a higher degree, which included MSc Maritime Management. Of these, 4.2% progressed to teaching qualifications and 3.5% came into the 'other' category, leaving 8.9% reporting unemployed.

What occupational sectors did they go for?

Engineering professionals is the majority destination, with 38.8% working as systems or electrical engineers with employers such as Scottish Power and Network Rail. IT professions absorbed a further 19.1%, with jobs including software engineer. 3.6% went into management in the commercial or public sector. It is interesting to note that a greater proportion, 5.9%, came under arts, design and media professionals. Business and finance professions took 3.5%, 7.1% went into retail, catering, waiting and bar staff, including sales assistant with ASDA and 8.2% went into 'other occupations'.

3.4 Mechanical Engineering

Range

A range of specialism and sector is reflected in the degree titles included here: Road Vehicle, Automotive or Automobile Engineering; Rail Vehicle, Ship Propulsion, Marine and Offshore Engineering, Vibration, Acoustics, Fluid and, finally, Farm and Agriculture Engineering.

Response rate and destination percentages

A total of 3,470 graduates responded, 83.5% of graduates in these disciplines. There were 270 female and 3,200 male respondents, making Mechanical Engineering the most male-dominated of all the degree disciplines studied. Of these graduates, 73.4% were in UK employment, with a further 1.7% in overseas employment. 3.4% were combining work with studying. Added together, that makes 75.1% in employment. A total of 10.3% went on to further study, which included PhD Fluid Dynamics and MSc Subsea Engineering. 1.5% progressed to teaching qualifications and 4.2% came into the 'other' category, leaving 7.0% reporting unemployed.

What occupational sectors did they go for?

A very high proportion of these graduates (64.9%) secured engineering profession jobs with employers such as: Tata Steel, British Airways and Shell. 4.4% went into business and finance professions, including risk analyst with RBS. A further 3.4% opted for commercial and public sector management. There was a small tail of other professions at 7.7% and IT professionals at 2.2%. In total, 83.4% of these graduates secured professional jobs, impressively high and just behind Civil Engineering on this count.

4 Social Sciences

Social Sciences comprises six disciplines: Economics; Geography; Law; Politics; Psychology; and Sociology. Only Economics and Politics have more male than female graduates and this is most pronounced in Economics, where males outnumber females by roughly 3:1. The other four subjects all have a majority of female students. This is roughly 2:1 in Law, 3:1 in Sociology and over 4:1 in Psychology.

brilliant example

'Originally I had chosen to study Psychology with Counselling Skills as a time-filler. It was meant to be a hobby only, or, at the very most, something which would improve my knowledge, giving me a head-start when it came to becoming a counsellor. Instead it changed my view of psychology and counselling quite dramatically. This changed my career path from becoming a counsellor to a health psychologist. Now working as a health promotion specialist . . . I am able to take the lead on many areas and have a huge amount of independence. The job is quite special in that way.'

Christopher, BA (Hons) Psychology with Counselling Skills

4.1 Economics

Range

The range of degrees included as Economics is pretty restricted, and simply reflects the various aspects of the discipline: Microeconomics, Macroeconomics, Econometrics, Capitalism, Keynesianism, Monetarism. It also includes topic-related degree names: Political, Financial, International or Agricultural Economics.

Response rate and destination percentages

A total of 4,805 graduates responded, 79.9% of graduates in these disciplines. There were 1,325 female and 3,480 male respondents, making Economics one of only two degree disciplines within the Social Sciences where men outnumber women (the other being Politics). Of these graduates, 63.1% were in UK employment, with a further 2.2% in overseas employment. 8.0% were combining work with studying. Added together, that makes 65.3% in employment. A total of 13.3% went on to further study, which included MSc Public Administration and MSc Petroleum Energy, Economics and Finance. Of these, 5.3% progressed to teaching qualifications. 5.6% came into the 'other' category, leaving 7.7% reporting unemployed.

What occupational sectors did they go for?

More than half of economics graduates, 54.2%, secured employment as business, HR and financial professionals, working variously as accountant or assistant auditor with employers such as HMRC and Goldman Sachs. A smaller proportion was found in marketing, PR and sales professionals, some 9.8% employed here, for example, as software salesperson with IBM. A total of 2.7% secured professional jobs within the catch-all 'other professions', including as a shipbroker. Turning towards commercial and public sector managers, 5.5% found work. 8.4% went into other clerical, secretarial and numerical jobs and 7.3% went into retail, catering, waiting and bar staff.

4.2 Geography

Range

Geography degrees include Human and Social Geography, plus study by area, e.g. Europe, Australasia, Africa or the Americas. Study of Geography by topic includes Cultural, Historical, Political, Transport and Urban.

Response rate and destination percentages

A total of 2,355 graduates responded, 82.2% of all graduates in this category. As with most of the disciplines in Social Sciences, there were more female respondents than male respondents, but with 1,275 female and 1,080 male respondents, this makes Geography a balanced discipline in terms of female:male participation rates. Of these graduates, 60.4% were in UK employment, with a further 3.0% in overseas employment. A total of 17.8% were combining work with studying. Added together, that makes 63.4% in employment. A figure of 17.8% went on to further study, which included Masters in China and Globalisation and CIPS Diploma in Procurement. A quarter of those studying opted for teaching qualifications. A total of 7.4% came into the 'other' category, leaving 5.8% unemployed.

What occupational sectors did they go for?

In stark contrast to Economics, graduates in Geography go into a wide variety of occupations, some professional, others not. Business, HR and finance professionals is the biggest destination with 20.2% of employed graduates. A smaller proportion recurs approximately in two further occupational clusters.

Marketing, PR and sales account for 14.1% and include PR manager for a water company. A total of 13.9% went into retail, catering, waiting and bar staff, 10.5% went into other clerical and secretarial and 7.4% into other occupations. Other professions included a number of jobs where the subject discipline was clearly relevant, such as store location planner with Sainsbury's. Finally, education professionals took 4.9% and engineering and building professionals 4.3%.

4.3 Law

Range

The range of Law degrees is not extensive, but does include degrees in Torts and Jurisprudence, and in topic areas such as Property, Medical or Criminal Law. There are also degrees on Law within a defined area: Scottish; English; EU; or Comparative Law.

Response rate and destination percentages

The response rate was 76.0% with a total of 9,975 graduates responding. As with several other disciplines in this section, there were more female respondents than male respondents, with 6,290 female to 3,685 male respondents. Of these graduates, 51.6% were in UK employment, with a further 1.3% in overseas employment. 10.8% were combining work with studying. Added together, that makes 52.9% in employment. This relatively low employment rate is balanced by a relatively high study rate, which accounts for 26.3% of all respondents. This is because many Law graduates undertake the vocational training needed for legal practice, typically the Legal Practice courses for Solicitors and the Bar Professional Training for Barristers. Of those who study, about a third do professional training, with another third taking higher degrees. These included LLM Criminal Justice and LLM Oil and Gas Law. A total of 2.6% were studying for a teaching qualification and 4.6% came into the 'other' category, leaving 5.4% unemployed.

What occupational sectors did they go for?

Given that over a third of these respondents proceeded to further training on graduation, there are relatively modest percentages in the employment sectors. It is interesting to see 28.8% working as legal professionals, doing jobs such as CAB adviser and paralegal with various law firms. The relevance of the degree studied is evident in jobs such as legal secretary with a law firm and in-court adviser with a charity. A total of 12.7% went into business, HR and finance professional jobs, including tax inspector with HMRC and auditor in financial services. Commercial and public sector management accounted for 4.8% and other clerical, numerical and secretarial work accounted for a further 14.1%. Finally, 7.7% went into other occupations, and 14.5% into retail, catering, waiting and bar work.

4.4 Politics

Range

Politics courses include the study of politics in a given area such as the Commonwealth, the EU or simply International Politics. Courses also include the study of Political Systems and Theories in general or, in particular, for example, Fascism, Socialism or Anarchism. Courses can focus on the constitutional, including UK Government, Parliamentary Studies or Public Administration. War and Peace as a degree is also included here.

Response rate and destination percentages

A total of 4,690 graduates responded, a response rate of 76.8%. There were fewer female respondents than male respondents, with 2,000 female and 2,690 male respondents. Only Economics and Politics show this gender balance with males, in contrast with most of the disciplines in this section. 58.4% of these graduates were in UK employment, with a further 3.8% in overseas employment. 6.8% were combining work with studying. Added together, that makes 62.2% in employment. A total of 17.8% went on to further study, which included MSc International and European Politics and MA Broadcast Journalism. Of those studying, 7.9% progressed to teaching qualifications. 5.8% came into the 'other' category, leaving 7.3% believed to be unemployed.

What occupational sectors did they go for?

Politics graduates went into a wide range of professional and managerial jobs. 5.9% went into commercial and public sector management, securing employment in the Ministry of Defence and Majestic Wines. The biggest employment sector, at 20.8%, was business, HR and finance professions. A further 11.9% went into clerical, numerical and secretarial occupations and 8.3% were categorised as 'other occupations'. Marketing, PR and sales professions absorbed 15.7% of the employed graduates. Other professionals, at 7.1%, included assistant to a Member of Parliament and campaign organiser for a political party.

4.5 Psychology

Range

Psychology degrees include subjects that reflect the range of applications in practice: Clinical, Educational, Health and Occupational Psychology, and the particular focus given to one aspect of the overarching discipline, such as Cognitive, Developmental, Experimental or Social. Neuropsychology and Psychometrics are also included here.

Response rate and destination percentages

Psychology is the largest student population within Social Sciences (Law being the second) and, with a total of 11,455 graduates responding, their response rate was 77.4%. There were 9,240 female and 2,215 male respondents; along with most of the degree disciplines in this section, women are in the clear majority. Of these graduates, 62.5% were in UK employment, with a further 1.3% in overseas employment. 8.4% were combining work with studying. Added together, that makes 63.8% in employment. A total of 15.7% went on to further study, which included PhD Social Psychology and Masters in Psychology specialisms such as Organisational and Mental Health. Of those studying, 21.5% went on to teaching qualifications. 5.9% came into the 'other' category, leaving 6.2% reporting unemployed. It is interesting to note that, compared with other Social Sciences, a high proportion (16.6%) opt for part-time work.

What occupational sectors did they go for?

The British Psychological Society advises that only 15–20% of all those who graduate with a qualifying degree in Psychology will go on to become professional psychologists. Many of those professional postgraduate training courses demand relevant work experience before admission, so it could be that graduates in these occupations are working to meet that requirement. Childcare, health and education occupations took 16.9%, including teaching assistant. A similar proportion, 17.1%, took up retail, catering, waiting and bar work. A further 3.5% worked as health professionals, including assistant psychologist for the NHS. Legal, social and welfare professionals absorbed 13.5%, including support worker with an autism charity. A total of 4.2% were in other professions, 8.7% in business, HR and finance professions, 5.8% in marketing, PR and sales professions, 11.4% went into other clerical and 3.4% secured work in commercial and public service management, with jobs including operations manager with Royal Mail.

4.6 Sociology

Range

The range of courses included in Sociology is very wide indeed. It includes the sociology of science, of politics and of economics, the study of social theory, social hierarchy and of disability in society. Courses such as Men's Studies, Women's Studies or Gender Studies are here too, along with Applied Social Science.

Response rate and destination percentages

A total of 6,340 graduates responded, 74.8% of all graduates in this discipline. As in most of the Social Sciences, there were more female respondents than male respondents, with 4,700 female to 1,640 male respondents. Of these graduates, 68.7% were in UK employment, with a further 1.1% in overseas employment and 5.4% who were combining work with studying. Added together, that makes 69.8% in employment. A total of 11.4% went on to further study, which included PhD Sociology, MA Criminology and MSc City Planning. Of those studying, 27.7% took teaching qualifications. 5.8% came into the 'other' category, leaving 7.6% reporting unemployed.

What occupational sectors did they go for?

Sociology graduates go into a wide variety of occupations, some professional, others not. Retail, catering, waiting and bar staff is technically the biggest destination with 21.0%. Other occupations account for 10.6%. Clerical and secretarial occupations took 14.0% and a smaller proportion (11.7%) went into legal, social and welfare professions, including domestic violence adviser with Women's Aid. A total of 6.7% went into other professions, including work as a probation officer. Business, HR and finance professionals accounted for 8.6%. At 3.9% commercial and public service managers was a minority destination. A further 6.2% went into marketing, PR and sales professionals, and 2.8% into education professions.

5 Arts, Creative Arts and Humanities

Seven disciplines are included here, namely: Fine Arts; Design; English; History; Media Studies; Languages; and Performing Arts. From the respondents included in the sample, employment rates are highest in Design at 81.8%, followed by Media Studies at 78.0%.

You will notice that many graduates go into non-graduate jobs as their first destination; this year has seen a welcome decrease in retail, catering, waiting and bar work now accounting for anything from 13.9% of employed graduates from Languages to 24.1% in Media Studies. If it means anything, it means that these are just the first destinations, that graduates can use these jobs to develop skills and competence for leverage, that graduates might just enjoy this kind of work or that graduates might simply want to earn enough money to allow them to be creative – certainly the story of someone waiting on tables one day and being discovered the next has been a dream come true for more than one successful artist down the ages.

brilliant example

'After my first year at a London dance conservatoire, I chose to transfer my studies to university, in order to gain a more academic and theoretical knowledge of the performing arts world. Whilst being able to continue building on technique and performance quality through practical classes, the course also allowed me to take an in-depth look at current practitioners and newly emerging dance makers, whilst being pushed to take my particular research interest (dance in education) further and further at each step of the course. Since graduating, I have worked as a performer, choreographer and company manager on UK tours, danced on cruise ships, and have recently taken over as principal of two part-time theatre schools in London.'

Dan, BA (Hons) Performing Arts

5.1 Fine Arts

Range

There is a range of disciplines under the Fine Arts umbrella including: Painting; Printmaking; Illustration; and Sculpture. More theoretical courses are included, such as Fine Art Theory and Visual Communication.

Response rate and destination percentages.

A total of 2,990 graduates responded, 76.4% of graduates in these disciplines. There were 2,200 female and 790 male respondents. Of these graduates, 68.4% were in UK employment, with a further 1.8% in overseas employment. 4.9% were combining work with studying. There were 70.2% altogether in employment. A total of 10% went on to further study, which included MA Fine Art and MA Photography. Of those studying, 35.5% chose teaching qualifications. 7.0% came into the 'other' category, leaving 7.9% reporting unemployed.

What occupational sectors did they go for?

Of the graduates who went into employment, 27% went into arts, design and media professionals, the destinations here clearly reflecting the degrees studied: artist in residence in a primary school and art gallery consultant. Retail, catering, waiting and bar staff accounted for a further 25.4%. A total of 12.5% were classified as 'other occupations' and 7.4% went into other clerical and secretarial work. Other professional and technical destinations (16.7%) included marketing assistant in a hospice and online quality assessor with Google. Commercial and public sector management accounted for 4.1% and included department manager for a fashion retailer.

5.2 Design

Range

The design umbrella includes: Ceramics; Clothing; Fashion; Furniture; Graphics; and Industrial.

Response rates and destination percentages

A total of 11,030 graduates responded, 78.7% of graduates in these disciplines. There were 7,405 females and 3,625 males. Of these graduates, 79.7% were in UK employment, with a further 2.1% in overseas employment.

1.9% were combining work with studying and 81.8% secured employment. A total of 3.7% went on to further study, which included MSc Ceramics and MDes Design. Of those studying, 17.9% chose teaching qualifications. 4.8% came into the 'other' category, leaving 7.8% reporting unemployed.

What occupational sectors did they go for?

Of the graduates who went into employment, 41.1% went into arts, design and media professions. The destinations here clearly reflect the degrees studied: 3D designer in an advertising company, cabinet-making intern for a furniture maker and consultant designer with a DIY chain. Retail, catering, waiting and bar staff accounted for a further 19.6%, 8.7% were classified as 'other' occupations and 4.8% went into other clerical and secretarial work. Other professional and technical destinations (3%) included architectural assistant in an architect's firm. Commercial and public sector management accounted for a further 2.9% and business, HR and finance professionals took just 1.8%.

5.3 English

Range

Degree courses in English cover English Language (including English as a second language), English Literature (including literature written in English as a second language) or a combination of both. Literature can be studied by period, by author, or by topic.

Response rate and destination percentages

A total of 9,785 graduates responded, 78.2% of all graduates in this category. As with every other discipline in this section, there were more female respondents than male respondents, with 7,245 female to 2,540 male respondents. With a female:male ratio of almost 3:1, English and Fine Arts are the most gender imbalanced disciplines in this broad sector. Of these graduates, 59.4% were in UK employment, with a further 2.5% in overseas employment. 7.6% were combining work with studying. Added together, that makes 61.9% in employment. A total of 18.1% went on to further study in the UK. Higher degrees included MAs in Creative Writing and English Language. Of those studying, 33.7% chose teaching qualifications. 5.8% came into the 'other' category, leaving 6.6% reporting unemployed.

What occupational sectors did they go for?

The biggest single employment area is retail, catering, waiting and bar staff, at 19.3%. Next is clerical, numerical and secretarial occupations accounting for a further 14.1%, including here work as a charity administrator. Turning to professional jobs, 8.0% went into education. Commercial and public management took 3.4%, and included a pub manager. A total of 13.9% went into marketing, PR and sales professions, with jobs such as marketing coordinator for a student union and 8.7% went into art, design and media professions, including copy editor for a newspaper. Business, HR and finance professions took 7.6% of those employed, 8.5% chose childcare, health and education occupations, and 3.2% went into other professions.

5.4 History

Range

History can be studied by period (e.g. Medieval, Ancient or Modern), by area (e.g. Welsh, Russian or New Zealand) or by topics such as Military History, Economic History, Social or Oral History.

Response rate and destination percentages

A total of 9,270 graduates responded, 79.6% of all graduates in this category. As with every other discipline in this section, there were more female respondents than male respondents, with 4,775 female and 4,490 male respondents. This makes History (along with Media Studies) the more balanced disciplines in terms of female:male participation rates. Of these graduates, 57.4% were in UK employment, with a further 2.5% in overseas employment. 6.8% were combining work with studying. Added together, that makes 59.9% in employment. A total of 20% went on to further study; higher degrees included MA Journalism and MSc Cultural Anthropology. Of those studying, 19.2% opted for teaching qualifications. 6.8% came into the 'other' category, leaving 6.6% unemployed.

What occupational sectors did they go for?

History graduates went into a wide range of professional jobs: 4.6% went into commercial and public sector management and 14.2% opted for business, HR and financial professions, with employers here including JP Morgan, PWC,

KPMG and Deloitte. Other professions, at 5.1%, included being a civil servant with DWP. A small proportion, 3.8%, secured employment as arts, design and media professionals, jobs here including broadcast assistant at the BBC. The biggest employment sector, at 19.1%, was retail, catering, waiting and bar work, followed by 14.6% in clerical, secretarial and numerical occupations. A total of 10.2% of employed graduates found work within other occupations.

5.5 Media Studies

Range

The range of courses within Media Studies includes: Broadcasting; Film Production; Radio Production; and both TV and Screen Production. The focus of other courses is more towards what might be called the infrastructure behind the media production, including Electronic Media and Media Technology. A final segment within the subject area is degrees that take a critical overview through the study of: Film; Media; Culture; TV; Radio; and Communication. Typically, the degree title would be Media Studies.

Response rate and destination percentages

A total of 4,735 graduates responded, 75.9% of all graduates in this category. There were marginally more female respondents than male respondents: 2,460 female and 2,275 male respondents. Of these graduates, 76.7% were in UK employment, with a further 1.3% in overseas employment. 2.4% were combining work with studying. Added together, that makes 78% in employment. A total of 5.3% went on to further study, which included MAs in Film and Scriptwriting. Of those studying, 19% opted for teaching qualifications. 4.6% came into the 'other' category, leaving 9.7% believed to be unemployed.

What occupational sectors did they go for?

At first glance, seeing 24.1% of graduates in this subject area going into jobs in retail, catering, waiting and bar staff might confirm the idea that these degrees don't necessarily lead to graduate-level jobs. But remember that the data looks only at the first job on graduation, and remember too that many such graduates may be using their wages in this occupational sector to support themselves whilst working on breaking into their chosen field. If they do, they follow in the footsteps of many fellow graduates, as 21.5% secured professional jobs in arts, design and media. Jobs included producer at an Internet radio station, editorial assistant in a publishing company and freelance sound engineer. A total of 14.7% found a profession in marketing, PR and sales, including communications assistant for the NHS, 3.5% went into commercial and public sector management roles and a relatively small proportion (4.3%) went into business and accounting professions.

5.6 Languages

Range

The range of languages includes the more familiar, e.g. French, the more exotic, e.g. African, and the more unexpected, e.g. both Cornish and Manx. As well as the study of foreign languages, the study of language itself is included, e.g. Phonetics or Phonology. It also includes the appreciation of what language can do, e.g. Latin Literature in Translation.

Response rate and destination percentages

A total of 7,315 graduates responded, some 79.8% of all graduates in this category. There were more than twice the number of female respondents than male respondents: 4,985 female to 2,330 male respondents. Of these graduates, 52.3% were in UK employment, with a further 10.1% in overseas employment. 6.2% were combining work with studying. Added together, that makes 62.4% employed. A total of 18% went on to further study, which included MAs in Translation and in European Studies. Of those studying, 24.4% opted for teaching qualifications. A figure of 7.0% came into the 'other' category, leaving 6.4% believed to be unemployed. The overseas employment rate, at 10.1%, is far and away the highest percentage of all degree disciplines. Could it be a case of 'have languages, will travel'?

What occupational sectors did they go for?

Looking more closely at those graduates who secured employment, the biggest proportion (17.1%) became business, HR and finance professionals, with marketing, PR and sales professionals just behind at 16.1%. Jobs in these categories included accountant with Grant Thornton and sales support executive in a logistics company. Arts, design and media professionals accounted for 6.6% and included European content editor with a news agency and foreign rights assistant with a travel publisher. Managers accounted for 4.2% and included an area manager for Aldi. Retail, catering, waiting and bar staff absorbed 13.9%.

5.7 Performing Arts

Range

It will come as no surprise that many of the degree disciplines included here cover performance: Acting; Dance; Musicianship or Performing; and Performing for the Theatre. There is another cluster of named degrees where the focus is on the creative input to a performance as a whole. These include: Directing for Theatre; Choreography; Stage Design; Theatre Design; Wardrobe Design and Theatrical Make-up. The final grouping focuses on the critical study of one or more of the performing arts within its context and history, namely History of Dance; History of Music; Musical Instrument History, and Theatre Studies.

Response rate and destination percentages

A total of 9,665 graduates responded, some 77.6% of all graduates in this category. There were more female respondents than male respondents: 5,695 female and 3,970 male respondents. Of these graduates, 71.4% were in UK employment, with a further 2.1% in overseas employment. 5.8% were combining work with studying. Added together, that makes 73.5% in employment. A total of 10.9% went on to further study, which included MA Arts Management and MA Directing. Of those studying, 31.5% opted for teaching qualifications. 4.1% came into the 'other' category, leaving 5.7% believed to be unemployed.

What occupational sectors did they go for?

A satisfying 29.9% of these graduates secured work as professionals in the fields of art, design and media. Individual destinations included working as a self-employed vocalist. A total of 21.5% went into retail and catering, a further 9.6% went into 'other occupations', and 7.6% into other clerical and secretarial occupations. 7.5% found work as education professionals. Other professions, at 1.8%, was a minority destination.

6 Business and Administrative Studies

There are four subject areas included in this section, namely Finance and Accountancy, Business and Management, Hospitality, Leisure, Tourism and Transport and Marketing. Compared with average employment rates for all graduates covering the full spectrum of degree courses, employment rates in two of these disciplines are considerably higher, at 81.5%, compared with 71.2% across all degree subjects. For the most part, there is a clear relationship between the subject studied and the destination by occupational sector, e.g. 54.3% of the Finance and Accountancy graduates who reported finding employment went into business and finance professions, many as accountants. Beyond the predictable destinations there is a huge variety of occupations, though small percentages in each domain. The gender balance across the four areas is interesting: in Finance and Accountancy there are more males than females; in Marketing there are marginally more females than males, and in Business and Management it is pretty evenly balanced, with males tipping the balance by a margin of about 20%. In marked contrast, there are twice as many females as males in Hospitality, Leisure, Tourism and Transport.

 example

'I thoroughly enjoyed my course; it combined both the theory and practical elements of the subject with lecturers that have both academic excellence and industry experience. A highlight for me was the work-based learning module – I found the exposure to the "real world" invaluable. Following graduation I used the confidence I gained to do the stereotypical post-university student activity: travelling. After seeing some of the sights the world had to offer, the job market was my destination. I secured a position with one of the world's biggest banks on their executive management graduate scheme, aimed at creating the next generation of company leaders.'

Phil, BA (Hons) Business Studies

6.1 Finance and Accountancy

Range

The range here is not extensive. Beyond Accountancy and Accounting, there are professional divisions including Cost and Management Accounting, and Public Accounting. Other specialisms include Book-keeping, Auditing of Accounts, Financial Reporting and Accounting Theory.

Response rate and destination percentages

A total of 5,860 graduates responded, 78.8% of all graduates in this category. There were fewer female respondents than male respondents: 2,375 female to 3,480 male respondents. Of these graduates, 69.5% were in UK employment, with a further 1.4% in overseas employment. 12.9% were combining work with studying. Added together, that makes 70.9% in employment. A total of 6.9% went on to further study, which included MSc Accounting and Finance and professional qualifications ACA, ACCA, CIMA and ICAEW. Of those studying, 7.5% opted for teaching qualifications. 4.2% came into the 'other' category, leaving 8.6% believed to be unemployed.

What occupational sectors did they go for?

As could be expected, a very high proportion (54.3%) of these employed graduates secured employment as business and financial professionals. Job titles included trainee management accountant, trainee actuary and tax adviser. Employers included Deloitte and Rolls Royce. Another 19.1% became numerical clerks and cashiers; while these were not graduate jobs, they would, nonetheless, provide valuable experience for graduates to move into a trainee professional role in due course. A further 4% went into commercial and public sector management, and 3.5% into the marketing, PR and sales professions. A total of 8.9% went into retail, catering, waiting and bar occupations and 4.6% fell into the catch-all category of 'other occupations'.

6.2 Business and Management

Range

This grouping spans Business Studies degrees, including European and International Business Studies. Management degrees include Management Studies and Management Techniques, followed by a spectrum of management specialisms and sectors: Change; Creative; Strategic; Domestic; Land; Project; Property; and Retail. Valuation and Auctioneering caters for more of a niche market.

Response rate and destination percentages

A total of 15,790 graduates responded, 76.3% of all graduates in this category. There were fewer female respondents than male respondents, with 7,155 females and 8,635 males. Of these graduates, 73.8% were in UK employment, with a further 2.1% in overseas employment. 4.9% were combining work with studying. Added together, that makes 75.9% in employment. A total of 6.0% went on to further study, which included MSc Organisational Behaviour and MBA. Of those opting for study, 10.6% chose educational qualifications. 5.5% came into the 'other' category, leaving 7.6% believed to be unemployed.

What occupational sectors did they go for?

A high proportion of Business and Management graduates found employment as either business, HR and financial professionals (23.7%) or marketing, PR and sales professionals (20.0%). Jobs included finance manager and project manager with Network Rail. A further 11.2% went into commercial and public sector management as, for example, marketing manager with a hotel chain. Clerical and secretarial occupations took a further 12.4%. A total of 12.2% went into retail, waiting, catering and bar staff, with 7.4% going into other occupations, including ride operator in a leisure park.

6.3 Hospitality, Leisure, Tourism and Transport

Range

The range of degrees included is explained in the title of this section, namely Hospitality, Leisure, Tourism and Transport.

Response rate and destination percentages

A total of 4,235 graduates responded, 76.3% of all graduates in this category. There were twice as many female as male respondents, with 2,830 females to 1,405 males. Of these graduates, 77.8% were in UK employment, with a further 3.2% in overseas employment. 2.6% were combining work with studying. The total in employment was 81%. A total of 3.5% went into further study, which included MA Conservation Management. Of those choosing to study, 19.9% opted for teaching qualifications. There were 6.5% in the 'other' category and 6.4% unemployed.

What occupational sectors did they go for?

The most common employment destination for these graduates was marketing, PR and sales professionals, which accounted for 25.2% and included an events duty manager in a national museum. The 'other professionals' group included a range of interesting and relevant jobs, namely travel adviser with a holiday company, a yield executive for British Airways and an adventure training instructor in the Army. A significant proportion (16.5%) went into retail, catering, waiting and bar staff, followed by 15.9% into 'other occupations'.

6.4 Marketing

Range

The range of degrees included is not wide, comprising Marketing, International Marketing and Market Research, also: Advertising; Promotion and Advertising; Sponsorship; Corporate Image; Sales Management; and Distribution.

Response rate and destination percentages

A total of 3,295 graduates responded, 76.4% of all graduates in this category. There were more female respondents than male respondents, with 1,960 females to 1,335 males. Of these graduates, 80.4% were in UK employment, with a further 1.9% in overseas employment. 2.3% were combining work with studying. Added together, that makes 82.3% in employment. A total of 2.8% went on to further study, which included MSc in Management with Marketing and in Insurance and Risk Management and Communication. Of those studying, 13% opted for teaching qualifications. 6.2% came into the 'other' category, leaving 6.1% believed to be unemployed.

What occupational sectors did they go for?

The most common employment destination for marketing graduates was marketing, PR and sales professionals, which accounted for 49.5% of the employed graduates, with employers ranging from a hotel chain to a professional body. A total of 5.4% went into commercial and public sector management. Business, HR and finance professions took another 8.9%, including graduate analyst with Barclays. Other clerical jobs accounted for 8.9% and 6.3% went into 'other occupations', including a soldier. A significant proportion (13.8%) went into retail, waiting, catering and bar staff.

7 Foundation degrees (all subjects studied at this level)

Defining characteristics of a Foundation degree

Foundation degrees were introduced in 2001. Although recognised as a qualification in its own right, a Foundation degree is designed to make it easy to lead on to an Honours degree. This means that a successful graduate from a Foundation degree may progress to level three (the final year for students studying full-time) and graduate in due course with Honours. Foundation degrees were intended to combine work-based learning with degree-level study and so include significant amounts of work-based learning. Students successfully completing HND courses are included as they follow a similar learning pathway. It is hardly surprising that the destinations data show roughly equal proportions of students (a) studying for their first degree, and (b) working full-time. Destinations data are collected for all Foundation degree and HND students but are not disaggregated by subject discipline.

 example

'As well as the huge variety of academic knowledge I gained on my Foundation degree, I also made a lot of personal developments which have really helped boost my confidence. I thoroughly enjoyed a work-based placement, learning a lot about the skills needed when working with animals, and experiencing the different issues that arise. My current role involves working with animals and continuing my learning of the technical side of animal management. I really enjoy my current role and look forward to continuing to work with animals and continuing my professional development.'

Jessica, FdSc, Animal Management

Response rate and destination percentages

There were 14,200 responses, 76.5% of all qualifiers in this category. There were more female respondents than male respondents, with 8,355 females to 5,845 males. Of these graduates, 39.3% were in UK employment, with only 0.7% in overseas employment. A total of 22.3% were combining work with studying. Added together, that makes 40% in employment. 2.5% come into the catch-all 'other' category. Only 2.2% were unemployed and 30.2% went on to study for a Bachelor's degree. Degree courses included Business Studies and Social Work.

What occupational sectors did they go for?

Because the destination data are collected from the full range of Foundation degree and HND courses studied, the destination occupations cover an extremely wide range of occupational sectors. Childcare, health and education occupations absorbed 21.7% of these graduates, with a further 10.1% going into health professions.

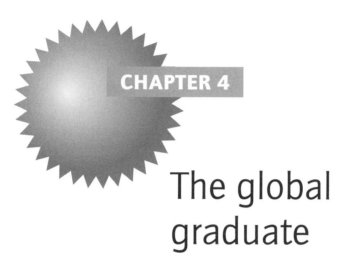

CHAPTER 4

The global graduate

This chapter picks up on the earlier theme of broadening your horizons, first mentioned in Chapter 2, which suggested keeping an open mind and looking at the whole range of jobs and career paths undertaken by other students who have graduated in your discipline (which is exactly what Chapter 3 does). As the title indicates, one way to broaden your horizons is to consider working or studying overseas, and this chapter will help you to think it through, whether you are setting your sights on global leadership of a multinational organisation, or just wanting to take off on your travels.

The chapter will consider what the demand is for the global graduate and how employer and employee both stand to gain. We look at where you can find opportunities, and cover some of the practicalities involved in travelling and living abroad, drawing on brilliant case studies to show how others have fared overseas. Crucially, we show you how to frame your own overseas experience in terms of adding value to your skillset and mindset, even if that was the last thing on your mind when you headed off, passport in hand. So whether you're working as a cleaner in a hostel in South America or as a high flier for a multinational, whether you're about to head off or even if you are reading this now you're back home, this chapter has something for you.

Demand for global graduates

The concept of supply and demand is an important one for the graduate jobseeker. Chapter 2 explains it in detail but all you need to know here is that you (as a graduate looking for work) are the supply and it is the employers who are the demand. So let's look at the demand for global graduates.

Employment overseas as graduate choice

The latest published figures confirm that overseas employment is very much a minority destination, accounting for only 3.4% of all graduates across all disciplines. Although that is a very small proportion, it is interesting that this proportion has increased in the last few years, which means more UK domiciled graduates have secured work outside of the UK than before. Roughly four in ten went to Europe, about two in ten went to the Far East and only one in ten went to North America.

Underneath this overall figure are different types of overseas employment, which are likely to include both graduate and non-graduate work. Graduate level entry could be either to a UK multinational company (e.g. Tesco) which then sends the employee to work overseas as part of its international operations, or where a multinational company based outside the UK (e.g. BNP Paribas) takes on a UK graduate and sends them to work as part of its operations which are based outside the UK. Or a graduate might simply seek out graduate work in an overseas location, perhaps to gain job-specific experience, as you will see from our brilliant examples. A graduate may well accept non-graduate work because working overseas is their key driver and the nature of the work is of less importance to them at that time in their career.

Although nobody can predict the future labour market with certainty, it is entirely possible to use economic modelling to get a good sense of how things might turn out over the next few years. Research into future demand across the European Union indicates that between now and the end of the decade, demand for managers, professionals and associate professionals is likely to increase – and these jobs are firmly at graduate level. The same research expects an increase in the employment rates of highly qualified workers within Europe. We need to be cautious here, because this could mean that highly qualified workers (which of course includes graduates) are taking jobs which may not necessarily be at graduate level. Of course that does not mean a graduate stays forever in a non-graduate job; they could easily use the experience of working overseas to develop the skillset and mindset required of a global graduate.

Specific demand for 'global graduates'

Increasing globalisation and internationalisation of business enterprise and organisations is starting to create a demand for a global graduate. Here's one definition: 'A global graduate is equipped with the skills and competence to succeed in a global marketplace and enable them to perhaps one day become a global leader of a multinational organisation' (CIHE, 2011). Global graduates in this context need to demonstrate that they have all the transferable skills (discussed in full in Chapter 2) but particularly teamwork, communication, resilience and self-management. If we picture a team of employees pulled together from the far reaches of a global organisation for a specific task, then think through what skills they need to work effectively, teamwork and effective communication would of course be top of the list. Resilience and self-management are also going to be in demand for the individuals in that team, because they will be dealing with the new and the unfamiliar, and they are going to have to get on with the job – and with fellow workers.

Multinationals are big organisations and they demand a great deal from their employees, which is why the skillset has to be at high levels; not surprisingly, the multinationals want to attract and retain highly qualified staff so these jobs can be very well paid. Clearly, not everyone is going to fit that specification, and not everyone is aiming for that career goal. Nevertheless, the global skillset is prized by all employers with global connections, not just the big transnationals, which means it is worth considering how you can enhance your total skillset through overseas experience.

Employment which demands working abroad

For some people, their career goal is to take up a role which will, by definition, involve working abroad. Examples include teaching English abroad, working for the European Union, or simply working in the profession for which they have been trained, but in another country. A growing number of people are choosing to work in international development, an interest that may start through volunteering and develop into a paid role. Our next brilliant example, Rachel, spent half of the second year of her degree as an English language assistant in Réunion and Madagascar. She returned to Madagascar as a volunteer soon after graduation, working on building and reforestation projects. After a spell back home to earn some money, she returned to Madagascar, and she continues her story.

 example

'I led a community health team in a remote region. I did a lot of translating as I was the only French speaker . . . I followed an ecology course as an independent student, being taught by non-government organisation (NGO) professionals . . . on my return to the UK I applied to an international relief and rehabilitation organisation. After a week-long assessment process, I was offered my present post in the Democratic Republic of Congo. I work in French every day, working in medical logistics.'

Rachel, BA (Hons) French and International Development Studies

Demand for language proficiency

For many people, over and above the desire to travel, learning a language is a big draw. Even language students who have studied a specific language to a high level want to deepen their proficiency and immerse themselves in the relevant culture. There is no doubt that learning a language (even at the most rudimentary level) requires you to see things differently and as such increases your cultural agility and sensitivity. But how highly do employers actually value language proficiency?

Employers canvassed by the Confederation of British Industry (CBI, 2011) for their opinion on key issues to do with education and skills reported some concerns about finding people with appropriate skills levels to fill their professional and managerial jobs in the future. This is encouraging for graduates aspiring to such jobs, provided they are prepared to develop their skills base.

As a population, the British are not known for their language ability and the prevalence of English as a common language in business may well have contributed to this. But that does not mean language proficiency is not needed. When asked specifically about the demand for foreign languages as part of the desired skillset, only 27% of the employers in the CBI survey said they had no need for languages; which means 73% do have a need for languages at some level. Only 8% of employers required language fluency. This is a small proportion but a high skill demand because fluency assumes mastery of spoken and written language, which requires constant upkeep and updating.

Even if your language levels are less than perfect, they are still a useful addition to your skillset; employers see their value in making new contacts and building relationships, and of course for international working. There is one final, very important point to grasp about language ability: although it adds value to a skillset, just on its own it offers very little.

brilliant example

'Working at the anti-landmine charity as a translator, interpreter and administrator was a significant learning experience . . . rewarding and challenging in equal measure. (But) I felt I wasn't really helping as much as I had hoped and with my lack of medical, psychological or sociological knowledge it seemed to me I didn't have a place in a charity.'

Claire, BA (Hons) Modern Languages (Arabic and Spanish),
MA International Journalism

brilliant example

'I also thought I was always going to get somewhere with the sheer intellectual kudos of being able to speak foreign languages. It might have been useful if someone had encouraged me to see the merits of business and to appreciate the interesting aspects of jobs that may seem quite boring at first glance. But I was far too concerned with analysing French Occupation literature and learning vocabulary to worry about such piffling things at the time!'

Simon, BA (Hons) French and German, MA Translating

Looking at travel from the employer's perspective

Employers value the transferable skills you will develop abroad

Once you're putting your travels behind you and are applying for work or postgraduate study, it is not about where you went and what you saw: it is about how you expanded your professional repertoire and how you can apply what you learned on your travels to your new work situation. It is highly likely that you develop valuable transferable skills through your overseas experience. Chapter 2 takes a detailed look at what transferable skills are, but the most likely skills you will develop as a direct result of your overseas experience are:

- **Self-management:** you will have learnt more about yourself, about how you handle stress and being out of the familiar, or being out of your comfort zone. You may also have had time to think through what is important to you in your life and therefore in your career.

- **Problem solving:** no doubt your overseas experience threw up challenges and problems that you had to solve. Even relatively simple challenges inherent in travel (planning journeys, making connections, getting to the right place at the right time) will make you think through what you are doing and how you are doing it. You may well have found yourself dealing with the unfamiliar and perhaps the unexpected; this in turn demands you find a way through problems.

- **Resilience:** this is the capacity to keep going even when the going gets tough. Living, working, studying and travelling overseas can all be delightful, but can also be challenging. Resilience is how you handle yourself when things seem to be relentlessly challenging. This calls for hope, optimism and being prepared to re-frame things mentally.

- **Foreign languages:** frankly, if you come back from an overseas experience with absolutely zero development in your language ability, that's disappointing. Even if you have mastered nothing but very basic language (greetings, thanks, requests) you will have had the valuable experience of realising how limited you are without language. And for many, the overseas experience allows you to develop fluency and understanding of the language in question and, through that, to develop an appreciation of that country's culture and customs.

Employers value subject-specific skills

Our next brilliant example is interesting because she already has a job, as a lecturer in animal management at a college of further education. She is travelling in order to enrich her subject knowledge.

 example

'During the summer I plan to travel to Africa to work on an animal conservation project. I am so excited! I look forward to visiting this extraordinary country and working with fellow conservation lovers, caring for wild animals and helping to maintain their environment. I can put my passion into practice and continue to learn in breathtaking surroundings with some of the most magnificent animals.'

Katie, BSc (Hons) Animal Behaviour and Welfare

What opportunities are there abroad?

Erasmus+: short-term study abroad as part of your degree

Erasmus+ is arguably the best-known university exchange programme: over one million students have participated in the last 20 years. Under the Erasmus+ scheme, students spend at least one semester studying in a different university in another country. The scheme has operated in at least 28 countries across the European Union (EU) and Switzerland and has expanded beyond the EU to other countries all over the world under the Erasmus Mundus scheme.

Erasmus+ eligibility requirements

In order to participate, you must be: enrolled as a student (undergraduate, postgraduate or doctoral); eligible to participate (which means broadly speaking that you should have the right to study in the EU); and your home university (here in the UK) must have a bilateral agreement with the host university (overseas). Your course tutor would know if a bilateral agreement with another university is already in place for the course you are on. Your own department might also have some information, but do look both at departmental and university level for the fullest possible information. Even if nothing is in place for your course, your university might already have a bilateral agreement with another university for other courses, and it could be possible for your subject simply to be added to that bilateral agreement.

So if you are interested, the best place to start is the international office or possibly the Erasmus[+] office in your own university. They should be able to advise you on what you can study where, and whether you can apply for a grant. Of course, what you make of those opportunities, and how you transfer your learning to your brilliant jobsearch is very much up to you. Most of what we discuss in this chapter would apply to people taking part in an Erasmus[+] programme: studying abroad gives you a unique opportunity to learn another language, to learn about another culture and to broaden your outlook.

Work experience as part of your degree

Some courses, especially language degrees, include a chance to spend a year working abroad in a role which will complement the academic content of the course, for example as an English language assistant in a school or college. Others may offer a shorter period of time – the kind of experience Joanne talks about.

 example

'One of the modules I undertook on my course was called experiential learning. I had the opportunity to work in Romania, delivering drama workshops in communities and schools there. This opened my eyes to all sorts of valuable experiences and taught me so much about education in another country.'

Joanne, BA (Hons) Drama and Theatre Studies

Vacation work while you are a student

Most students need to work in the summer vacation, so why not think about working abroad? There are useful reference books on the subject which you will find in your university careers service or library, and some employers come onto campus to recruit.

 example

'The university careers team were instrumental in helping me secure a vacation job coaching football in the USA for the summer of my first year, something which undoubtedly benefited me and increased my employability.'

Phil, BA (Hons) Business Studies

How to get what's out there

Check if you are allowed to work

You can either secure employment and then travel to your new job – or travel to your destination first, then sort out employment. In some cases, you'll have to get the job first because that's what the law requires. You will find there are restrictions to employment depending on the country of employment and the nationality of the employee, so your normal country of residence is important.

There are, however, many opportunities: European Union (EU) nationals are free to live and work anywhere in the EU; some labour markets allow fixed-term work visas for temporary work, or specialised work which can't readily be filled by a local employee; and some international employers can secure work permits for employees who need them.

 tip

European Union nationals are free to live and work anywhere in the European Union. In addition, temporary work visas are sometimes available for specified workers, either with key skills or in hard-to-fill sectors.

Before taking on employment you will need to check (a) if there are any restrictions and (b) if these restrictions apply to you. This information is readily available by country – though of course it may not be available in English. The best source of reliable information is the Embassy or High Commission of the country you are interested in. There are also compendium books which pull together a number of destination countries. Your university careers service should have these for reference.

Check out job opportunities

Chapter 1 takes you through the process of finding out what jobs are on offer in great detail, and everything in that chapter applies here. Broadly speaking, you need to look at what's on offer in terms of paid work, and you need to let employers know that you are available for work. You can use printed media (newspapers, bulletins and directories) and online (websites, social networking). Online is particularly useful for overseas work.

 tip

Make full use of online resources when looking for work abroad. Use websites, including national newspapers which publish job adverts online. Use social networks to find out about working abroad.

You can also look for work on location. If, for example, you are an EU citizen you can travel anywhere within the EU and then look for a job. You can try the usual labour market channels: local newspapers; employment agencies; speculative applications (i.e. going into an organisation and asking them if they have any vacancies) or word of mouth. It is worth expanding your jobsearch to include some sectors and occupations you wouldn't normally think of; this is particularly useful if the experience of living and working abroad is more important than developing a particular set of job-related competencies.

The problem with looking for a job once you're abroad is that you'll need to stay somewhere, and to fund yourself during your period of jobsearch.

This takes money – almost always more than you expect. And it probably takes a fairly good idea of the local job market, and maybe even a bit of luck once you get there to secure the kind of job you want, as shown in our brilliant example.

 brilliant example

'I started off looking for a job on the Mediterranean coast, because I'd got the chance of accommodation there. So basically I got a load of CVs and went round pretty much every restaurant; that was where I had had most experience, through my Saturday job and work experience at school. It was horrible, really scary, because I didn't really know what I was saying. One place phoned back, invited me for an interview, and gave me a job as a runner.'

Hannah, (Undergraduate) Economics, Politics with International Studies

Check out whether casual work is worth the risks

Beware that you might be offered casual work that is not legitimate. This can be very tempting: often the pay is cash in hand, and at first sight it does look so much easier to get started working straight away, rather than wade through the hassle of bureaucracy. But working illegally can end up being way more hassle. With no legitimacy and therefore no employment rights or protection, you would be on your own if you had to deal with some of the potential problems of unregulated employment: under-payment; accidents at work; bullying or discrimination.

brilliant tip

Take the bureaucracy of labour laws (work permits) seriously: protect yourself from the potential problems of unregulated work.

What you need to know before you go

The Foreign and Commonwealth Office (FCO) spearheads the 'Know Before You Go' campaign, which aims to help British nationals be safe (and in good health) when abroad. It covers a number of key areas – some of which could save your life:

- get adequate travel insurance;
- check the FCO's country travel advice: this is updated very frequently, to take account of emergency situations, e.g. natural disaster or political unrest;
- research your destination – know the local laws and customs;
- visit your GP as soon as you know that you are travelling;
- check your passport is in good condition and valid and you have all necessary visas;
- make copies of important travel documents and/or store them online using a secure data storage site;
- tell someone where you are going and leave emergency contact details with them;
- take enough money and have access to emergency funds.

 tip

Use the Foreign and Commonwealth Office (FCO) website (**www.gov.uk/knowbeforeyougo**) for good information and advice about your destination.

Once you're away from home

Enjoying the overseas experience

brilliant example

'I eventually decided to do TEFL in Germany, especially as I had missed out on the country during my uni year abroad (I had only gone to France) and saw it as a great opportunity to learn the language properly and get some teaching experience. It went really well for me. I really took to teaching and was extremely enthusiastic about living abroad. The Business English context I teach in in Germany has given me a great and interesting insight into so many different companies. I'm very positive about my time in Germany. I've done translating and proofreading work here also, helped set up a website and have worked for a disabled foundation. I had initially thought I could never move back to the UK but lately I've felt more open to it.'

Simon, BA (Hons) French and German, MA Translating

You might find the whole experience of working and living away from home is enjoyable from day one: that's brilliant! However, you also might have to put a bit of work into making the experience enjoyable. Having some language is going to help – and acquiring language once you are there will help even more. Being ready to try new things, eat new food, do things in a new way is also going to help you adjust quickly and fit in. You might also need to make more of an effort to make new friends than you would do at home, just carrying on with your normal social circle. People may well make the first approach to include you in what they are doing, but you'll need to show that you are interested in what's going on and are prepared to fit in. So, try to say 'Yes' to any invitations – even if they turn out to be a less than brilliant time, you will at least have clocked up one more experience.

tip

Be prepared to put a bit of effort into fitting in: try to pick up some language even if you feel self-conscious. Rather than dismissing an invitation or a suggestion, try to give new things a go.

Surviving the overseas experience

Thanks to social networking sites, you can learn a huge amount, both positive and negative, from other people's experiences. Use them to post questions in advance of your trip, and once you get to your new place. And once there, you can readily tap into the online community, which itself can be a mixture of local people and a more international crew. Your new work mates may also have good advice, which can cover really basic stuff (where to buy food at local supermarkets or markets) to blending in as a local. See what Claire has to say on this:

brilliant **example**

'Before I went to Damascus people asked me if I'd have to wear a hijab (headscarf) in order not to offend, or to try and fit in. But I didn't want to wear one, I felt it would be somehow lying, so I decided I wouldn't, and it was absolutely fine that way. The main thing is to dress conservatively, covering elbows, knees and chest, but in a comfortable way. It's important to maintain a level of confidence in how you dress and it's really good to have clothes that suit you and that you like, even if they're not what you'd wear at home. Having said that, even covering yourself from head to toe will not prevent the comments and the staring. It's just something that you have to put up with, walking around as if you're no longer anonymous. Once a young girl of about 10 tapped me on the shoulder and asked incredulously, "Are you from here?" So whether it's men or women doing the staring, it's best to assume it's a harmless sense of wondering.'

Claire, BA (Hons) Modern Languages (Arabic and Spanish),
MA International Journalism

Bureaucracy and accessing key documents wherever you are

Once you are away from home, there are a number of really vital documents which if lost, you would have to replace. Some of these are official: National Insurance documents; passport; visas. Others are personal but equally important: insurance policies; tickets; bank details. You can easily create a document which records all the detailed information you would need if the worst were to happen. It will help enormously if you have someone back home who can access the things you need which you have forgotten to bring: your contact lens prescription; your birth certificate; your European Computer Driving Licence certificate. You could also scan these, and other important documents, and save them on an Internet-accessible website account that you can then access from an Internet connection anywhere in the world. Here's Hannah again.

brilliant example

'The bureaucracy (for working abroad) was tedious, but not impossible. Both my employers did what they could to help. If I needed something I didn't have with me, I phoned home and got it faxed out, or went to an Internet café and accessed stuff that way.'

Hannah, (Undergraduate) Economics, Politics with International Studies

Keeping going when the going gets tough

Even if you have really been looking forward to going abroad, you will have difficult times, when you might feel lonely or homesick. You might feel you have made a big mistake and just want to go home. You might feel you are doing everything you possibly can to get work, make friends and join in with people and it's just not getting you where you want to be as fast as you want to get there. This is perfectly normal, and part of any successful transition from one phase of your life to another. Here is another brilliant example: Claire spent six months in Africa before going to university (three months working in Uganda followed by three months travelling in East Africa), a whole year abroad between her second and final years of undergraduate study (six months at Damascus University and six months working in Colombia for an anti-landmine charity) and now works in Cairo. She shares her experience of feeling low, and what works for her.

brilliant example

'I learnt to deal with homesickness (in Uganda) – there was just one bout of it, about a month and a half in, and I found the best thing was to go and see friends, or acquaintances, and do something local. To live in the moment and the place, and try and detach. But there's also an element of riding it out. Certainly having had that introduction to living far away from home comforts helped a lot on my (undergraduate) year abroad though. I settled into life in Colombia without too much trouble, and by the time I went to Syria I was a pro at packing and dealing with airports, visas and foreign currency. Settling in, for me, comes with a routine, and I think it's important to feel settled in order to get the most out of a place.'

Claire, BA (Hons) Modern Languages (Arabic and Spanish),
MA International Journalism

Positive steps to take

Try to keep a sense of perspective: is the setback you're experiencing going to be such a big deal in five days' or in five months' or even in five years' time? When you feel you've had a really rubbish day, just take five minutes on your own and identify three positive things that have happened. These can be quite small steps, for example:

I got off the bus at the right bus stop/I understood my colleague when he asked me to do something.

Positive things can also be outside of work, for example:

I smelt the gardenia in blossom/I felt so warm in the heat of the day.

It can help to write these moments down in a notebook, so that you build up a store of positive experience, which can help to give a sense of perspective when you're feeling down. Try to keep going: put a bad day behind you and rather than starting the next day convinced things are going to keep going wrong, try to be positive and open to this day going a little bit better.

 tip

Try to put negative experiences and feelings to one side and focus on the positive. Take five minutes, each and every day, to identify three positive experiences, no matter how small they may seem.

Returning

Securing something to come back to: study or work

Update your CV in the light of your experience abroad

Try to capture, on your CV and in your job applications, the ways in which you have expanded your skills and competence. If you have been working, your new skills may well be specific to the work you did, for example.

I learned to speak fluent Spanish; I can cash up a till; I can operate tools and/or machinery and/or programmes.

Have a look at the kind of employability skills all employers want, but also look at anything an employer specifies in a job advert or person specification.

 tip

Rethink your CV in the light of your travelling experience. Think it through from an employers' perspective so you are ready to explain how your travels have added value to you as a prospective employee.

Include soft skills: look at it from the employers' perspective

You may also have developed the so-called soft skills, which are just as sought after by employers. These include:

- communication;
- problem solving;
- self-management and resilience.

It is highly likely that you will have found yourself in situations abroad where you had to be flexible, and perhaps also where you had to keep going when things weren't plain sailing. Teamwork skills, such as persuading/negotiating and respecting others are undoubtedly skills you had to develop for a good experience abroad. Try to sell your experiences in terms that are of interest to an employer.

Foreign language ability

Many employers are not satisfied with foreign language fluency in graduates. But before you claim you can negotiate high-level deals in another language, appraise your language levels. And if your newly polished language is restricted to ordering food and drink, you might think about picking up some more commercial language applications as part of your jobsearch.

Get your return destination sorted before you go abroad

Securing a job or place on a postgraduate programme to pick up on your return is exactly the same procedure you followed to get your job abroad – but in reverse. You might be able to get this all sorted before you even go off on your travels, which means you don't have to think about it at all once you're away from home. Or you might decide to apply from abroad before you return. This is certainly worth exploring for postgraduate programmes, as an interview is not always necessary.

How to be interviewed at a distance

Even if you are expected to have an interview you could explore the possibility of doing the interview at a distance – by Skype, for example. This would mean you would miss out on the chance to visit the campus and to meet other people applying for your programme, so it does have its drawbacks.

But the distance interview does have the major advantage of sparing you the expense of travelling a long way. If you do manage to organise a cyber-interview, treat it exactly as you would a face-to-face meeting: prepare for it thoroughly, and present yourself well. Dress formally, look professional. You can always head for the beach once the Internet interview is over.

 tip

If you need to be interviewed while you are abroad, ask if an online interview is possible, e.g. using Skype. Remember this is still a formal interview, so dress professionally and present yourself well.

Aftermath

 tip

Don't be too shocked if home seems unfamiliar when you first return: you will adjust to the way of life here, just as you did abroad!

Reverse culture shock

Coming home after a spell abroad might seem like the easiest thing in the world. But you need to be aware of reverse culture shock. Quite simply, what has always seemed familiar becomes unfamiliar when you go back to it, having experienced something quite different. You might even feel a bit homesick for your life abroad. This can come as something of a shock, and although it's not something people talk about very much, it is quite common. You can draw on the same techniques as you did when you were away: look for the positive in your experiences, however small they may at first appear. You will adjust, and in time, things will fall into place again. Just hold on to everything that was good about your experience. Here's a final word from Hannah.

example

'The best thing about working abroad is when you realise that this is your life. You really do have friends here that you care about. You can go out with them and you can really talk to them in French. And it's as real a relationship as if it was in English. It's just very satisfying, and it's what I wanted. Would I recommend working abroad? Yes, definitely, one hundred per cent.'

Hannah, (Undergraduate) Economics, Politics with International Studies

 recap

- Working abroad can be both enjoyable and useful.
- Just a few simple steps will help you to be safe and healthy.
- There are opportunities before, during and after your degree course.
- Make sure that you show clearly how your experiences add value to you as a prospective employee, using the language of employability and skills.

What to do next

Have a look at the Erasmus[+] programme (**https://www.erasmusplus.org. uk/about-erasmus**) to get an idea of what it does. You could also find out what your university offers under the Erasmus[+] scheme, by talking to your course tutor, or the international or Erasmus[+] office in your university. Use social networks or ask friends who have worked abroad what they made of the experience. Ask employers (at job fairs or alumni events) whether they value overseas experience. Simply think about travelling to enhance your employability, and keep it in mind as a possible option.

CHAPTER 5

Graduate training schemes

This chapter covers one of the better-known options for graduates, and for many graduates it's the option they aspire to. In case you are not quite clear about what's involved, we will start with a definition, before looking at some examples. Finally, we will show you how to be a strong contender, if a graduate training scheme is your preferred option.

What is a graduate training scheme?

 definition

A graduate training scheme is a graduate entry position where there is a planned programme of training and development. Usually associated with large organisations of the kind you will meet at careers fairs, they are increasingly also offered by SMEs (small to medium-sized enterprises).

Sectoral growth and decline

Graduate training schemes can be found in a whole range of job areas, or sectors. Vacancies are currently on the increase in retail, manufacturing and construction, IT and telecommunications and banking.

Note that the term graduate training scheme is sometimes used in professions like law, accountancy, teaching and psychology. In this chapter we are looking at more generalist schemes where the subject of your degree may be less important and the training more broadly based.

Direct entry

Many smaller organisations or SMEs offer the same kind of opportunity for a graduate entrant, but may not always label it a graduate training scheme. Remember that in Chapter 2 we defined an SME as an organisation with up to 250 employees. These organisations cover almost 60 per cent of the private sector employment in the UK and this includes graduate-level roles, with training.

On the other hand, be aware that many larger organisations also recruit people, who happen to be graduates, to what are called direct-entry jobs, where a degree is not a requirement. This might give you a route in, if your application for a graduate training scheme has been unsuccessful, and you could still work towards a position similar to someone who has come through the graduate training scheme route.

Three key features

The key defining features of a graduate training scheme are:

- You need a degree.
- You will follow a planned programme which will enable you to sample different work areas and identify your particular strengths and interests.
- You will be employed and therefore paid a salary.

. . . and three myths

- Graduate training schemes usually lead to a job – but not automatically. You may have to apply for internal vacancies, or wait until a suitable role comes up. In some cases, especially in the public sector, graduate training schemes are offered on a fixed-term contract and offer no guarantee of a job.

- You have to go straight into a graduate training scheme as soon as you leave university. Not so – many graduates apply in the year following graduation – or even later than that. Employers are fine with this, as long as you can show some benefit to yourself, and potentially to the employer, deriving from the time since you graduated. Typically, around half of all graduate trainees recruited across the UK will not be straight from university.

- You have to have a first class or upper second class Honours degree. Not so – although some companies have such a requirement, many do not.

Some typical graduate training schemes

These examples come from recently advertised graduate training schemes, and help to illustrate the features they have in common, and where the differences might be. You will see that even this small sample covers a range of occupational areas and includes an SME.

 examples

A national pub and restaurant company

- Offers a two-year, fast-track retail management scheme, combining on-the-job experience and formal training, leading to general manager posts with progression to area manager or head office roles.

- The company looks for applicants with strong leadership and team-building skills and the ability to motivate their team, and the self-motivation to develop a business.

- Graduates must have a 2:2 or better and a minimum of 12 months' supervisory experience in a customer-facing environment, and be flexible within two geographical regions (excluding London).

A global business consultancy

- Offers trainee technology or management consultants a two-year programme with analysts, a balance of workplace, project-based learning and 250 hours of formal training, including online courses, together with the support of buddies and mentors.

- Applicants need 340 UCAS points and at least a 2:1 in any discipline and a strong interest in technology.

- You'll need to be fully mobile to work on client projects that could be anywhere in the country – or even the world – though you would have a UK base.

- An interesting additional requirement is that candidates must prove that they have achieved high performance in other areas of their lives, i.e. outside academic performance. (If you were applying for this training scheme, what evidence could you offer?)

A regional housing association

- An intensive two-year training programme working in different functions to provide a breadth of experience as a basis for choosing a specialist area after training. All placements will be real business roles. The first year will involve discrete projects lasting 2–4 weeks. In the second year there are two placements lasting six months each in either development, operations or care and support housing.

- Graduates from any discipline may apply. They need to be able to demonstrate energy, enthusiasm and a 'can do' attitude together with good verbal and numerical reasoning, report writing and communication skills.

- You would need to show an understanding of the work of a housing association and be able to explain why you have chosen this area of work.

A multi-national engineering company

- Offers a structured development programme over the course of 18 months, travelling across various global sites and accessing key training and development modules.

- Training on-site will focus on developing your technical expertise as well as interpersonal skills such as communication, team working and leadership.

- Trainees will be helped to gain appropriate professional accreditations such as IMechE or similar and will be offered a permanent position in an appropriate area of the business.

- Applicants need a minimum 2:2 in mechanical, civil or marine engineering, maths or physics.

Is a graduate training scheme right for you?

Meeting the selection criteria

The harsh reality is that, in order to deal with large numbers of applications, recruiters to graduate training schemes set the bar high in terms of degree classification and sometimes, like one of our brilliant examples, even use UCAS points. Sometimes the initial selection is done using computer software. This is highly likely to be the case if you apply online. If you don't meet an essential requirement (for example, you have a 2:2, they want a 2:1) you will be selected out. And all this will happen well before anyone reads your well-crafted personal statement. So you need to consider if, and how, you can achieve what is being asked for. If you can't, then look for other routes.

brilliant example

A large, multinational business consultancy has an alternative graduate training scheme for people who have fallen short of the academic standards normally required but can demonstrate achievement outside their studies.

In large organisations you need to be prepared for, and willing to commit to, the full range of selection methods. The entire selection process could last a full day or more and may even require an overnight stay. Have a look at Chapter 10 'Dates and deadlines: your timeline for action' for managing all this alongside your study, and Chapter 12 'Succeeding in selection', for more about what might be involved.

A chance to find your strengths and interests

You may know that you would like to work in a large organisation of a particular kind – public sector, logistics, retail, finance – but not yet be clear about a specific direction. Many graduate training schemes offer a programme of rotation through various functions and, while you will be expected to make a contribution in each area you work in, you do have the chance to experience different roles first hand.

Are you flexible?

Large, multi-site organisations will expect you to be prepared to work at different locations. Even if the head office is in your home town, it doesn't mean that you will work there. Make sure you are aware of any requirements to move or work away, and that they fit with your own circumstances.

Can you commit?

A graduate training scheme is long term – think two years minimum, and that's just for the training programme. So, if you plan to work for six months and then travel, it's not for you at this stage. A recruiting organisation wants a return for the cash investment it's making in selection and training – and you will be giving a lot of yourself to get the most from the experience. So be sure that the time is right for you.

How to be a strong contender for a graduate training scheme

Much of what we say elsewhere in this book, about researching the labour market, job opportunities, applications and interviews, applies to graduate training schemes as well as to other options you may be considering, so we will assume that you will dip in to the relevant chapters as you need to. What we will do here is look at the particular demands of graduate training schemes on you, the applicant.

Know the business in context

For every organisation you apply to, you need to know how they generate their revenue, who their competitors are, how they adapt to changes in the market, their strengths, what they are developing, and so on. This knowledge will help you with your application and certainly with your interview. Visit careers fairs, look at websites, talk to anyone who might know anything about the organisations or the sectors they belong to.

Know about recruitment timescales and where to find vacancies

Some graduate training schemes have an annual or twice-yearly intake, others a rolling programme. For the first group, being ready to apply at the right time is critical. Deadlines can be as early as October of your final year. Sign up for careers fairs, pick up your free copies of graduate directories from your careers service, use your university's online graduate vacancy service and sign up to graduate recruitment websites.

Know about selection methods

We said earlier that graduate training schemes often use the full range of selection methods, in particular assessment centres, so make sure you know what these are, what to expect and how to prepare for them. Read Chapter 12 'Succeeding in selection', for lots more information about this.

Be creative

If you don't meet the academic requirements, is there another way you can gain access? You could look for companies like the brilliant example earlier in this chapter, or you could try a direct approach with a good letter or personal contact at a careers fair. Alternatively you could go for direct entry and aim to progress once you are in the organisation.

Manage your applications

You will almost certainly be applying to more than one graduate training scheme, so keep your applications in order – create a schedule of closing dates and interview dates, make an electronic or paper folder to keep copies of applications, CVs and interview information. Read Chapter 10 'Dates and deadlines' for more about managing your time to hit closing dates and keep your academic work going at the same time.

Seek and make use of feedback

An unsuccessful application can help you to get the next one better. We talk about this in Chapter 11. If you get as far as an interview you should be able to ask the employer for feedback – but do listen to what is said. The employer is telling you how you presented at interview, so try not to defend or justify, because it really doesn't matter – what matters is what the employer saw and heard.

 timesaver

Keep track by making a paper or electronic folder for copies of application forms, CVs and interview information.

brilliant **dos and don'ts**

Do

✔ find out about the business and its competitors;

✔ learn about selection methods;

✔ get and use feedback;

✔ look for different routes to where you want to be.

Don't

✘ leave it till the last minute to look for vacancies;

✘ lose track of your applications.

What are the benefits?

We think there are three key benefits of graduate training schemes, and we are not alone. Have a look at the three real-life graduate stories that follow.

In our first example, Paul highlights the benefits of learning to work in a big organisation.

brilliant example

'My role as a trainee manager on the graduate training scheme of an international car rental company provides me with valuable training on running a business, working as a manager and working your way up a big organisation. The experience has given me such a big insight into the workings of a big company.'

Paul, BSc (Hons) Sport and Exercise Science

In our next example you can see that a good graduate training scheme will support you in further learning, sometimes leading to specialist qualifications.

brilliant example

'I secured a position with one of the world's biggest banks on their executive management graduate scheme. At university we were introduced to the concept of lifelong learning and with the bank I have the chance to further my studies with qualifications in financial services.'

Phil, BA (Hons) Business Studies

Our final example illustrates the longer-term benefits. Victoria's experience helped her to develop strengths and preferences that enabled her to work out the next stage of her career plan. She is now in her third job after graduating.

brilliant example

'I joined the graduate programme of a consulting company. In two years I learned masses and I still use the tools and skills I gained with them. I use their methods as a mark of what good looks like in my present company. The IT projects I worked on were for a range of blue chip retail companies. However, after two years I wanted to try a move away from IT so I moved to another consultancy for more analysis and strategic projects . . . after another two years I realised that I wanted to work in retail, and within the industry rather than through consultancy. Because of my experience I found the job market very responsive, and I got my present job as a business systems analyst with a multinational retail organisation. I get to travel and work with different cultures, teaching and shaping how countries do business.'

Victoria, MA Geography

 recap

Graduate training schemes are great for developing your skills and experience. They help you to refine your career plans, and often include the chance for you to gain a specialist qualification.

What to do next

- Remind yourself of the key features of a graduate training scheme. Could you see yourself as a graduate trainee?

- Think about a job area you might like to work in – marketing, finance, research and development, HR – and see if you can find a suitable graduate training scheme being advertised. Visit websites; useful ones include **www.milkround.com** and **www.prospects.ac.uk**.

- Get hold of a copy of a directory of graduate training schemes from your careers service and look at their online list if they have one. Have a browse and look for similarities and differences among different schemes.

- Sign up for the next graduate careers fair in your area. Find out more from your university website or from **www.prospects.ac.uk**.

CHAPTER 6

Entrepreneurship, intrapreneurship and self-employment

Introduction

Self-employment is a real option for some graduates, particularly in creative industries but also in less obvious areas like counselling or animal behaviour. Our brilliant examples in this chapter come from graduates who have recently set up businesses in ethical clothing, recruitment, counselling and digital multimedia. In this chapter, while we don't have space to give you the nuts and bolts of setting up your own business, we will give you some pointers to help you explore this career option in more detail. We'll begin by looking at two related concepts, entrepreneurship and intrapreneurship. Any or all could be part of your working life, for some people immediately after graduation, for others at a different career stage.

The number of people in the UK who are self-employed has risen steadily in the last five years to around 4.4 million. This is believed to be due in part to the reduction in the number of full-time jobs that are available, and the choice made by some to become self-employed rather than unemployed. However, there is also a steady rise in the number of business start-ups, with new enterprises setting up at the rate of 435,000 per year. This rise is impacting on graduates too; of those who graduated in 2013, 4.8% were self-employed six months later (around 7,000 graduates), compared with 3% of those who graduated in 2007. The percentage is higher in subjects such as Art, Design, Drama and Multimedia/Computing. But before going into any more detail, let's clarify what we mean by entrepreneurship, intrapreneurship and self-employment.

Entrepreneurship

What do you think of when you see the word entrepreneur? Probably due to its original use in the entertainment industry, you might think of glamour, drive, ducking and diving, imagination, success. But put simply, an entrepreneur is a person who organises and operates a business or businesses, taking on financial risk to do so. The Business Zone website fleshed this out:

> 'An entrepreneur sees an opportunity which others do not fully recognise, to meet an unsatisfied demand or to radically improve the performance of an existing business. They have unquenchable self-belief that this opportunity can be made real through hard work, commitment and the adaptability to learn the lessons of the market along the way.' (**www.thebusinesszone.co.uk**)

So while self-employment describes a status, entrepreneurship says more about the style and approach. In other words, to be successfully self-employed you need to be entrepreneurial.

Nature or nurture?

Many studies of well-known entrepreneurs draw attention to the personality characteristics they appear to share, such as a need to achieve, a desire for autonomy, a capacity for risk taking, high creativity and a glass-half-full outlook. Some researchers extend this observation to the belief that entrepreneurs are born, not made. However, most studies of this kind are based on a small sample, and it would be easy to identify people with these characteristics who are not successful entrepreneurs, and vice versa. During the last twenty years, many schools and universities have introduced 'enterprise education' – you may have experienced this yourself – in response to policymakers believing that equipping students and graduates in this way will help organisations to operate more effectively during times of rapid change. So this approach assumes that entrepreneurship can be learned.

'A challenge (of entrepreneurship) is to handle and integrate knowledge from several different fields – for example marketing, operations, human resources, accounting and finance.'

From *Exploring Entrepreneurship* by Richard Blundel and Nigel Lockett (2011)

Intrapreneurship

If the idea of being entrepreneurial appeals to you, but you have reservations about going it alone, here's an alternative. Intrapreneurship refers to the process by which employees are supported to create and develop new products, services and systems, with necessary resources and the freedom to bypass or shortcut the organisation's usual routines and procedures. The term derives from an abbreviation of 'inside entrepreneurs'. Here's a simple example to illustrate how it works.

 example

A final-year student aims to work in retail management as a graduate trainee and has a part-time job in the local branch of a global fashion brand. She knows that students perceive the brand to be too dressy and business-dress focused, even though there is a good range of more casual clothing, but the window displays are determined by head office and must be the same in every store. She believes that if part of the window display could be used for more informal clothes, it would attract more students into the store and sales of these products would increase. She makes her case to the store manager, pointing out that the success of the scheme would be measurable using the stock control system, and asks if special permission could be given for a two-month experiment. The store manager is persuaded and manages to get approval from area office, who allocates a design colleague to work alongside our student on an eye-catching and targeted window display. The student is encouraged to talk about her idea at a morning staff briefing so that colleagues will be receptive to new customers. The scheme becomes a success and is rolled out to other branches in university towns.

So, being part of a large, formally structured organisation need not prevent you from being innovative and creative. Intrapreneurs transform ideas into social or economic capital through ventures which are consistent with the goals of the organisation. So the benefits to the organisation are clear, but what does the intrapreneur get out of it?

Evidence from organisations which actively encourage intrapreneurship suggests that there are two key gains for employees. First, there are gains in motivation and job satisfaction for the intrapreneurs themselves. And second, because staff can use entrepreneurial skills and techniques such as persisting until successful, and learning from failure, without the risks associated with operating alone, the organisation can be less static and livelier as a place to work. And, of course, intrapreneurial success is a great basis for setting up a new enterprise later on – according to the Office for National Statistics, people over 50 account for 84 per cent of the increase in self-employed workers during the last five years – using their amassed capital and experience.

Self-employment

You might be surprised to know that, even though there are legal and financial implications, there is no clear definition of self-employment. However, according to government advice, you are likely to be self-employed if you:

- run your own business (including as a franchisee) and take responsibility for its success or failure;
- have several customers at the same time;
- can decide how, when and where you do your work;
- are free to hire other people to do the work for you or help you at your own expense;
- provide the main items of equipment to do your work.

Note that there are some employers who require their staff to be technically self-employed, even though none of the above criteria apply. This is a technique for managing human resources and while legal, can have drawbacks for the staff concerned. In media and IT the term freelance is often used – usually meaning contracted by an organisation or series of organisations for a particular task or role and for a fixed period of time. You may be called a contractor and there is a useful graduate guide to contracting at **www.contractoruk.com**. For the purposes of this chapter, however, we are staying with the accepted understanding of self-employment covered in the bullet points above.

 brilliant definitions

Entrepreneurship – identifying and taking forward an opportunity to meet an unsatisfied demand or improve an existing business

Intrapreneurship – applying the skills and techniques of entrepreneurship within an organisation

Self-employment – running your own business and taking responsibility for its success or failure

Setting up and running your own business

So now let's focus on what self-employment might mean for you as a new graduate. According to a recent report by the UK Commission for Employment and Skills, there are three main reasons why running your own business might be a serious option: opportunity, lifestyle and necessity.

First, opportunity – because in the sector you are interested in, it's the norm, or because you have spotted a gap in the market for a product or service. Second, because you see yourself doing it – perhaps it's in your family, or you are attracted to the idea of working independently and 'being your own boss', so it's a lifestyle choice. Third, out of necessity – you see fewer opportunities to be an employee in your chosen field, and you see self-employment as a better option than unemployment. Of course, it may also be a combination of these reasons.

So you have your motivation. What else do you need? An idea, obviously. But in addition to technical or sector-specific knowledge and skills, you will need to know how to set up, promote, operate and resource your business. Here are just a few of the questions you will need to be able to answer:

- **Market research**: how do I know there's a demand, who are my customers and who are my competitors?

- **Marketing, publicity and promotion**: how will I promote my product or service, both to launch the business and to keep it going? Am I aiming for repeat business or will I have to keep finding new customers?

- **Financial management**: setting up income and expenditure accounts, following tax regulations by keeping records and completing returns on time, budgeting, setting a fair price which will generate demand and income, sourcing and costing materials and equipment.

- **Premises**: do the planning regulations permit me to operate from home? If I rent premises are there health and safety considerations? Are the premises secure?

- **Resources**: what finance, equipment and materials do I need to start off with? What are my renewables, and what will they cost? Can I get supplies quickly when I need them? Do I have anyone to call on if I get urgent work?

- **Operating**: do I have insurance for when things go wrong? Am I clear about what I am offering and what I am not offering?

Skills and knowledge

The list of questions above may have given you an idea about the skills and knowledge you need to be a successful entrepreneur, but we will list the most important here.

Skills

- Creativity
- Communication (oral and written)
- Resilience

- Confidence

- Project planning and management

If we look more closely at just one of these skills, confidence, it's partly about how you feel and partly about the confidence others have in you, as Gemma, who has a multimedia development business, describes.

brilliant example

'When I first started out, it was quite difficult to get potential clients to look past the fact that I was just one person, working from home. Although I was basically just a sole freelancer, I think it was massively helpful setting up as a proper limited company. It only costs around £60 and meant I could give the impression of a more professional, serious setup. And I found it was always best to refer to the company as "we" and not "I". Of course, when a client had worked with me once, they could see I was capable of delivering so it became easier as it went along, together with word of mouth recommendations. I think that acquiring office premises helped boost our company image further.'

Gemma, BA (Hons) Multimedia Computing (Multimedia Development Company)

Knowledge

- Market research

- Marketing

- Finance

- Business planning

- Business awareness

- Sector-specific knowledge

Here's Gemma again, talking about developing her own business awareness.

'I have become much more business savvy as the company has grown. Things like making sure that you get a 35% deposit and setting out clear terms and conditions before starting the project have been important lessons learned along the way. It's so important to have a clear set of terms agreed in writing so that both we and the client know what needs to be delivered for the agreed price. In the early days it was easy to get pushed into adding lots of extras as the project went along, all for the same price. Also some people would talk you into doing projects for nothing in order to "gain experience", but this is never a good idea.

Even if you are starting up from scratch as a sole graduate, you are still highly qualified in your field and clients should pay for your skills.'

Gemma, BA (Hons) Multimedia Computing (Multimedia Development Company)

Help is at hand

You might have been put off by now by that list of questions – but don't be. There is growing support for would-be entrepreneurs and much of this is focused on undergraduates and graduates. Here are some of the ways by which you can learn.

Take a course or module as part of your degree

You may be able to choose a course or module within your degree which focuses on entrepreneurship. Around 80% of UK universities offer credit-bearing awards and modules related to entrepreneurship and, like Alex in our brilliant example, it might be a way to discover if running your own business appeals to you.

brilliant example

'I thought I was destined to be employed as a graphic designer, but my third year at university really changed things. We had a module called business management and production and it was the highlight of my third year. It completely absorbed me. We had the opportunity to develop a business plan and then pitch it to professionals. Our pitch was successful and we were invited to develop the idea. Two of us took it forward.'

Alex G, BA (Hons) Graphic Design (Ethical Clothing Company)

Research and develop your idea

It's a statement of the obvious, but you need to identify a product or service in which you have some interest, skills and knowledge. The book *Start Your Own Business* (Welsted and Whiteling, updated regularly) identifies 'shoe-string start-ups' which can be set up with minimal capital and resources, including eBay business, tutoring, personal training and web design. This book also contains ten great questions to ask yourself before launching a business, to test for demand and viability in the market.

Many entrepreneurs build on the knowledge they have acquired as employees in setting up their business, but research is still needed. Our next brilliant example, Katie, worked for almost four years in recruitment consultancy before deciding to explore setting up on her own.

brilliant example

'I decided in the February to start looking into my own business. I bought the *Financial Times Guide to Starting a New Business* and other similar books, including one which was specifically made for recruitment. I started writing lists of what I would need, for example, a name, telephone number, a domain email address and website, insurance, database, job boards etc. and then started looking into these specifically. Eventually, by July, I had done all my research and chosen the company name. I know ▶

it will be a hard slog as after a non-compete clause I had to find all new clients and candidates and in the current market this may not even work . . . I was investing a considerable amount of money from a house sale.'

Katie, BSC (Hons) Psychology (Recruitment Company)

You may have noticed the reference to a 'non-compete clause'. This is something to look out for if you are already working and then setting up in a similar field, and protects employers from having their business taken away by the new company. It can also apply to a franchise, e.g. for exercise classes, preventing a former franchisee from running a similar business in the same locality.

Gain experience

Many entrepreneurs start out by working for someone else and being employed by an SME offers a chance to experience life in a small business at close quarters. You might even be able to arrange some work-shadowing of an existing small business, though perhaps not if you are proposing to become a competitor! Access to a business mentor can be valuable, as Zoe, our next brilliant example, found.

brilliant example

'At university I was matched with a business mentor. This was extremely useful as I had not thought about how to run a business before. My mentor set me goals such as finding out about counselling rooms and advertising, and how to budget for such things. It really made me think about the business side of setting up a counselling practice.'

Zoe, PGDIP/MA Counselling and Psychotherapy (Counselling Practice)

Business start-up support

Look for business start-up support at your university – over 90% of universities provide extra-curricular support – or in your local area. Even if your course isn't directly relevant to setting up your own business, you should be able to access local, regional and national information, advice and support. Alex, our brilliant example earlier in the chapter, developed his idea by attending an intensive training 'boot camp', then successfully bidding for funding and office space, all provided through his university. Our brilliant example below contains a local, regional and national initiative – see what you can find near you.

 example

- A university in the north of England offers intensive 'bootcamps' and 'boiler rooms' for interested undergraduates and graduates, in which they develop a business plan, meet local entrepreneurs and experts in finance, market research and publicity, and have the chance to bid for funding and workspace.

- A group of universities in the Midlands offers students and graduates interested in starting their own business a programme which includes mentoring, tailored training, networking opportunities, access to business incubation space, and the opportunity to bid for financial support.

- Shell liveWIREUK provides online support and the opportunity to apply for start-up funding to young entrepreneurs aged 16 – 30 (**www.shell-livewire.org**).

Taking the first steps: three ways forward

Start your business immediately at full strength

This can work if you have done your research and feel reasonably confident of success – or have a financial cushion to protect you while you put all your energy into your new business. As a new graduate, Alex had nothing to lose by committing himself full-time to his new business, particularly as he had been awarded £1000 start-up funding and a year's free office space. His location meant that he also had access to legal and financial advice and networking events. But note what he says here about attitude and mindset.

 example

'You need to be highly self-motivated and competitive, in order to push yourself to work those long hours and possibly weekends. You also need to have confidence in yourself and your ability to make your business work. If you don't believe in yourself, and your idea, no one else will – confidence is key. You need to grasp every opportunity, even if it's things that scare you, like public speaking. If it could help you and your business, it's worth doing.

Furthermore, make mistakes, as you don't learn from success, but from the mistakes you make – don't be afraid to fail, as this will lead to you getting it right next time. . . . Determination is the backbone to it all.'

Alex G, BA (Hons) Graphic Design (Ethical Clothing Company)

Start with a micro-business using evenings/weekends to try out, then expand if successful

For some people, either because of funding or because of the nature of the business, it makes sense to start on a part-time basis. This helps to grow the business at a rate you can manage, and also gives you the chance to decide if it's for you before you make a full commitment. Our next brilliant example, Gemma, faced exactly this decision. Towards the end of her degree in multimedia computing, she was offered a job at the same university, working on the development of a Second Life project. After six months, she felt that the job was not 'techy' enough for her, so she left and started a PhD. She takes up the story.

brilliant example

'I was hoping to do some freelance work alongside the PhD, to bring in some extra money, so I set up a company with just myself on the roster. I was contacted by someone from another university I had met during my employment, asking if I knew anyone who could work on their 'Second Life' development. I explained that I was just starting up a small business for this kind of thing . . . My quote was accepted.

After a few weeks, other enquiries came in and I realised it was going to be too much to balance this new venture and a full-time PhD. I had to decide which one to pursue. After much deliberation I realised that running my own multimedia development business was my ultimate ambition, so this had to be my choice. That was four years ago and I have been running the company ever since.'

Gemma, BA (Hons) Multimedia Computing (Multimedia Development Company)

Be employed in an innovative organisation

If the idea of running your own business appeals to you but the time isn't right just now, make it your aim to work in a small company which is itself innovative, and perhaps just beginning to take on staff. This way you will get to experience the commitment, risk-taking, multi-tasking and long hours which characterise successful small businesses, and you will develop some of those skills for yourself. Small businesses advertise in all the usual places, covered in Chapter 2. Be proactive; look out for networking events, work experience and work-shadowing opportunities and make some speculative applications.

brilliant dos and don'ts

Do

✔ carry out your market research;

✔ devise a business plan;

✔ get access to financial and legal advice;

✔ make sure that you have the drive and commitment to see your plan through.

> **Don't**
>
> ✘ set up in competition with your current employer without checking your
>   contract first;
>
> ✘ borrow more than you can pay back;
>
> ✘ think self-employment is an easy option.

Look to the future

Finally, remember that entrepreneurship and enterprise training, even if it's
not used to set up a business, increases your employability by making you
more enterprising, creative, innovative, commercially aware and self-motivated. And you may find that there's an opportunity later on in your career
to set up your own business, using your experience and any capital you may
have been able to put aside. While just 9% of small business owners are
under 35 (though this percentage is growing year by year), 56% are aged
between 35 and 54, many working in the field in which they were previously
an employee. So running your own business might just be part of your future
career plan.

Self-employment – a life-changing choice

Many people choose self-employment because it offers a different quality of
life – a key benefit to set against the hard work and dedication essential to
success, and a factor to take into account in any plans to expand. So the last
words in this chapter go to Gemma and Katie.

 example

'For the four years that I have been running Gemixin, I have been making enough
money to support my own salary and freelance staff when required. This is great as
it means that I have spent four years doing what I enjoy doing, working for myself
during the days and hours that I choose. However, I want to take this further and

become a large company with full-time staff, creating our very own mobile apps and games. This is my ambition.'

Gemma, BA (Hons) Multimedia Computing (Multimedia Development Company)

'Whereas before I was out of the house at least 22 hours a day, I now work from home and am flexible, so if I go for lunch with a friend I can make up the hours in the evening. Financially the company did well in the first year, billing just over £115,000. I enjoy managing my own time and not having so much pressure from managers, though I still set myself targets. The next decision is whether to grow the company or keep it as just me. Some days I want to grow the company by recruiting more recruiters and giving us a bigger presence, other days, like today, I realise that I made the move for a better quality of life rather than for the money!'

Katie, BSC (Hons) Psychology (Recruitment Company)

Next steps

- Check out your business idea – is it viable?
- Ask yourself if you have the right characteristics to work independently and develop your business.
- Find your local sources of expertise and support.

CHAPTER 7

Postgraduate study: choosing a course and making a good application

We've already identified postgraduate study as one of the options you can choose from on completing your first degree. This chapter considers this option in more detail and, even if you have already made the decision to progress onto postgraduate training, you'll still find some of the later sections within this chapter useful.

Firstly, we consider the range of postgraduate courses on offer: academic and professional; full-time and part-time; distance, online and blended study modes; in the UK or overseas. Then we work through your decision-making process: the advantages and disadvantages of studying beyond an undergraduate degree; thinking through timing – whether to undertake postgraduate study immediately after your undergraduate degree or a few years into your career; finding out what you need to know before you commit to a particular programme; how to fund yourself as a postgraduate student, and how to make a good application. The final section talks you through presenting your postgraduate qualification in a positive light to an employer when making a job application.

Postgraduate courses – what's the range on offer?

The undergraduate degree as the basis for postgraduate study

It is safe to assume that you now know that an undergraduate degree is usually the first level of study you can undertake at a university. On successful completion you are awarded a Bachelor's degree, most commonly Bachelor of Arts (BA), Bachelor of Science (BSc) or a protected, specialist title such as Bachelor of Laws (LLB) or Bachelor of Medicine (MB). There are some slight distinctions within undergraduate degrees (foundation, ordinary and honours) but they are all undergraduate or first degrees. Once you have successfully completed your undergraduate degree, you can progress onto a higher level. It is worth noting that some postgraduate courses will consider an applicant without a first degree. This is more common on vocational courses where relevant work experience counts for a lot.

Higher-level degrees: Masters and Doctoral

Masters degrees

There are two higher degree levels, namely: Masters and Doctoral. Masters degrees are awarded after a programme of teaching or research, or a mixture of the two. Typically, a Masters degree takes at least one year of full-time study. This can often be a full calendar year, lasting 12 months, as opposed to a full academic year. Students may work through the summer period (June/July/August) to produce an extended piece of independent work. The nature of their finished product will vary according to discipline, but it could be a research dissertation, an industrial or design project, or a performance piece.

Academic and professional Masters

A Masters degree can be designed as an academic programme, which allows you to study your chosen subject in more detail and depth, e.g. French Studies or Violence and Conflict. It might also be designed to satisfy a professional body's requirements for a qualifying examination, e.g. Architecture. Or it could be a programme of advanced study, with the possibility of researching an area of professional practice for qualified professionals who want a higher degree, e.g. Renewable Energy and the Built Environment. Some subjects are offered as a four-year programme, where students spend the first three years getting their first degree, and on successful completion progress onto their Masters, e.g. Civil Engineering courses leading to a Master of Engineering (MEng).

tip

If you are thinking of a professional career, check what qualifications you need with the relevant professional body. They usually list courses they have approved.

Masters titles

Research-based programmes lead to the award of MPhil. Taught programmes most commonly lead to the award of Master of Arts (MA) or Master of Science (MSc), with specialist designated awards for professional qualifications such as Master of Engineering (MEng).

Postgraduate Certificate and Postgraduate Diploma

Studying at Masters level can also lead to the award of a Postgraduate Diploma or a Postgraduate Certificate. A diploma course typically takes one academic year studying full-time and a Postgraduate Certificate typically takes one term studying full-time, which equates to one academic year if you study part-time. Postgraduate Diplomas and Certificates are frequently awarded for programmes of study that are approved by a professional body. This means that, on completion of that programme, students will have reached a level of competence, making them equipped for professional practice. For example, the Postgraduate Diploma in Information Management at the University of Strathclyde is recognised by the Chartered Institute of Library and Information Professionals.

 definition

Higher degrees can be academic or vocational/professional. Study at Masters level can lead to the award of Masters degree, Postgraduate Diploma or Postgraduate Certificate.

Doctoral degrees: research and taught (professional) doctorates

Research doctorate

Doctoral studies are research-based, and a doctorate is awarded, broadly speaking, for the creation of knowledge. The degree awarded would typically be a DPhil or a PhD, and would normally take three years of full-time study. It can of course be studied part-time.

Taught or professional doctorate

Where a doctoral programme includes a research component, but has a substantial taught element, this would lead to an award that specifies the discipline in the title, e.g. Doctor of Education (Ed D). These kinds of programmes are often referred to as 'taught' or 'professional' doctorates, and they normally take three years of full-time study.

Taught doctorate for professional practice

If you want to practise in some professions, the qualifying route is by professional doctorate, e.g. Clinical Psychology or Educational and Child Psychology. So if you want to be a Clinical or Educational Psychologist, you will have to complete a professional doctorate. Again, these normally take three years of full-time study.

European doctorate

A European doctorate can be awarded where part of the research has taken place in another country, and where the examiner team spans more than one EU country.

brilliant definition

Doctoral-level degrees can be research-based, taught or a combination of both. Those with a substantial taught element are professional doctorates. Some professions demand a taught doctorate in order to be included on the register and practise in that profession.

Where and how to study

Full-time or part-time?

You can see that there are several different types of postgraduate programmes to choose from. They can be offered in two attendance modes: full-time and part-time. Any course will have a mixture of teaching delivery and self-directed learning. Full-time courses might require attendance most days of the week or only a couple of days. This often depends on the nature of the subject studied: Engineering and Science degrees need you to put a lot of time into laboratory work, which obviously can only be done in the university. Art and Design courses also demand long hours in the studio, which could be done at home but is more likely to be done on campus. You will need to check with individual courses how much attendance is required; you can't assume that all full-time courses have the same classroom hours. Courses that lead to professional qualification will require practice or placement hours that can take up several weeks each semester. So the decision to study full-time might be made for you if the programme you want is only offered in full-time mode. Once you start to look at the courses on offer, you'll get a feel for what can be studied flexibly and what must be studied full-time.

 brilliant definitions

Full-time study normally expects attendance on several days each week, with significant self-directed study.

Part-time study might involve only one day of teaching per week, along with self-directed work to be undertaken by you during the week.

On campus, at a distance or online?

There are also three recognised ways of teaching a programme, sometimes called 'modes of delivery'. They are: campus-based, distance-learning or online learning. You may already be familiar with these distinctions from your undergraduate course.

brilliant definitions

Campus programmes are based at the university. You will meet your lecturers and tutors face to face and they will deliver lectures in person.

Distance learning programmes do not necessarily involve any attendance at university. Teaching is delivered through module guides or study handbooks, which can be in print or accessible online. Tutorials are delivered by email, phone or online.

Online programmes make extensive use of information communication technology for teaching and learning. These include: virtual learning environments; online teaching materials; video and podcasts; discussion boards; wikis; facilitated chatrooms, and forums. Tutorials are delivered by: email; phone; video conference, or Skype.

Blurring distinct modes of study

These clear distinctions do get blurred in practice, particularly as developments in new technology and mobile communication make it ever easier to pick up online materials. It is true that a student on an online programme might never set foot on campus, but it is equally entirely possible that they do visit from time to time and might arrange to meet a tutor if that is mutually convenient. By the same token, a student studying on campus may well pick up a pod- or videocast of a lecture, or access online teaching and learning materials in a virtual learning environment. It can also be a really interesting peer learning experience to invite a mix of students (online, distance, part- and full-time) to participate in a facilitated online chat, or to contribute to a discussion forum, as this can lead to a powerful mix of experience and insight.

brilliant tip

Lecturers are making greater use of mixed media. Even if you're an on-campus student, check out online material for your modules, e.g. podcasts or films posted by your tutors.

Study in the United Kingdom or venture abroad?

Postgraduate study abroad

You might already be thinking about doing your second degree at a different university, but what about doing it in a different country? You will of course need to work through all the issues around postgraduate study that are in this chapter. However, it is worth mentioning here the possibility of studying abroad for your second degree. You are probably more confident now than you were when you started your undergraduate course, so you might be prepared to widen your horizons at this stage.

brilliant example

'Biological Psychology opened my eyes to a world of scientific knowledge and curiosity. To my delight, this course integrated aspects of Comparative Psychology focusing on the behaviour of non-human primates. This inspired my final-year research project, studying the self-directed behaviour of chimpanzees at Chester Zoo. In 2008, I continued my studies at Bucknell University in the USA to study for my Masters degree in Psychology, where I studied the behaviour of squirrel monkeys for my graduate thesis. After a two-year exceedingly rigorous programme and adjusting to some differences between the British and American education systems, I recently graduated with my MSc degree.'

Sam, BSc (Hons) Psychology, MSc

Language of instruction can be English, even in Europe

You would normally be expected to have sufficient fluency in the language of instruction (i.e. the language in which the postgraduate course is taught and examined) before you are admitted onto a study programme. However, if your language levels are not yet sufficient to cope with postgraduate study, you can follow our brilliant example of someone studying in the United States, where the language of instruction was no problem.

Even across Europe, you can find a way across the language barrier because many postgraduate programmes are offered in English. This is particularly so where the programme wants to attract a range of students of different nationalities, which means English can be used as the common language. Examples of this would include the Master of Business Administration (MBA) offered at the Copenhagen Business School in Denmark, or at the University of Oulu in northern Finland. Doctoral-level programmes are also offered in English medium, e.g. PhD Chemistry and Materials Technology at the Tomas Bata University in the Czech Republic or PhD in Strategic Information Systems Analysis at the Open University of Switzerland. A growing number of UK universities have overseas campuses, e.g. Nottingham in Malaysia and Heriot Watt in Dubai. This allows you to study for a UK degree, delivered in English, whilst living abroad. Even if your foreign language level is modest at the start of a postgraduate programme, by virtue of living overseas, you will have plenty of chance to develop it. Choosing to study abroad would also help you develop a wider perspective, which could be of interest to employers when you look for work. Take a look at Chapter 4 'The global graduate' for more on this.

 Increasingly, employers will look for some more interesting skills: things like cultural sensitivity and what makes a global graduate.

Carl Gilleard, Chief Executive, Association of Graduate Recruiters

Why study beyond an undergraduate degree?

It is important to ask yourself why you are even thinking of continuing your studies beyond an undergraduate degree, and it is highly likely that many other people will be asking you that very question: fellow students; family; friends; possibly your bank manager or any potential funding body; and perhaps, most critically, the admissions tutor for the programme you want to go onto.

There are many possible responses to the basic question: why study at a higher level? Each one takes a slightly different perspective, so you don't need to respond positively to all of them, but you do need to respond positively to at least one.

Because you really enjoy your subject

Intellectual curiosity and deep enjoyment of your subject are both important drivers if you are thinking of an academic degree. If you are thinking of a research degree, either MPhil initially or PhD eventually, they are both absolutely essential. On a research degree, you are going to study one small aspect of one specialist area of one discipline. Just look back at our brilliant example: Sam studied Psychology, took an option in Biological Psychology, which narrowed into Comparative Psychology and focused on non-human primates, which led her to work on the behaviour of squirrel monkeys. Once you have narrowed your own focus to your own research inquiry, you are then going to work for 12 months solid at the very least to reach Masters level. If you continue to PhD, you will be working on it for another two years full-time, and perhaps for several years if you study part-time. Your interest is what will pull you through, month after month, perhaps year after year. If you just feel very strongly that you want to delve further into your specialist area, don't worry if this seems irrational: it's probably a good sign.

brilliant example

'My ambition for the future is to complete my doctorate – something I hope to be embarking on in the very near future. Long term – who knows? I have been trained as a therapeutic practitioner and use a narrative therapy approach in much of my work. I hope to publish, to continue developing this way of working and to reflect on my practice as much as possible. I might end up in a lecture theatre near you!! Whichever way, I hope very much to be developing my personal practice in psychology until I retire. Psychology for me has been one of the most amazing and life-changing subjects to study. I have been studying it for seven to eight years and still it is ever changing, moving and posing me constant questions. I could not ask for more.'

Rhona, BSc (Hons) Psychology, PGCE, MSc

Because it's the main route to a career as either lecturer or researcher

If you are drawn to a career as a lecturer in higher education or a researcher, you will need to get a doctoral-level qualification, probably a PhD. There are some exceptions to this, but they really are the exceptions to the rule. Most universities now, when advertising for a lecturer or researcher post, will expect you either to have been awarded your doctorate or to be very far advanced, with perhaps only weeks to go before you formally complete your doctoral degree. This doesn't necessarily mean that you have to go straight from being at school to being an undergraduate to being a doctoral student to being a lecturer. You might undertake doctoral study as a mature student, perhaps even part-time while you are working. This is by no means unusual and would not be viewed adversely by selection panels. But you will still need to secure the doctorate in order to secure a sustainable career in higher education.

 example

'I now work in academic support as a research and development officer, having completed an MSc in Mathematics. My role utilises the statistical knowledge I gained on my course for evaluative research. I also use the IT knowledge I gained on my course, to support the work of the department. I have recently begun a PhD and I hope eventually to use my knowledge and experience to become a lecturer in higher education.'

Nicola, BSc (Hons) Mathematics with Computer Science and Information Systems, MSc Mathematics

Because entry to a profession demands an M-level qualification

Some jobs, particularly professional jobs, demand a postgraduate qualification. These professional (sometimes called vocational) courses are awarded by universities, but can also be recognised by professional bodies. Professional bodies set standards and regulate practitioners. Examples include the Institution of Civil Engineers or the Chartered Society of Physiotherapy. So you are awarded a postgraduate degree which can also give you access to a profession and licence to practise as a named professional. It is important to check (with the professional body) whether you need to have a recognised qualification, and then to check (with the university) whether the course you want has got professional body accreditation.

Thomas, our next brilliant example, completed a law degree and did a relevant academic Masters programme before undertaking the course required by the professional body as the first part of training to be a barrister.

brilliant example

'After completing my degree, I decided to continue my studies in order to give me a more specialised knowledge. So I completed a Masters degree in Law, Medicine and Healthcare. Completing the Masters degree has provided me with more in-depth knowledge on a subject which I enjoy and ultimately wish to practise in.

Following my Masters degree, I completed the Bar Professional Training course. I found the course extremely interesting as I was using the legal knowledge gained from my degrees in a practical context.'

Thomas, LLB, LLM

Because M-level qualifications give you leverage in the labour market

You'll realise by now that we use 'leverage' to mean gaining the necessary skills and know-how that enable you to move to a better job. Taking a Masters-level qualification can be the transition from one occupation to another. This can be within the same occupational sector, but extending your professional repertoire, e.g. an architect taking a course in Renewable Energy in the Built Environment. This can be to facilitate a move between two related occupational sectors, e.g. from mental health nursing to psychoanalyst. Or it can be a career change to something completely different, e.g. from laboratory technician to librarian. The training might be a requirement to practise in the new occupation, or it might help to formalise a particular interest within your own professional domain, as this example shows.

brilliant example

'After completing my BSc Honours degree in Sports and Exercise Science, I started my full-time career in the fitness industry and worked my way up to achieve a position in the NHS as a physical activity advisor . . . my personal ambition was to enhance my knowledge and expertise around cardiovascular disease, treatment, therapy and post-rehabilitation. I decided that, despite working full-time, I wanted to continue my studying career and found the MSc was ideal . . . I have continued to work with the regional cardiac rehabilitation service, and have found that postgraduate qualifications not only give you the opportunity to boost your knowledge but give you that edge to show you are a committed individual who is willing to work hard.'

Jennifer, MSc Cardiovascular Rehabilitation

Because you can develop specialist know-how for niche sectors

You can use a Masters degree not only as an academic qualification, but also as a time-limited space in which you will develop know-how that will put you in a better position for getting into very specialist or niche sectors. Some Masters programmes, particularly in the creative industries, will build in a lot of time for you to develop your own professional repertoire: some creative writing programmes, for example. On many specialist Masters, the university lecturers will make great efforts to bring in specialist lecturers from the relevant industry. Indeed, your lecturers themselves may well be practising in their industry. So, as well as extending your knowledge and understanding, you are given privileged access to valuable contacts within your chosen field. You need to be proactive here. Access and opportunities are very much the start of the story. It is up to you to seize chances and do everything you can to make the most of them. Networking is particularly important here, so have a look at Chapter 1 'Accessing job opportunities', which gives you practical help on how to network.

brilliant example

'During my second year studying Civil Engineering I started to realise I had doubts about whether Civil Engineering would be right for me. I wondered if it might be possible to transfer the engineering skills I was gaining to another part of the industry . . . motorsport. I realised I would need a more relevant degree to appeal to potential employers (in motorsport). I also thought it crucial to finish my Masters in Civil Engineering . . . in case I need to fall back on it . . . The Motorsport Engineering MSc was the only specialist qualification available in the UK at that time, with strong links to the motorsport sector. If I was to get a career as an engineer in motorsport, I felt I had to get on it! It has taken a great deal of determination, but now I am a systems engineer in a Formula One racing team.'

Oliver, MEng Civil Engineering, MSc Motorsport Engineering and Management

Because now is a good time

We have seen that you don't need to take a Masters qualification immediately on completion of your first degree, and we already know that not everyone starts an undergraduate career immediately after leaving school, so M-level qualifications can be taken at any stage in your career or, indeed, at any stage in your life.

brilliant dos and don'ts

Do undertake postgraduate study because

✔ you're passionate about your subject;

✔ you want to gain access to a profession;

✔ you want to progress in your sector;

✔ you want to move into a new sector;

✔ you are at a point in your life where you have time.

Don't undertake postgraduate study because

✘ you've no idea what else to do;

✘ you want to put off starting your career;

✘ your mates are doing it;

✘ your tutors think your talents would be wasted on the job market.

How to choose the right course for you

Be clear about why you want to study beyond an undergraduate degree

The earlier section in this chapter has explained that postgraduate degrees can meet a range of different demands: to satisfy intellectual curiosity; to satisfy professional body requirements; to help you break into a niche sector; or to prepare you for a career in higher education. Once you have clarified what it is you want to get out of postgraduate study, you can focus your search on the appropriate type of course.

Work out where you want to do your postgraduate study

Do you have a free choice of where you want to study? Perhaps you are constrained in terms of location, because of family commitments or housing arrangements. Before you restrict your search to a very limited geographical area, look at online or distance programmes. Or check out just how much attendance is required on campus: could you manage to stay overnight just for the study days?

If you do have the luxury of free choice, make the most of it! When compared to other segments of the labour force, graduates are more likely to move around for their jobs and graduate employers are more likely to expect them to relocate. So now is your chance to try living in another place or even another country.

How to find out more

Look at what individual universities offer

There are lots of postgraduate courses on offer, and lots of help in accessing information about them. There is plenty of online material: universities will have websites and, certainly within England, Wales and Northern Ireland, they are expected to publish clear and fairly detailed information about their courses, often called a specification. You can also request printed prospectuses from universities you are interested in: they often produce a separate postgraduate version which is less bulky than the undergraduate version. If you're not sure where to start, the postgraduate study section of the Graduate Prospects website (**www.prospects.ac.uk**) lets you search by region and subject.

Look at professional body course listings

If you are applying for a professional or vocational programme, you can turn to the relevant professional body to check what university courses offer accredited programmes. This can really help to focus your search.

Look beyond the UK

If you are thinking of studying outside the UK but in the European Union, don't be put off by the breathtaking amount of choice on offer. There are some very nifty websites with useful search facilities that allow you to set clear parameters for your search. The studyportals site **www.mastersportal.eu** is useful because it includes different sections on Masters, PhDs and scholarships, but is limited to Europe. There is a whole world out there beyond the EU, so look online for them too.

Probe beneath the glossy brochure

Ask people what they think: tutors, postgraduates, online contacts

Obviously, universities want to attract the best talent, so the course information they publish shows things in the best possible light. You can probe
beneath the surface by asking people what they really think. Your tutors may
have a view, so ask them about a programme's reputation. What do they
think of the people who teach on the course? If your tutors are themselves
qualified professionals, what advice would they give about where to study?
Do what we did, and ask people who have undertaken postgraduate programmes. You can start this in your own department by finding out who the
postgrads are and asking them about their courses. (Don't worry, they don't
usually bite!) You can also make use of social networking sites to post questions and learn from other people's experience. See Chapter 1 'Accessing
job opportunities' if you need help getting started on social networking sites.

Go and visit

As you may know from your undergraduate experience, universities run open
days where you meet students and tutors from the courses on offer, and have
a look at the facilities. One of the very best things about physically going to
a university open day is that you get a feel for it. So it may be a bit inconve-
nient, and it may cost you money to get there, but going to an open day is
always worth it. Even if you come away convinced it is not the right course or
location for you, you are better informed, which is definite progress in your
decision making, even if it doesn't feel like it at the time.

Of course, it may not be practical for you to visit the campus, especially if it
is overseas. You can still interact with students there, but online rather than
in person. See if there is a webcam or a 360-degree tour. Or maybe you could
Skype someone there to get a feel for the location.

brilliant tips

Questions to ask:

- What kind of jobs did last year's completers go on to?

- Do you have any links with the industry/profession?

- How much time will I spend in lectures and tutorials?

- How much self-directed study should I expect to do?

- What makes this course different from others?

- What kind of specialist teaching space do you offer?

What kind of a student am I?

As well as asking course tutors and postgraduate students some probing questions, you also need to ask yourself some probing questions too. While there are different types of postgraduate courses on offer, there are also different types of postgraduate student. You are, of course, a complex human being, and to pin you down by asking only a couple of questions is only to scratch the surface of what makes you the unique individual you are. However, thinking about two fairly basic behaviours can help you to interrogate whether a particular course mode is right for you. So just try to answer these two questions:

Are you (a) self-disciplined in your study or (b) more easily diverted?

Are you (a) happy in your own company or (b) do you seek out the company of others?

If you are opting for the (b) answers, maybe you shouldn't be opting for a distance-learning programme where you will have to structure your own study timetable, and will be working alone for the vast majority of your time. You know yourself better than anybody, so make use of that self-knowledge to identify the kind of course that will allow you to do your best.

Funding postgraduate study

You will realise very quickly that one stark difference between funding your postgraduate study, compared with funding your undergraduate degree, is that there isn't a unified system for funding that you just slot into. The sources of funding are out there, and there is good signposting.

People who can advise you

Tutors on your undergraduate programme can be helpful; remember that they probably had to go through the same process themselves. Admissions tutors on postgraduate courses are also a very good source of information and, as it is in their interests to get funded students on their courses, they are likely to be helpful.

Grants, loans and bursaries

Funding can be in the form of grants, bursaries or loans. Grants and bursaries are where the money online is given to you and you don't need to pay it back. You will, however, have to satisfy the conditions attached to the grant: if the grant expects you to complete the postgraduate course successfully, you'll need to do just that. Loans, however, do need to be repaid and the repayments will be with interest, so you end up paying back more than the amount you borrowed. Graduate Prospects produces an annual guide to postgraduate funding which comes out in September. This is an invaluable starting point, and you would do well to access this online at **www.prospects.ac.uk** at the very start of the academic year *before* the year you hope to start your postgraduate course.

 timesaver

Access the Graduate Prospects annual online publication: *The Postgraduate Funding Guide.* Published in September, **www.prospects.ac.uk.**

Funding yourself: combining study with employment

All of these sources of advice will merely signpost you; it is very much up to you to track down sources and follow up leads and, if you don't do it, it is unlikely that anybody else will do it for you. This section will outline all the sources of funding that might be open to you. A further alternative is to fund yourself, perhaps by mixing part-time study with part-time work. Official statistics show that about half of postgraduate students do this. The problem here being that you will need to find the balance between these two competing demands on your time and brain power. One good way forward is to find employment that enhances your area of study, for example working as a lab or teaching assistant if you are doing doctoral study, or doing sessional youth work if you are studying youth work.

 example

'As the course was so limited in its hours (something that had originally attracted me) it meant that I carried on working a lot of hours and was therefore unable to give my studies the time and attention I feel they needed for me to have gained the most from the opportunity. It is difficult to come straight from work into an academic environment and just switch from one role to another and really reach your potential.'

Lesley, MA Fine Art

Be resilient and resourceful

For most people, accommodation is their biggest single expenditure. Rather than looking for sufficient funding to pay rent, could you find some way of getting a rent reduction or even a job with accommodation? Perhaps you could be a warden in a university hall of residence if you are a postgraduate student, or maybe you could ask family or friends to let you have a room rent free in exchange for helping around the house. The chances are that you will end up stitching together a patchwork of funding to get you through. Resilience and resourcefulness come into play when funding postgraduate study. If you find you are getting disheartened, remember that many people before you have somehow found a way, and so can you.

Sources of funding for postgraduate study

Universities themselves fund postgraduates

You may be surprised to find that universities themselves sometimes offer funding direct to postgraduate students. Often this comes about because the course tutor (or someone in the university administration) has secured funding (from public money or from employers) to meet the demand for training or research. This is more likely to be limited to designated programmes, rather than applying to the individual student irrespective of the course chosen. There might be a brilliant fit between the course you want to do and the courses that are funded. Or you might be thinking about modifying your course choice in order to follow the funding. That's fine, but do think this one through so you are confident you have the enthusiasm and ability you will need in order to succeed on the funded course, rather than your original choice.

Research councils

A small part of the work of research councils is to fund postgraduate students through grants. Soon to be reorganised, at present there are seven research councils in total: Arts and Humanities Research Council; Biotechnology and Biological Sciences Research Council; Economic and Social Research Council; Engineering and Physical Sciences Research Council; Medical Research Council; Natural Environment Research Council; and Science and Technology Facilities Council. The big advantage of research council funding is that it is a grant rather than a loan, and it should be enough for you to pay course fees and live on, albeit modestly. The funding can be for either a Masters degree or doctoral study, and successful applicants would normally have a good first degree, that is either a first class or upper second class honours degree. Eligibility is usually restricted to UK or EU nationals. You need to be aware that competition is intense: research council funding is keenly sought and hard won.

Public funding

You might be eligible for public funding outside the research councils. For example, students in Northern Ireland and in Scotland can apply to particular schemes for postgraduate funding, and the European Union is another source worth considering. As eligibility criteria are different for each funding stream, and can also change from year to year (particularly when there is pressure on public funding in general), you will need to pick your way through the details of each of the various funding streams to find one that could work for you.

Postgraduate loans

Loans of up to £10,000 per student for postgraduate study are available through the Department for Business, Innovation & Skills (BIS). It is non-means tested and is paid directly to the student.

 tip

Check out what loans are currently on offer. Banks can withdraw or launch new products, and schemes using public money can be subject to change of government policy.

Charities

Charities vary enormously in scale and scope, so some will offer big grants to cover tuition fees and living costs for full-time postgraduate study, where others will make only a modest contribution to your overall needs. On the principle that any money is better than no money, even the modest sums are worth applying for. Each funding scheme and every different charity will have its own procedures. They are, however, all likely to set clear eligibility criteria and to have a set procedure for funding applications. All of this will take time, so applying in the September of your final undergraduate year will not be too soon. You need to be aware that some charities will award a grant only once they are satisfied that you have exhausted all other possible sources of funding, so you'll need to show that you have made applications to some of the other funding streams outlined here as well as applying for charitable funds.

Employers can sometimes be persuaded

If you are already employed, perhaps in a graduate job, it is worth looking to your employer for funding. There may already be a company scheme in place, in which case you'll need to check out eligibility and application procedure. If it is a big company, the human resources department should be able to advise here. If it is a small to medium-sized enterprise (SME) it is worth having a look at government or EU funding for workplace development. If there is nothing like this already in place, it is still worth exploring this option with your employer, but you will probably have to make a proposal. Think about this from the employer's side: what's in it for them? How will you be able to add value to the company once you have the postgraduate qualification? Could the postgraduate study itself be of value to the company – for example if you are doing some kind of research, could this help the company be more productive or competitive? Even if the company can't pay all your fees, could they make a contribution, or could you share the cost between you? Or could they pay the fees up front with you paying them back through salary sacrifice, a bit like an interest-free season ticket loan? Although it may seem daunting to approach your employer for help with funding your career progression, the very fact that you are taking the initiative says a lot about you as an employee: it shows you are resourceful, proactive and business-minded. So, prepare your case well and go for it.

Which comes first – getting a place or getting funding?

Clearly, there are two key challenges that you face as an aspiring postgraduate: you need to secure a place on the course of your choice, and you need to secure the funding that will enable you to take up the place and succeed on the course. Don't worry about getting a place before you get funding, or indeed getting funding before you get a place. Certainly don't get so stuck worrying about doing things in the wrong order that you don't actually take any action. Pursue these twin challenges at the same time. The worst thing that can happen is that you end up with more than one source of funding and more than one offer of a place. That's quite an enviable position to be in, so risk it.

brilliant tip

Don't worry about the sequence of securing a place on a course and securing funding. Pursue both at the same time: you'll probably need to apply to more than one course, and you'll probably need to consider more than one source of funding. Just get started with both challenges.

Making a good application

Everything that applies to job applications applies to applications for post-graduate courses. Chapter 11 takes you through this in more detail, but here are a few key pointers to get you started.

Dates and deadlines

Some postgraduate courses run to strict deadlines by which applications must be received. You need to check if this applies to your chosen programme and, if it does, you must be sure to get your application in on time or it simply will not be considered. You'll need to give yourself enough time to work through your application so you don't have to rush to meet the deadline.

Even if programmes don't publish a deadline, if an admissions tutor has received sufficient good applicants to fill the available spaces, they may well stop making offers (conditional or unconditional) and start a waiting list. This means you'll get a place on the course only if someone who is holding an offer of a place turns it down. So it is better to apply early than to risk the course filling up without you.

Personal statement

Make sure that your personal statement shows that you have got what they are looking for: go back to the course literature and see what they say about the kind of student they want. You will need to show motivation, ideally by including examples of how that motivation has shown through already. You will also need to show ability to study at postgraduate level: this includes the ability to write effectively, so take care to structure your work and to check spelling and grammar are correct.

Referees

You will need to provide references. For postgraduate courses, it is usual to request two referees, both of them academic. You will need to talk to your referees and get their agreement before you include their names on your application. You need to be clear with them that this is an academic reference, which means you are going to need to approach people who can actually comment on your academic ability. This might be your personal tutor, a tutor from your first couple of years' study, or your final-year dissertation supervisor, but should include someone who is familiar with your academic record right now. If it has been a while since you have been studying, this can be difficult. However, you will need to try to find someone who can comment on your ability. This might mean going back to your last place of study, even if that is some time ago. Or you could use someone more recent, but they will need to say something about your potential for postgraduate study based on their observation and judgement. It is helpful here if your referee has personal experience of postgraduate study, so they can use their understanding of what postgraduate study demands to inform their judgement of your potential to achieve a postgraduate degree.

 brilliant tip

Make sure you have two academic referees. Both should be able to comment on your potential to achieve a postgraduate degree. If you have been out of study for a long time so can't readily locate an academic referee, try to find someone who has personal experience of studying at postgraduate level, even if they are not a tutor.

Applying even if you don't have a first degree

You don't necessarily need to have a first (undergraduate) degree in order to be accepted onto a postgraduate course. Vocational degrees have a long and noble tradition of taking on people with relevant work experience. However, in addition to that experience, you will need to show that you have the capacity to achieve at a higher level of study. So it is important to showcase any steps you have taken to increase your knowledge and know-how in the field of study. This may have been practical experience, but may also have been through work-shadowing a professional, or doing some work experience or volunteering in the field. Your written work will be very important in making a first impression, so do spend time on your application form and get someone to have a look at it and give you constructive feedback. That can be nerve-racking, but better to get feedback from someone so you can improve it before you send the application off unchecked and not even get invited to interview for a place on the course.

Applying without a 'good' degree

A 'good' degree means a first class or upper second class honours degree. Research degrees normally demand a good degree as a minimum for entry. Whilst it is possible to be offered a place on a research degree without a good first degree, it is very unusual. Don't despair if you can't go immediately from undergraduate to research degree because of this hurdle. You can go step by step; by progressing from undergraduate to postgraduate degree and from there to doctoral-level study. It takes longer, but that time allows you to develop your scholarly performance, which will stay with you for the rest of your learning days, so it is never time wasted.

Applying to jobs once you have your postgraduate qualification

If everything goes right, you'll get a place on the postgraduate course you want, and you'll make a brilliant success of it. And, before you know it, you'll be making applications yet again, this time for a job. Present your postgraduate studies as a thought-through career choice, not the result of procrastination, or a reluctance to enter the world of work. Check back through earlier parts of this chapter for good, positive reasons for choosing postgraduate study. Show the employer very clearly what you yourself have gained through your postgraduate study. It should have enhanced your skillset and mindset (if that means nothing to you, have a look at Chapter 2) and so you are offering added value to the employer. Be confident: you have travelled further for having undertaken higher-level study.

 recap

- Make sure you have a positive reason for going on to postgraduate study.

- Choose a course that plays to your personal strengths and circumstances.

- Consider studying outside the UK.

- Don't worry in what order to apply for a place and to apply for funding: the important thing is to apply early.

- Be resourceful and resilient in funding your postgraduate study.

- You'll need an academic reference, so talk to your tutor about your plans.

- Be positive in selling your postgraduate qualification to an employer; it should add value to you both.

What to do next

If you do nothing else, access the Graduate Prospects publications about postgraduate study online and read through them for ideas. See if there is a postgraduate fair or open day either at your current or target university: register for it and go there to get a feel for what's on offer. Talk to your personal tutor (or a tutor whose judgement you trust) about your plans. See if there are current postgraduates in your department who you can talk to about their experiences.

PART 2

How to make the most of what's out there

CHAPTER 8

Knowing who you are: skills, interests and values

There are two important perspectives when planning your brilliant career. One is what's out there, which we explored in Part 1; the other is who you are, which we cover in this chapter. It's good to try and have both of these perspectives in your mind. Both have enormous value – a sound knowledge of graduate opportunities helps you to be realistic in your plans, while an understanding of your own strengths and preferences will make you a more successful applicant. Even more importantly, this understanding and its application to your career plan will make you a more fulfilled person. When jobs are scarce it's easy to focus on getting whatever is available – and certainly it may be necessary to compromise or to plan for the longer term – but even in a restricted job market there is still scope for choice.

Skills, interests and values

In this chapter we will help you to analyse your own skills, interests and values.

Here are three fundamental questions: spend a little time thinking about them, making a note of your answers – just words or phrases will be fine. We are giving you some prompts to help.

What are you good at?

Think about:

- technical skills associated with your degree subject, such as using specialist equipment or software;

- generic or transferable work skills, such as cash handling, working under pressure, meeting targets, supervising others, report writing;
- soft skills, such as working in a team, communication, time management, showing initiative.

What are you interested in?

This question covers the kind of physical and social setting you want to work in (office-based, a variety of locations, outdoors, production, laboratory, in a team or alone) as well as the subject matter – would you like to use your degree subject in your job? Remember that around half of graduate jobs don't specify a particular subject, so, while it's not necessary for you to use your subject, it might be something you would like to do.

What do you believe in and how does this fit with your career plan?

At first sight this is less straightforward than the other two questions. To help you, think about which of the following is something you care about:

- protecting the environment;
- improving the life chances of people who are disadvantaged;
- contributing to the economy through provision of goods or services;
- being creative, with words or materials;
- sharing, creating or discovering knowledge;
- achieving a high standard of living.

These are examples of values, or beliefs that guide the way we live our lives. Some people live out their values outside their working life, for example a high-flying business executive whose work role is to contribute to the economy and who gives time and money to a local charity for the homeless; others look for a working life that is consistent with their values, for example an international development worker. Thinking about what matters to you is another way to identify suitable job opportunities.

Make a note of your answers to our three questions.

 tip

Think about these three questions:

● What are you good at?

● What are you interested in?

● What do you believe in and how does this fit with your career plan?

Why does it matter?

Firstly, knowing yourself better helps you to get started if you have no particular preferences about your future career. If you can think and learn about
what you are good at, what you are interested in, and what you believe in,
you will begin to identify job choices. You will also be able to eliminate jobs
from your career plan and this is just as useful, as it helps you to narrow
down the possibilities. It also helps you to identify the underlying factors
in the jobs you are both choosing and eliminating, which in turn helps you
to broaden your range of choices. As you learn more about the detail of job
opportunities you will be able to fit this knowledge with what you know about
yourself. Remember to refer back to Part 1 of this book to revisit the kinds
of opportunities open to you as a graduate.

Secondly, career success and satisfaction are more likely to be achieved if
there is a good match with what you are good at, what you are interested
in, and what you believe in and believe to be important. Have a look at this
brilliant example to see what we mean.

⏺ brilliant example

'There was so much that my course taught me, including skills that I can use in all aspects of my life. Doing Drama and Theatre Studies encouraged me to be myself and show the world what I had to offer, and this began opening up so many opportunities for me. As well as the content of the course, I developed skills like working to deadlines and self-organisation, which brought with it self-discipline and an increase in my independence. I feel that all these skills have stood me in good stead for the world of work.

Using the wealth of experience I gained at university, along with the academic knowledge, I am now working as an Arts & Cultural Positive Activities Officer for an amazing community interest company delivering activities to children in deprived areas. Workshops range from DJ-ing through drama and graffiti to film production, to raise the aspirations of young people in those communities. The children have the opportunity to work towards an arts award, a nationally recognised certificate which boosts their confidence and gives them something to be proud of. I thoroughly enjoy this role and the satisfaction it gives me in seeing young people, who once may not have had many aspirations, achieve and build in their confidence and outlook on life.'

Joanne, BA (Hons) Drama and Theatre Studies

Now read this example again and look for evidence of Joanne's skills, interests and values in her story. All three are critical to her success in, and enjoyment of, her brilliant graduate career.

We noticed her references to:

- working to deadlines;
- self-organisation;
- self-discipline;
- increased independence;
- satisfaction at seeing young people with low aspirations grow in confidence and broaden their outlook;
- her interest in using her degree subject.

Each of us is unique

Although we referred to Joanne's achieving a good match between her own skills, interests and values and the job she has chosen, this doesn't mean that we are trying to put square pegs in round holes. Two students on the same course, getting the same grades, doing the same kind of part-time work, will each make their own unique and valid sense of their experience – which in turn will impact on their career planning. A skilled careers adviser will help you to 'make meaning' of your own particular experiences and ambitions. So, in addition to considering your skills, interests and values and how these might be fulfilled in particular job roles, you might also think about key turning points in your life so far, how people or events have influenced you, and the extent to which you take a logical, rational approach or an intuitive approach to planning your future. These are all factors that contribute to your uniqueness.

The skill of reflection

To understand more about your skills, interests and values you need to develop your personal insight and self-awareness. Some people are comfortable describing what they think, feel and believe, others less so – it might not have been encouraged in their upbringing, or they might not find it easy to put such concepts into words. It often takes someone else to tell us what we are good at – perhaps we fear sounding big-headed or overconfident. As far as interests and values are concerned, we might need help in generalising from the specific example to the broader category – 'I really enjoy the voluntary work I'm doing and believe it is making a difference, but I don't know of any paid jobs like this.' Tests, questionnaires and inventories are a great help in learning more about ourselves and we will come to these later. But first let's look at what we can learn just by taking time to reflect on what has happened.

How reflection works

Watch any post-match discussion of a big football game and you will see the experts taking the game apart, reviewing the successes as well as the weak points of the game and analysing the performance of every player in great detail. If you are a football fan, you might well have evaluated the game in the same way. If not, you might be amazed at the perception of the experts, at the extent to which they notice and interpret what's going on in the game. We can be sure that the manager, coach and players use the same process of review soon after the match, in order to make improvements for next time. What has this got to do with career planning?

- Firstly, the experts and professionals take time to reflect.
- Secondly, they know what they are looking for and can describe what they see.
- Thirdly, they know what this means for future performance.

So let's apply this to something you might do, say working in a group of other students to complete a project. You get an average mark for the work. Which of the following do you do?

1   Say, 'Great, that's a pass', and think no more about it.
2   Take time to read your feedback, talk to your tutor, think about what went well and why, what went badly and why, what your own role was in the group, how you could behave differently next time to get a better result, and then make a note somewhere to remind you.

Option 2 might sound like a lot of trouble – but the gain is that you will have an insight into how you work as a member of a team (a classic area for you to cover in an application and for employers to explore at interview) and a sense of how to become more skilled. You will also find that, if you get into this way of thinking, it will become part of your behaviour and much less of an effort. Your university may have an electronic framework, or e-portfolio, to help you to keep your record. Otherwise, just devise a simple template that you can update as significant events occur.

Try this yourself

Now try this one for yourself, this time focusing on your communication skills. Take an example – giving a presentation to your seminar group or handling a difficult customer in the workplace – and answer the following questions.

1   What happened? (Describe the setting and the activity/incident.)

2   What went well? Why? How do you know?

3   What went less well? Why? How do you know?

4   What would you do differently next time? What do you need to help you to do this?

Notice that there is a new question here – how do you know? The answers to this question are the evidence you need to show that you have the skill in question. Employers will seek evidence – it's not enough to say, 'I'm really good at communicating with people.'

Where's the evidence?

Let's go back to the example of giving a presentation. Evidence can come from:

- your own self-reflection ('although I covered the ground, I was running out of time and I felt as if I rushed the last part');

- the response of the audience (they looked interested/stayed awake/asked questions/told me afterwards they understood it); and

- feedback from your tutor (informal comments, written feedback, an actual grade or mark).

Gathering this evidence and being willing to listen to feedback will make a real difference to what you do next time – in other words, it will improve your performance.

So go back to those four steps – what happened, what went well, what went less well, what will you do differently next time and try to apply them. You will learn more about your own skills, and you will get better. Best of all you will develop a skill employers really value, because you will be a person who learns from experience and who actively seeks opportunities for learning.

Most graduates now are expected to do regular evaluations of where they are at and where they are going . . . developing the individual to the point where they can take control of their life, their learning and their career.

Carl Gilleard, Chief Executive, Association of Graduate Recruiters

More techniques to help you to know who you are

Let's go back to those three questions at the start of the chapter:

● What are you good at?

● What are you interested in?

● What do you believe in and how does this fit with your career plan?

For some people, thinking about their skills, interests and values is enough, especially if they have developed the skill of reflection we discussed earlier in the chapter. However, many people need some help in structuring their thoughts, from talking to someone, e.g. a careers adviser, to completing a questionnaire.

Talk to people

If your university offers one-to-one careers consultations, you really don't need to know what you want to do before you book your slot! Careers advisers use skilful questioning to guide you through these three areas as a way to help you to develop a career plan. It's surprising how often 'I don't know what I want to do' really means 'I've got a few ideas but I'm not sure . . .'

If you can't get access to one-to-one consultations with a careers adviser, talk to your personal tutor, or a tutor you get on with who knows you well. Just thinking aloud with a good listener can move you forward. Also, try other people you know who might have some time – friends, family, someone you know through a part-time job or work experience. Get them to help you to answer our three questions. If they are in a position to give you feedback, ask them, so that you get a better insight into your skills.

brilliant example

'With an idea in mind of the type of career I was interested in, I visited the university careers service to talk to a careers adviser about my options. With the use of interactive software I was able to analyse my skills and get possible career ideas which I was then able to discuss with the careers adviser. She also referred me to a really good website, Graduate Prospects, which contained a wealth of different information for me to research. I found all these processes really useful and realised that my strengths were in communication and teamworking, and that I enjoyed a competitive environment.'

Paul, BSc (Hons) Sport and Exercise Science

Use psychometric tests

In Chapter 12 of this book we will be looking at how tests and questionnaires are used by employers during selection. In this chapter we will tell you how to use them to learn more about yourself. Tests used in career planning or selection are often referred to as 'psychometric' tests. This simply means tests that 'measure the mind'. We will look more at the detail of psychometric tests in Chapter 12 and have a look at our companion book, *Brilliant Passing Psychometric Tests* (Mulvey, 2015); for now, here are some quick definitions.

brilliant definitions

Psychometric test – a set of questions that measure an aspect of mental performance or behaviour. The word psychometric means measuring the mind.

Aptitude test – a measure of a particular aptitude or ability consisting of questions with right and wrong answers. Scores are compared with others to assess performance.

Personality test – a set of questions designed to explore and describe aspects of personality, or what kind of person we are. There are no right or wrong answers, though when employers use a personality test they may be looking for certain characteristics.

You can use aptitude tests to check out your ability with logic, numbers and words. They may not tell you anything you don't already know – but you might be surprised.

Personality tests, on the other hand, can give you real insight into your characteristics and preferences. They are particularly useful because they contain statements – often multiple choice – that act as prompts. So instead of asking yourself, 'How do I contribute to a team?', a personality test will give you a set of situations to choose from, which, taken together, will indicate how you usually behave. Personality tests and questionnaires are not magic – they only reflect back to you information you have put in, but in a systematic and logical way.

'Career Planner' is a readily accessible and career-specific questionnaire, which can be found on the Graduate Prospects website. Questions are in four sections: first steps; skills; motivation; and desires. Complete 'first steps' and you will see a list of matched occupations; as you complete each further section the list is refined and edited, and there are links to help you to explore the best matches in more detail.

Employability skills

Skills that have particular currency in the job market are often referred to as employability skills. They are the skills and behaviours that enable you to interact and work with a range of different people, and they can be learned. Here is a reminder of the employability skills we listed and defined in Chapter 2 – look back if you need to remind yourself what some of these terms mean.

● self-management;

● resilience;

● teamwork;

● business and customer awareness;

● problem solving;

● project management;

- communication and literacy;

- numeracy;

- application of IT;

- foreign language skills.

It may not be obvious at first glance, but most degree courses provide opportunities to develop skills that transfer to the workplace. A connection between a degree in Theology and a career in the police might seem unlikely, but read what Andrew says.

brilliant example

'My degree encouraged me to think beyond the expected norms, to challenge ideas and express that thinking. My work certainly demands that I look closely at any given situation and try to look beyond the glaringly obvious . . . whether working with a prisoner or developing new working practices. The close study and intricate dissection of theory, particularly in Theology, was responsible for developing these skills.'

Andrew, BA (Hons) Theology and Psychology, MTh postgraduate student

Find out more

Your university may offer sessions or online materials on how to develop your employability skills. Sometimes these sessions form part of your subject timetable; in other cases they are an optional extra. See what you can find out about what's on offer where you are. Check your university careers service website or Facebook page regularly, or follow them on Twitter. An Internet search for employability skills will also bring up useful questionnaires and checklists.

tip

In addition to the skills needed for a particular job, employers of graduates look for competence in a range of employability skills, so look for opportunities to learn about, develop and show evidence of these skills.

Making the connections

If you have followed this chapter through, you should now have a clearer idea about those aspects of yourself that help to determine your future choice. You might even have drawn up a summary of your own skills, interests and values. It may be important to add other information about yourself, for example your health and fitness, your family situation and your finances. In the final chapter of this handbook we will explore the impact of these other factors on your career plan. For now, let's think about how to make use of your new insights.

 dos and don'ts

Do

✔ keep up to date with how your skills, interests and values change over time;

✔ seek out opportunities to develop your skills, through formal and informal learning;

✔ develop your interests with new experiences;

✔ examine job information for skills, interests and values as well as for the activities involved in the job.

Don't

✘ stand still – keep on learning, whatever the circumstances.

Try this exercise

Looking at your own skills, interests and values will help you to look at jobs in a new way. Think about your last part-time or vacation job – you might have taken it 'because it was there', or because you always work there in the vacation, or because your friend works there. For a few moments, think about this job and answer the following questions:

- What skills did you need, or use?

- In doing the job, what did it help to be interested in?

- What values did the organisation hold, either in a mission statement or in everyday working practice?

Now answer these questions for a graduate job you might think about doing:

- What skills will you need?

- What will it help to be interested in?

- What values are likely to be important?

You can find information about skills and interests in the entry requirements or person specification for the job. Information about values is harder to pin down. Though a company website will often quote the organisation's values, you need to think about the detail of a particular job to work out what the associated values might be.

 recap

- Knowing more about yourself, especially your skills, interests and values, will help with your career planning and jobsearch.

- Use the skill of reflection to develop your self-awareness and build your evidence.

- Employability skills are important in all jobs – work on yours.

- Get an in-depth insight into job opportunities by using the 'skills, interests and values' headings.

What to do next

- Use the ideas in this chapter to identify your skills, interests and values.

- Complete the 'Career Planner' on the Graduate Prospects website.

CHAPTER 9

Work experience: making it purposeful

Work experience offers enormous benefits to you in your career planning and job seeking. It sometimes has a poor image – it's associated with school, it's boring, or it's exploitation. We will show you in this chapter that it need be none of these. You can choose and manage your work experience to suit your needs, and make it work for you.

Firstly, we need to be clear what we mean by work experience, and how it differs from work and employment.

brilliant definition

Work – a purposeful activity that could be done as a paid job.

Examples from your everyday life include fixing a computer, delivering or collecting something for a friend, decorating a room, braiding someone's hair, giving some sports coaching. Reasons you might do this: to save money, because you enjoy it, are good at it, because friends will return the favour with something they can do, because you want to get more practice. Employment is simply work you get paid to do. So how does work experience fit in?

brilliant definition

Work experience – work that you do in order to develop your skills and knowledge. It is usually unpaid but, in some circumstances, such as sandwich placements and some internships, work experience is paid.

In the rest of this chapter, we will look at different kinds of work experience, how to access them and how you can benefit from them, and we'll show you how to get the best out of your work experience.

Five kinds of work experience

What you choose to do will depend on a number of factors, including how much time you have, what you want to achieve, and whether you really need to get work experience as an entry requirement for a graduate job or course. Later in the chapter we will look at the overall benefits of work experience, but first we need to be clear about the different kinds of opportunities covered in our definition. There are five main categories, each with its own particular benefit, or impact. We will illustrate some of these with real-life stories from graduates.

Volunteering

Volunteering is, by definition, something you offer to do without being paid. You might think it's about working for a charity, or fundraising for a good cause, but it also includes spending a couple of weeks in a law firm or a primary school in order to learn more about what goes on while making yourself useful. It could be one day a week, a block of time, or just a one-day event like beach cleaning or marshalling for a charity bike ride. A particular benefit is that employers see you as motivated because you are choosing to use your spare time constructively.

brilliant example

'In my second year I had to choose between studying abroad or having a work placement. I went abroad but realised at the start of my third year that I had missed out. I joined the local tourist board as a volunteer for two days a week, and learned many valuable skills which helped me to apply my studies to real-life situations. Towards the end of my third year a full-time job in the tourist board came up – I got it!'

Caroline, BA (Hons) Marketing and Tourism

How to get in

Some organisations are highly dependent on volunteers and may recruit on your campus with posters and display stands, but other opportunities are less visible. Follow our suggestions to find a really good volunteering opportunity.

brilliant dos and don'ts

Do

✔ find the student volunteering organisers in your university. They help to 'match' volunteers to opportunities – you tell them what you would like to do and how much time you have, and they will make you an offer. You may need a DBS (Disclosure and Barring Service) check, which they will help you with. Be aware that having a criminal record may not rule you out entirely but it may restrict the opportunities open to you;

✔ contact the volunteer bureau in your nearest town or city if you have already graduated – they will do the same job of matching you to what's available;

✔ make a direct approach by letter or email if you have an organisation in mind that isn't on the university's list of opportunities. This works especially when you want to spend a short block of time observing and learning – but make sure that you offer to do some work too. You need not be specific, just show willing! Help them by saying why you want to spend time there and what you hope to gain;

✔ ask people you know. We discuss networking in Chapter 1 'Accessing job opportunities'. Friends and relatives are useful as a way in, but remember firstly, that you will be in a work role in the organisation, not as a niece, godson or next-door neighbour; and secondly, that they may have stuck their neck out to get you in – so don't let them down.

Don't

✘ let people down. Many organisations rely on volunteers, so if you have made a regular commitment, keep to it. If there's a day when you really can't make it, for a good reason, let them know.

Work placement as part of your course

Some courses include a work-based or employability module that can either be compulsory or optional. The extent to which you can choose what you do varies according to the university and the subject – but if you have the chance, it's well worth taking. Assessment may be based on the tasks you have carried out for the employer; or it may be about your own learning during the placement. This means what you have learned about yourself – your skills, interests and capabilities – as well as what you have learned about the organisation. The personal insights you get from this process of reflection will help with your career planning, and the particular benefit of a work placement is that it might lead to a job.

brilliant example

'As part of my Animal Behaviour and Welfare course I did a six-week placement with a charity that trains dogs to assist people with disabilities so that they are able to live more independently. The placement gave me the skills and experience to improve my chances with future job applications, as well as reconfirming that this was the area I wanted to pursue. A year later, the charity contacted me to offer me a temporary post for maternity cover. Four months after that I was offered a permanent post as the charity was expanding.'

Anna, BSc Animal Behaviour and Welfare

How to get in

Some universities have a department or team whose job it is to find placements for all students. This works well because relationships are built up between the university and employers over time and approaches are centrally coordinated. If this is the case at your university, make sure that you provide all the information you are asked for, within the deadlines set. This way you are more likely to get the kind of placement you want.

Other universities expect you to find your own placement. This offers you greater flexibility to tailor the placement more closely to your preferences, but it does also mean that you'll need to be proactive. Here's what to do.

brilliant dos and don'ts

Do

✔ think about the kind of experience you want, based on your career plans, your interests, and the gaps you would like to fill. Do think about talking this over with a tutor or a careers adviser;

✔ identify the organisations that are likely to fit the bill – ask your careers service, your tutors and your contacts. For possible leads, get inspiration from job advertisements and business directories, both in print and online;

✔ write a good letter of application, setting out what you want and why, e.g. 'a four-week work placement to apply the learning from my course in a commercial setting', (don't say 'because I have to do this for my course') and what you can offer while you are there. Check for spelling and punctuation and include your contact details. If you don't hear within say a fortnight, follow up with a polite phone call;

✔ start looking in plenty of time – six months ahead, more for a one-year placement.

Don't

✘ settle for an easy option – your old school, your Saturday job, your uncle's firm – unless it really fits in with your career plan and adds value to your CV.

Work shadowing

This is usually a short spell, from one day up to a week, where you find out more about a job by accompanying someone who does that job in their daily work. The great thing is that you could spend time with anyone in an organisation, from a new graduate trainee to the chief executive. You're not expected to do their job, so you can really concentrate on observing, listening and learning about what they do, to build up your knowledge of a particular kind of work. It's low cost and relatively low effort for organisations, so it can be easier to set up than a longer placement or voluntary opportunity. The gain to you is that it opens up contacts and adds to your networking.

How to get in

Some universities offer work shadowing placements so check this out first. Otherwise, just look back at the dos and don'ts for getting your own work placement. The same principles apply, but this time you will be asking for the chance to shadow for a day, or a week, as a way to enhance your experience and knowledge. Also, remember that, for some roles in the public eye, you can observe informally, as Thomas's story illustrates.

brilliant example

'So that I could see what a career as a barrister is like, I contacted various chambers to arrange mini-pupillages, the name given to a few days shadowing barristers in court and in meetings with clients. Not only did this give me an insight into a career at the Bar, but it meant I met barristers at various chambers. In my days off at university or in the holidays, I often went to court and sat in the public gallery observing cases, giving me more opportunity to see barristers in action and sometimes speaking to those I had spent time with on mini-pupillage.'

Thomas, LLB, LLM and Bar Professional Training course

The next two categories are a little different as they may involve payment, but are still work experience according to our definition.

Sandwich and vacation placements during your degree

These placements are either the whole of the penultimate year of your degree, or they fit into a vacation – usually, but not always, summer. They may not be assessed as part of your course. However, a course that is designed to include a sandwich year will require you to carry out the placement in order to pass your degree. Some vocational degrees like Engineering will expect you to undertake relevant vacation placements.

Travel and international trade and commerce have led to a rise in the number of courses with a 'year out', though some of these offer a year of study abroad rather than work experience. Here, we are using the term sandwich course to refer to four-year degree courses, which include a one-year placement in industry, typically in science, business or vocational programmes, such as quantity surveying or dietetics. There are particular benefits – a substantial, one-year placement can make a real difference to your job prospects because you have evidence to demonstrate what you can do. A vacation placement adds to your experience and demonstrates that you are purposeful in choosing how to spend your time off.

? brilliant question and answer

Q What is the difference between a vacation placement and a vacation job?

A The difference is in the intention – the employer is offering you some work that will help you towards your degree, and may signal this with a clear 'vacation placement' label; and you are choosing to do it for the same reason.

How to get in

If your placement is a course requirement, there should be some help at the university, even if it's just the contact details of last year's placements. Otherwise, use websites such as Graduate Prospects, get help from your careers service and try personal contacts. Your part-time job in retail just might have something in management or buying if that's your interest.

Be prepared – more is expected of you at the application stage than for the shorter work placements in term-time, which we looked at earlier in the chapter. You may have to go through a full selection process, including application form and interview, so look at Chapters 11 and 12 'Making applications: getting past the first post' and 'Succeeding in selection' for pointers. On the plus side, a recent survey of one hundred top employers revealed that they expect one in three graduate jobs to be filled by applicants who have already worked for the organisation, on a placement or during the vacation. So the effort could pay off.

Internship after graduation

An internship usually refers to a period of planned work experience for graduates. The term is sometimes also used for vacation placements between your penultimate and final year. It was introduced partly to offer something useful to graduates feeling the effects of the recession on their jobsearch; job prospects have now improved, but internships have become established as part of the employment landscape.

Some internships are paid, others are not. Whether you're entitled to payment will depend on what you actually do for the organisation – not what your role is called. If you are performing as a worker, you must be paid at least the national minimum wage. If you are taken on as a volunteer, you're unlikely to receive payment. Even if your internship is unpaid, however, it's worth asking whether the organisation could cover your expenses, such as daily travel costs.

The particular benefit is that some employers use an internship as an extension of the selection process, so you can demonstrate your suitability for the job in the workplace.

How to get in

Internships are advertised on websites such as Graduate Prospects and Graduate Talent Pool.

brilliant example

'I came to realise that the people who get the graduate jobs are the people who had gained work experience during their time at university . . . I decided to take out a loan to support a political internship . . . Ultimately, it's all well and good having knowledge of a subject, but a practical ability to perform in a working environment is completely different. My eight-month internship involved working for three days a week in every imaginable part of political campaigning. What an eye opener! . . . after the election, I wrote to a dozen or so newly elected MPs explaining what I had been doing. Three days later I had an interview and was offered a job as a parliamentary assistant.'

Kevin, BSc (Hons) Politics

How you can benefit

Whichever kind of work experience you choose there are great gains to be had – and not only because you will be more attractive to an employer, though clearly this is important.

Personal confidence and transferable skills

Just being engaged in a purposeful activity that has clear outputs and helps other people out, either directly or indirectly, can give you a sense of achievement and a confidence boost. If you pick up some skills for employment, even better. The student in the following example volunteered within her university in a variety of roles, not obviously connected to her graduate job as an innovations researcher. Notice all the gains she made.

brilliant example

'One of the voluntary roles I took on was as a student ambassador. I introduced new and potential students to the campus and showed them what was available to them on campus and the services open to them. Having been a new student previously myself, I knew how they felt and the need to help them settle in as soon as possible.

I also worked as a volunteer one day a week in a university department. This gave me a chance to experience an office environment and to see the university services from the other side of the counter. I undertook lots of different tasks, including general admin tasks and statistical analysis as well as helping out at different events put on by the department. It was a very team-oriented department, which taught me so much about the need to work as a team.'

Jo, BSc (Hons) Mathematics

In this one example, you will have noticed how Jo developed her experience of:

- communication skills;
- administration;
- statistical analysis;
- event management;
- working in a team.

Sometimes you just have to look beyond the surface to find the opportunities for learning. Think about working as a volunteer in a charity shop – a popular choice for people who want to help others. Firstly, there are job-related skills to learn, such as sorting stock, pricing up articles for sale, display, handling money and customer service. Then there are the transferable or 'soft' skills of working in a team, acting responsibly by turning up when you say you will, and interacting with all kinds of people. So what starts out as doing a good deed also becomes a great chance to learn.

Improving your job prospects

You might have noticed Kevin, in one of our case studies, saying that the people he knew who got graduate jobs were the ones who got work experience at university. It might sound obvious, but why does it work so well?

It works because it enables you to do all of the following.

Try things out

Firstly, you can try things out so that, by the time you are applying for a graduate job, you are much clearer about what you want and why, and you can say so in your application form and interview. Deciding that you don't want to pursue something is just as valuable as confirming that you do, and you might discover a kind of work, or an interest, that you didn't even know about.

Get experience

This isn't as obvious as it sounds. For some professional training courses it's essential to have relevant work experience before you can be considered.

Examples are teaching, clinical psychology, physiotherapy; and for jobs and courses where it's not a requirement, it certainly helps to demonstrate your commitment and knowledge.

Collect and record evidence for your applications

We talk about the need for evidence in Chapter 11 'Making applications: getting past the first post', and work experience is one of your best opportunities. It's hard remembering in your final year the detail of that great work placement you did in your second year, so keep some kind of record of what you did, what you learned and what you achieved for each piece of work experience you have. It will make a real difference to your CV. Kevin, our brilliant example for internships, was able to replace his long list of part-time bar and retail jobs with a section headed 'Political work experience' and a much shorter 'Summary of other work experience'. His CV became targeted and relevant for the kind of job he wanted.

Enhance your jobsearch

Every work experience opportunity you take will give you some contacts, who may be helpful when you are looking for work. Even if they don't have a job to offer, they might know someone who does, or be willing to look at your CV.

Depending on how long you've been there and what you have done, work experience employers might be great for writing a reference for you. This is useful as most application forms ask for an academic and an employer reference. Remember to ask them first.

Give yourself structure and focus

This is particularly useful when you have graduated and you are still looking for your graduate job. Even if you are working, using days off or holidays to pursue your career goal with relevant work experience helps to remind you that your goal is still there. Thomas was our brilliant example for work shadowing, and this is how he is using work experience to keep in touch with his career aim of becoming a barrister.

example

'Since qualifying I have continued to apply for pupillage. In order to enhance my chances I have continued to complete a number of mini-pupillages at different chambers to broaden my experience and also make myself known to chambers before applying to them.

In order to gain more practical experience, I became a volunteer at an advice bureau. I conduct one-to-one interviews with clients weekly on a variety of different subjects. This has given me experience of dealing with different types of people as well as exploring a client's problem through questioning before advising them on the different options available.'

Thomas, LLB, LLM and Bar Professional Training course

How to make it work

If you have worked through this chapter you will now know about the different kinds of work experience, how to access them, and why work experience can be a real benefit in your career planning and jobsearch.

In this final section we tell you what to do, and what to avoid, to get the best from your work experience.

 dos and don'ts

Do

✔ take control – be clear what you want and what you can offer and negotiate with the employer so that you both gain;

✔ reflect and review – think carefully about what you are learning and record it somewhere, so that you can refer to your experience in job applications;

✔ be aware that there are limits on hosting work experience in some job sectors, due to factors such as confidentiality and child protection – it may be easier if you use your university volunteering scheme or local volunteer bureau to set up your placement in sectors involving children, vulnerable adults, health services or offenders;

✔ notice and absorb the discipline and protocols of the workplace – what to wear, how people are addressed, how the phone is answered.

Don't

✘ give up – if you think that you are not getting any benefit, talk to the person in charge of your programme to see if some adjustments can be made. If it's a placement that forms part of your course, get the advice of your tutor;

✘ assume there's no value in a work experience opportunity without really thinking about it and giving it your best shot.

 brilliant recap

- There are five different kinds of work experience, each with a particular benefit.

- There are also benefits that apply whichever kind you do.

- Work experience can help you to develop and learn about yourself as a person, and it can help with getting a brilliant graduate job.

- You can make it work for you – take control, be clear about what you want and what you can offer.

What to do next

- Think about how work experience could help you with your career plan.

- Consider what you want to (a) learn and (b) achieve?

- Use our 'How to get in' tips to get the work experience you want.

CHAPTER 10

Dates and deadlines: your timeline for action

Whether you enjoy planning, list making and target setting or whether you much prefer the adrenalin rush of a tight deadline or just letting fate take a hand, this chapter will help you to deal with the imposed deadlines and timescales involved in job seeking, and show you how to fit them into the other demands of your final year. We will tell you how to find out about critical deadlines, and how to manage application forms and interviews alongside academic assignments. It's never too soon to start – and, as you are reading this book, you are already under way.

Your time is your best resource

Your own time is one of your best resources; managing it well will not only help you achieve your graduate career, you will also develop a valuable skill for reducing stress at work and enriching your life outside work.

Managing your time is *not:*

- pre-planning every waking moment with lists and charts;
- losing out on spontaneous invitations;
- giving up the right to change your mind.

Managing your time as a student is about:

- having a sense of how much time you *need* to spend on: academic work; paid work; socialising; exercise and relaxing; and how much you *actually* spend – then making adjustments as needed to keep a good balance;

- knowing what your current projects are and when each deadline occurs;
- planning ahead to maximise performance and reduce pressure and unnecessary stress, as Kevin did in this brilliant example.

brilliant example

'First year was standard – just enough reading and scraping by on a couple of modules. Second year, I kicked on slightly – I wanted to go into my final year with a prospect of a 2:I, and I had seen friends with a backlog of failed modules – I didn't want that to happen to me.

I put extra work into my final year – it paid off and I achieved a first.'

Kevin, BA (Hons) Politics

Four critical factors

There are four critical factors you need to consider in creating a timeline for action while you are at university. These are:

1   devising a graduate job plan;
2   making the best use of your time at university to increase your employability;
3   early deadlines;
4   in your final year particularly, balancing job applications and interviews with the pressures of study.

Now let's look at each of these in turn.

Graduate job plan

Large or difficult tasks are more easily tackled if they are broken down into smaller tasks, so let's see what we can do with this very large task of getting a graduate job.

1 Decide what kind of areas you want to go for. If possible, book a one-to-one interview with your university careers adviser if you want to talk it through. You can also make use of online resources before you meet up – check out what your own university offers or visit some of our recommended sites.

  If you don't know where to start, other chapters in this book should help. Remember that Part 1 covers what's out there, so you might want to use it to remind yourself of what the options are.

2 Prepare your CV and LinkedIn profile and keep them updated. Use Chapter 11 'Making applications: getting past the first post' to help you get started.

3 Tell the people who will write references for you about your plans and give them a copy of your updated CV.

4 Check dates and deadlines, look at job advertisements, visit careers fairs, follow your careers service on Twitter.

5 Make applications for: jobs; postgraduate courses; internships.

6 Prepare for interviews: read (and act on!) Chapter 12 'Succeeding in selection'.

7 Get feedback – from employers who have interviewed you, employers who did not invite you to interview; friends and tutors.

brilliant tip

- Steps 1 and 2 are SLOW – they need the biggest investment of time, so you need to get started on this early in your final year or even sooner, perhaps in your first or second year.

- Step 3 is QUICK but important – you may need to provide updates from time to time; and

- Steps 4 to 7 are MEANDERING – less of a straight line and more of a cycle that you will repeat a number of times, and that you should spend some time on each week.

Note that time doesn't always pass at the same speed, and that some tasks are quick to do while others are slower. Anything that involves other people takes time to organise – for example, try to avoid getting someone to check over an application the day before it's due in – they may not be free, and you won't have time to make changes. You can't control other people, but you can control what you do and when you do it – so take advantage of that. Make sure that every week you do something, big or small, to advance your career plan.

 example

'The university can help in so many areas. The careers and employability team helped me to develop my CV before I started applying for graduate jobs, and the volunteering team helped me to organise some relevant work experience.'

Nicola, BSc (Hons) Forensic Biology

Increasing your employability

University life is full of opportunities to increase your attractiveness to graduate employers, while at the same time testing out your own ideas about your future career. If you struggled to think of something to say in your UCAS personal statement, then act early to ensure that you have plenty to say to a graduate employer about how you have spent your time at university and what kind of difference that has made to you as an employee.

In Chapter 9 'Work experience: making it purposeful', we talk at length about work experience, both paid and unpaid. Remember that, for some careers, relevant work experience is an essential requirement, so don't leave it too late. Your university careers service or job shop will help, and remember to use online resources too. There are useful opportunities within your university, such as representing your peers on a staff–student liaison committee, or being a student ambassador on open days. Think about the benefits of getting involved with a student society, too. All societies depend on events for their success, such as meetings, matches, competitions, trips and fundraising events. Consequently, if you're an organiser or officer of your society, you will develop lots of experience and expertise in event planning and organisation. In many societies there is an opportunity to learn about topics such as health and safety, finance, marketing, and aspects of the law, as well as developing strong interpersonal skills and the ability to take responsibility for money, equipment and people. Look at the following table in the brilliant example for the employability skills you could develop, and tell an employer about, with three of these examples.

brilliant example

Role	Skills for employability
Treasurer, film society	Using communication, initiative and persuasion to raise funds; using numeracy and integrity to manage a budget; contributing to committee meetings
Student rep., staff student liaison committee	Listening, questioning and summarising to obtain and represent views of others; understanding the protocol of, and contributing to, formal meetings; advocacy and negotiation skills
Open-day ambassador	Customer relationships; communication to a mixed group (students and parents); tact, diplomacy

If you are still a student, try to map out the opportunities you have between now and graduation for becoming more employable. Include vacation work, paid part-time work, voluntary opportunities, work placements and other student activities.

Think also about your life outside university, especially if you are a home-based student. You still have time to find and enjoy activities that will make a difference to you, the applicant. This is not just about employability, but about presenting yourself as a well-rounded person – and enjoying what that feels like.

tip

Map out the opportunities between now and graduation for increasing what you can offer to a prospective employer.

Early deadlines

Next, let's look at early deadlines for postgraduate study and graduate jobs. These take many students by surprise, especially those who, perhaps understandably, assume that the beginning of their final year is the time for action. If you habitually hand in assignments at the last minute, now is the time to break the habit if you want to maximise your chances of securing a job in a competitive labour market.

Some organisations have a cut-off date and candidates can apply up to that date. Others operate a first-come, first-served approach, which means that, once the places are filled with suitable applicants, no more will be considered. That means you can't predict when exactly the application process will close. Either way, if you know what you want to apply for, it makes sense to apply early. This will give the impression that you are motivated and organised.

Ones to watch

- Postgraduate teacher training applications in England and Wales, for both university-led and school-led schemes, are made through UCAS Teacher Training (UTT). The UTT/UCAS system opens in late October for training courses starting in the following autumn, and applications can be made right up to the beginning of the academic year. Individual training providers must open their programmes to applicants for a minimum of two weeks and can then decide when to close. Many providers will fill their places before Easter or even Christmas. Check the UTT website for guidance and aim to apply as early as possible.

- **Law:** applications to training courses to become a barrister (Bar Professional Training course) must be made between early December and early January; exact dates for each year are at **www.barsas.com**.

Application deadlines for training contracts (prospective solicitors) vary according to the law firm. There is a useful list on the website **www.lawcareers.net**. For the Bar, applications for scholarships via the Inns of Court close on the first Friday of November.

- **Postgraduate courses:** some have a specified and non-negotiable closing date, for example the clearing house for postgraduate courses in Clinical Psychology each year identifies a date in early December, but advises applying by mid-November to ensure processing before the Christmas vacation. Many have no published closing date, but will close when full. Don't be lulled into a false sense of security. Places are limited and, once a programme leader is sure that they have got enough applicants to fill all the places they have, they may well stop admitting to the programme or may only run a waiting list. Also, admissions tutors may well be away from the university over the summer. So, although it may be tempting to leave these applications until you have got through your finals, it may not be wise. You can find more information on **www.prospects.ac.uk** – go to postgraduate study, and look on the websites of individual universities if you know the course you want to do.

- **Graduate training schemes:** some have closing dates in the autumn term, so you need to be quick off the mark and well prepared in order to complete your application. Get early information from your careers service and ask for their advice about useful websites.

Keep checking your careers service website and social media sites for deadline reminders.

 brilliant tip

Know your deadlines and apply in good time – you will appear motivated and organised to employers and you will avoid last-minute panics.

Balancing job applications with final-year study

This is our fourth critical factor in managing dates and deadlines. We're not going to pretend that this is easy – but it is possible – and, somehow, you are going to have to do this. When the graduate job market is tough, you have to start earlier and keep going to get your job.

Having a clear schedule of your academic deadlines and workload is the essential first step. The next step is to carry out this work steadily and in good time. This way you will have some spare capacity for the unexpected job application.

Next, have the groundwork done in advance. In the next chapter we will look in detail at making applications. A key point to note now is to have a good, up-to-date CV to hand. It's great to refer to when you need to give details of qualifications and previous employment, with dates.

Next, be organised. Where possible, keep a saved copy of your applications, as many of the questions will be similar. This also means that you can remind yourself of what you said if you are called to interview.

Finally, be honest. Your tutors want you to get a good job and, while they might also expect full attendance in your final year, they will be flexible about time for interviews, so let them know if you are called for interview; ask them to help you to catch up with anything you missed. You also need to keep them informed so that if they are asked for a reference they can respond immediately.

brilliant dos and don'ts

Do

✔ know your schedule and academic deadlines;

✔ work ahead of your deadlines to create some spare capacity;

✔ carry out the groundwork for your applications in good time.

Don't:

✘ keep your tutors in the dark about your applications and interviews.

Skills to help you

Managing dates and deadlines is a skill, or more accurately a set of skills. While it's true that some people might have a more natural aptitude, or preference, for planning ahead and juggling conflicting demands, it's also true that you can learn and you can improve with practice. Good time management, project planning and fact-finding skills are all invaluable in dealing with dates and deadlines. You may cover some or all of these in your academic curriculum, especially if your course includes study or learning skills or a work-related module. Good reference material abounds and some examples are listed in our 'useful reading'; here are some key points to give you a start or a reminder.

Project planning

 definition

A **project** is a piece of work that is carried out within a set timescale, with predetermined goals and agreed resources.

During your course you may have learned something about project planning and project management, especially if your course includes a work placement. This knowledge will be useful in the workplace, but it can also be applied to assignments, job hunting and even planning a holiday or a spell abroad. You can see how easily the examples just listed fit our brilliant definition. There are excellent resources to help you get to grips with project management, including software and reference books. Even something as simple as a countdown on your computer will keep you aware of the number of days left to a given deadline.

 tip

Treat job hunting like a project and it will become more concrete, manageable and achievable.

SMART project goals

Firstly, good project goals are SMART – **s**pecific, **m**easurable, **a**chievable, **r**ealistic and **t**imebound. Test out your current career goal – is it SMART? What do you need to do to smarten it up?

Look at this example of a graduate career goal, and think about how you would improve it:

Specific	A graduate training scheme
Measurable	Earning £25,000
Achievable	In a blue chip company
Realistic	Without moving from where I live now
Timebound	By Easter of my final year

Here are some of the questions we would ask about this career plan – compare them with your own thoughts.

Specific	A graduate training scheme	*In what industry or sector?*
Measurable	Earning £25,000	*How does this compare with what is on offer? Is this your bottom line or would you start lower if the prospects were good?*
Achievable	In a blue chip company	*Are you clear what you mean by this? Do you know what proportion of graduate jobs are offered in SMEs?*
Realistic	Without moving from where I live now	*What do you know about your local labour market? Can you achieve the other parts of this career goal without moving away?*
Timebound	By Easter of my final year	*Why this deadline? Does it fit with what you know about graduate recruitment?*

Milestones

Secondly, projects have milestones, or steps along the way that help you to break up the project into something more manageable and give you a sense of progress as you achieve each one. Go back to the graduate job plan earlier in this chapter and think about how you could create milestones from this plan.

Quality standards

Thirdly, projects have quality criteria to ensure that each piece of work that is produced towards the final project is of a good enough standard. You will need to 'quality assure' your CV, your applications and your interview technique. You can get objective and experienced feedback from your careers service; think about other people who might help, especially those in senior positions in employment who are used to recruiting staff.

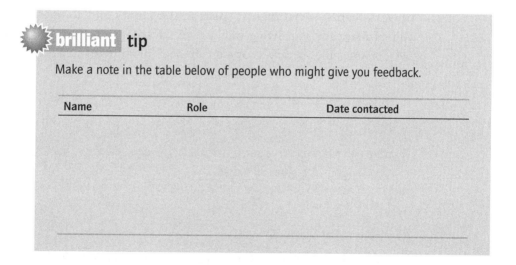

brilliant tip

Make a note in the table below of people who might give you feedback.

Name	Role	Date contacted

Managing your time

Earlier in this chapter we talked about time management: put simply, this involves balancing what you must do against what you enjoy doing. Even within work or study, some people spend more time than they need on aspects that interest them, at the expense of things they need to do but enjoy less.

How do you spend your time?

In the relative freedom of university life it's easy to get out of balance, reducing the time spent on academic work to the minimum, or prioritising your part-time job in order to keep your finances under control. So an honest assessment of how you actually spend your time each week, compared with what might be more reasonable, is a great start. As a guideline, full-time students are recommended to carry out no more than 16 hours per week paid work, in order to keep enough time for academic work (and a social life).

Getting your friends to help

A really good tip to help you to manage your time is to have a friend or friends who will work with you, and to agree among yourselves a pattern of work nights, social nights, spells in the library and so on. The evenings you earmark for socialising might take advantage of special offers, such as two-for-one cinema tickets or a cheap deal for students in a local restaurant.

 tip

Make planning your time into a shared activity with one or two friends, so that you can keep each other organised.

Knowing what works for you

You should now be able to identify the periods of time each week that are for your academic work and your job search. These should be built around your own productive times of day – or night. Some university libraries are open 24 hours a day, recognising some students' preference for working late into the night when there may be fewer distractions – but be mindful of the 9 am lecture or early shift at work the next day.

The next step is getting the most out of these time slots, and there are two techniques that many people find really helpful.

Use a to-do list

Using your schedule of academic deadlines and your graduate job plan, try starting each week with a list of jobs to be done. Then at the beginning of each day or study session decide what you will work on. Big tasks are daunting and difficult to start, so break them into smaller steps. For example, 'complete my application for Superstores Graduate Training Scheme' might have you staring at the screen or page, stalling at the more complex questions and putting it off until the day of the deadline. How might you break this task down into smaller steps?

You could:

- gather your factual information (qualifications, previous employment and so on, which should be to hand in your updated CV);

- research the company and the job information and identify aspects that you can include to indicate a good fit between you as an applicant and the company's values, aims and requirements;

- draft your personal statement/answers to open-ended questions and arrange for a careers adviser or tutor to have a look;

- set a day and time to clear away distractions and complete the form.

 tip

Break a large task into smaller achievable steps, each with a deadline.

Do the important/urgent test

The second useful tip is to use the important/urgent test. These two words don't mean the same! Urgent indicates a time deadline, while important refers to the impact of the task. So an assignment or a job application due in this week is both urgent and important, a decision early in your degree about your final-year dissertation topic is important but not urgent, signing up by 12 noon for a free coach for a night out is urgent but not important (you could get there on the bus, you could do something else), and deciding who'll do the food shopping next week is neither urgent nor important. So think about the tasks on your career planning list. Using the following chart, tasks can be graded A, B, C or D to indicate their urgency and importance.

	Important	Not important
Urgent	A	B
Not urgent	C	D

Looking back at the examples we have just given, you can grade them according to this table, so an assignment or job application due in this week is category A, both urgent and important.

Have a look at these tasks and grade them A, B, C or D.

- Returning four overdue library books.

- Doing your laundry.

- Meeting your tutor to discuss their feedback on your work.

- Drafting a CV for your booked appointment with a careers adviser tomorrow.

We would suggest in order of the list they are: B, D (unless you leave it till you have run out of everything, in which case B), C and A.

When you write your 'to-do' list, try to apply this grading to help you to prioritise.

It goes without saying that 'urgent and important' must be tackled first. In the workplace, 'urgent but not important' can often be dealt with by delegating; you probably don't have this option, but many tasks in this category are in any case relatively small and can be dealt with quickly and ticked off on your list.

'Not urgent and not important' tasks need to be kept under review in case they become urgent or important. In our earlier examples, next week's food shopping will become both urgent and important if the fridge and cupboards are empty; and your dissertation topic becomes urgent as well as important if it has to be formally approved in a week's time.

 tip

Your own time is one of your best resources – and you are in charge of it.

Key dates: knowing where to look

Whatever your degree subject, you are almost certainly involved in researching information and developing good research skills. You need to apply these same skills to accessing good, up-to-date job information. Make sure that you know how this information is communicated at your university, for example through social networking sites, text messaging, email distribution lists, careers service websites and even posters and notice boards, and keep up to date. Your careers service may give you a list of graduate job websites and you may find others. Be aware that the Internet is unmoderated and don't assume that all websites are accurate and reliable.

Check that the website you are using is:

- **well presented** – written in grammatically correct English and free from spelling mistakes;
- **relevant to you** – e.g. suitable for higher education students seeking jobs in the UK;
- **up to date** – containing current information and with active external links;
- **authentic** – can you check the author? Is the website address genuine or passing itself off as something similar? Useful suffixes for websites are .gov for a local or national government body; .org for a non-profit making body or charity; .co.uk for a commercial company; .ac.uk for a UK educational body, and .edu for a US educational body.

tip

Make sure that the graduate job websites you are using are accurate and reliable.

Tips for new graduates

If you have left university it doesn't mean that you have missed the boat for graduate jobs. Many employers have several recruitment points during the year, and many also recognise that there are some final-year students who choose to concentrate on getting a good result and defer their job search until after finals. However, compared with your situation when you were a student, there are some key differences that you need to tackle in order to manage your graduate plan.

- If you are working full-time you may find it more difficult to have time off for interviews, and consequently feel less motivated to keep on with your job search. Think about how best you can use days off, take unpaid leave or offer to work extra shifts to make up for lost time.

- Keep in touch with your university careers service. Are you on their email distribution list? Have you let them know that you are still working on your graduate plan and welcome their help? Are they running any workshops or bridging programmes to help you into work? Many universities have secured funding to run short programmes for new graduates. Have a look at our brilliant example.

brilliant **example**

A medium-sized university in the north of England offers a free 'graduate head start' for its graduates who are still seeking employment or striving to fulfil their career ambitions. A concentrated three-day programme, worth 20 credits at Masters level, includes: career planning, self-review, self-marketing and a mock interview. In addition, three optional elements cover the European Computer Driving Licence (ECDL), widely recognised by employers as evidence of IT competence; a five-week work placement; and three individual career coaching sessions. Recent participants say 'an opportunity to bridge the gap between university and real world employment'; 'a course to help develop your "soft" skills and make you more employable'; 'a real asset on your CV; a must-have for any student struggling to gain experience when jobs are hard to come by.'

If you have returned home after graduation, or moved to another part of the country, check out what your local university careers service might offer, for example information about local and regional opportunities. Don't forget to look online; check out the list of sites we recommend.

Keep a record of the skills and experiences you are developing through the job you are currently doing. Graduates in direct-entry jobs often get early responsibility, so think about what being a bar supervisor or shop manager means for your future employability.

In our next brilliant example, Paul shows that by being open to opportunities it is possible to turn your prospects around and take your career plan in an unexpected direction.

brilliant example

'I struggled to find a job I wanted after university, due in part to my lack of preparation for a career and also to the competition for graduate positions. I tried to gain interviews for a variety of graduate programmes with no success. My ambitions for my first job outstripped the preparation I had put in to that point. I had a large number of interviews but ended up temping at my local recruitment agency. Fortunately, at the time my father started a new company with a family friend and they needed an administrator. I started working for them expecting it to only be a short-term job and stayed with the company for two years. When I left I was a marketing executive and had enjoyed my time far more than I had expected. I had never considered a career in marketing before that job, but that position has shaped my career and my life since. Therefore I would advise graduates to be open to all opportunities that come their way.'

Paul, BA (Hons) English Literature, MA Publishing

The rescue plan, for when things go wrong, the unexpected happens or you leave things to the last minute

In the context of your jobsearch, things can and do go wrong. We've drawn up a list of nightmare scenarios – we haven't had to imagine these. They've happened to other graduate job seekers and that means they could happen to you. So what can go wrong?

- You miss a closing date.
- You are offered two job interviews on the same day.
- You're offered the job – but you have another job interview next week.
- There's a clash between a crucial piece of course work and the job interview of your dreams.
- You have two days to prepare a presentation for a job interview – and you are due to attend lectures.

Crises happen to the best organised of us – and in some of the situations above (two job interviews on the same day, for example) there's not much the individual jobseeker could have done to prevent it. It's how to proceed that's important. So here's what we would advise.

Honesty is the best policy

In these situations, honesty is pretty much always the best policy. Missing a closing date is of course to be avoided, but ask yourself what is the worst that can happen if you send your application form in late (if you can – it may not be possible online) with a note of apology. The worst that can happen is that you will hear nothing more, but there is just a chance that there were no other suitable candidates, or that the firm will advertise again in due course and suggest that you reapply.

If you are offered two interviews on the same day, then you do need to decide which job you actually do prefer, now it has come down to it. Accept your preferred interview, then contact the other organisation (your second preference) and say that you already have an interview, so wonder if they can offer you another date. The worst that can happen is that they say no – but they might say yes.

The 'job offer with another interview next week' scenario is the one many students worry about, though it rarely happens. When it does, then do remember that you have been offered job number one, but the second job is by no means yours. What not to do is to ask employer number one if you can let him know next week after your second interview. This never goes down well and employer number one may well withdraw the offer and give the job to someone else. If the job on offer is what you want (and you shouldn't have got this far if it isn't) then accept it and withdraw from next week's interview. This is the only fair and honest thing to do.

The last two examples in our list of nightmare scenarios concern clashes between academic work and job hunting, so the obvious approach is to talk to your lecturer(s) for their advice. If there is no flexibility in your course work, then contact the employer and explain the circumstances; you may be offered another date. If not, then you must let this one go – the course work is both urgent and important.

The final example calls for some really firm time management on your part. How much time is at your disposal outside your lecture time? You may need to cancel other plans, but the chances are that you can draft out your presentation on day one, and get someone to look over it early on day two before you prepare the final version in the evening. This, after all, is what will happen at work, so it's good practice.

The golden rule, if you have a crisis or setback, is to stay positive and talk to a tutor or careers adviser.

 brilliant recap

- There are four critical factors in managing your time at university: having a graduate job plan; increasing your employability; anticipating early deadlines; and balancing job applications with final-year study.

- Important skills to develop are: project planning; time management; and knowing where to look for key dates.

- When things go wrong, stay calm, be honest and seek advice.

CHAPTER 11

Making applications: getting past the first post

Your formal application to an employer, whether it's an online application form, an uploaded CV and covering letter, or another format, is the all-important first impression. In this chapter we will take you through the different requirements of the application process and help you to make the best possible job of this first step. You might be the best interviewee in the world but without a good application you will never get to the interview stage.

Just to clarify, when we refer to applications we are including application forms, both downloadable and online, and also CVs and covering letters, which are the preferred application method of some employers. (Very few employers now use paper application forms, though they are sometimes offered as an option – e.g. a university states 'download an application form or pick one up from our HR department'.) We will cover all of these, and share some tips for ensuring that you have made the best possible first impression. Special tips for applying for postgraduate study were covered in Chapter 7.

Which method of application?

A snapshot of 20 employers from diverse industries recruiting on the Graduate Prospects website indicated two different instructions for making the first approach. Three-quarters of the sample asked for candidates to complete an online application form; the remaining quarter asked for a CV and covering letter to be uploaded. Some of the first group asked for a CV to be uploaded alongside the online application. Only a few years ago there were still employers asking for applications by post, an option that has all but disappeared.

A third approach, which did not occur in our sample but which is used by some public sector organisations such as universities and local authorities, is the downloadable application form. Unlike an online application in which you are interacting with the employer's recruitment software (and from which you can be discontinued if you don't meet a particular criterion), a downloadable form stands alone. As the title suggests, you download it to your computer, complete it and send it back, usually as an email attachment.

In some specialist roles, particularly in the creative industries, applicants are asked to complete a task and submit it with their CV, or to apply only if they can bring a sample of work to the interview. Here are two recent examples.

 examples

- A technical magazine asked applicants for a piece of scientific writing aimed at a non-specialist readership.

- A film company stated that applicants must be prepared to demonstrate at interview a short film they had made or edited.

So the first message – and the first test – is to look carefully at what you are asked to do, and do it. If you attach your CV or a covering letter when it isn't asked for, you give the impression that you haven't read the instructions carefully enough or, even worse, that you think you know better than the employer. An error like this could mean that you are disregarded immediately.

 tip

Different employers have different requirements for the application process. Read instructions carefully and follow them exactly.

Getting started: information you need

Before you can start to prepare an application, you need the following information.

About yourself:

- **Qualifications:** what subjects, what grades, what year.
- **Employment:** dates of employment, job title, employer's name.
- **Voluntary and other spare-time activities:** dates, scope, location.
- **Skills and aptitudes,** with examples to provide evidence, drawn from your own experience.

About the job:

- Company information: not just facts and figures, check values and principles too.
- Information specific to the job, usually a job description.
- Information on their ideal candidate, usually a person specification.

We are going to start with your CV because once this is done it's an excellent reference document for completing application forms and, as we explain in the next section, it is often a vital part of the application process. Then we will look at using LinkedIn and gathering company and job information before getting to the nuts and bolts of application forms.

Preparing and updating your CV

 definition

A **CV** is a marketing tool that presents relevant facts about your life to date to prospective employers. CV is short for curriculum vitae, which means 'stream of life'.

Although not all employers ask for one, a full and up-to-date CV is a vital tool in your graduate job plan as is your LinkedIn profile, which we will come to later. Your CV is a central place for information about yourself that you can cut and paste into an application form; it's great for speculative applications (when you don't know if a job exists but you want to show interest in an organisation) and for taking multiple copies with you to careers fairs. And as you saw earlier in this chapter, a quarter of the graduate employers in our sample ask for CVs despite the rise in popularity of online applications.

brilliant tip

You should always target your CV to the job or job area you are aiming for, so you may need to make some amendments to your CV each time you use it. Save each copy with a separate file name to remind you.

There are many good books and online guides that will help you to write your CV; in this series, for instance, have a look at *Brilliant Graduate CV* by Jim Bright, Joanne Earl and David Winter, which contains some good guidance and useful examples of layout.

The big challenge for you as a graduate is to present yourself as a well-rounded individual with experience and interests outside your academic course, and with evidence of skills for employability and, where appropriate, business awareness. So we are going to give you some key guidelines here for strong graduate CVs.

Presentation

No more than two sides of A4; clear typeface such as Arial or Verdana at minimum font size of 11pt; good layout with white space, consistent use of heading style using larger, bold or italic type rather than underlining; good quality, plain white paper for hard copies. And remember that tailoring your CV includes changing the presentation to meet the employer's requirements. If they ask for a one-page summary of your education, relevant work experience and contact details, then that's what you must send.

Structure

Most important information first, most recent first in each section. Although you might find CV templates on your computer, they can be limiting and it's better to have a go at your own layout. Start with your name, address, phone number(s) and email – no need for a 'Curriculum Vitae' heading as it will be obvious that it is a CV.

Important: is your email address suitable for use by an employer? Recent real-life howlers in otherwise presentable CVs include: no1fashiondiva; igiveblondesabadname; pokeybabe; ibsexysam; and ratonthemat. Fine to use these for your personal emails, but not for job seeking. So either change your email or set up a new email account for job seeking (or use your university email address). Think about your voicemail too – don't be the graduate who almost lost a job in PR when the employer phoned her with the job offer to hear the voicemail message, 'Hi Babes, it's Juicy Lucy' (another real example – we didn't make it up).

 tip

Make sure that your email address and voicemail message are professional and suitable for employers to use to contact you.

Content

Your key headings in order are: Personal profile
                                   Qualifications
                                   Employment
                                   Skills and achievements
                                   Referees

However, if you are a mature student with previous work experience you might prefer to start with skills and achievements rather than with qualifications. Getting the content of your CV right can be tricky, so let's look at these headings in more detail.

Personal profile

This is a good way of telling a busy employer the key facts about you and is particularly useful for new entrants to the labour market. A survey of employers conducted by Bright and Earl and described in *Brilliant Graduate CV* suggests that this kind of statement has a positive influence on recruiters. The act of writing it also helps to focus and summarise your goals. A couple of examples:

> A mature student of Forensic Science with previous experience in laboratory work, now seeking a first post that will enable me to apply my academic knowledge in the workplace.

> A second-year Business Studies student aiming for a graduate career in financial management and seeking a finance-based work placement in which I can begin to build my experience while making an active contribution to the organisation.

Qualifications

The key information is *what, when* and *where.*

It's important to include your current degree course – the dates will make clear that you have not yet obtained the qualification. Relevant modules, final-year dissertation topic and work placements are all important in a graduate CV, so work at presenting this information concisely.

Working backwards in time, A level subjects are important and so are grades if they are good. You may need to state grades anyway in an application form, but remember that your CV is your marketing tool so keep it positive and don't include failed subjects. *Never* lie – it just isn't worth it and if you are subsequently caught out you could lose your job.

For GCSEs, you don't need to list each subject but it's useful to indicate if you have English and Maths, so you might state:

> 2005 Anytown High School   GCSE: 10 passes including English and Maths;
> 5 Grade A, 4 Grade B, 1 Grade C

Include all academic qualifications here. Anything else – IT, first aid, sport qualifications – can usefully go in your 'skills and achievements' section.

Don't ever lie on your CV – would you really want to be doing a job knowing that at any minute someone could suss you out?

Carl Gilleard, Chief Executive, Association of Graduate Recruiters

Employment

Your next task is to outline your employment record, giving dates, name of employer, role undertaken and achievements in the role. List with present or most recent first, and be sure to include work placements and work experience, as these may be particularly relevant. Don't dismiss part-time and holiday jobs as having no value on your CV. Over time, as your working life develops, these early jobs might be replaced by more relevant, graduate employment, but for now they might offer useful evidence of the skills you have developed. For example, your short outline of a job as a sales assistant might state:

> Contributed to company sales targets, operated electronic till and stock control system. I was the first part-timer to be promoted to acting manager for my shift, and I devised and implemented an effective staff rota system, which was adopted in other branches.

Skills and achievements

This is a much better heading than 'other information' or 'hobbies and interests', though it can include these, because it's positive and presents information in a way that an employer can grasp. It's helpful to group this section under four or five bullet points, each with a theme. Here's an example based on IT skills to get you started:

> Computer literate: proficient in Microsoft Office, Internet and email; obtained ECDL (European Computer Driving Licence) in [give date].

You can include both 'hard' topics – sport, languages, workplace qualifications like first aid, health and safety – and 'soft' skills – communication, teamwork, leadership. For example:

> Effective team player: demonstrated through group projects in my degree, representing my year on the staff-student liaison committee, and my part-time work in a busy student bar.

References, testimonials and referees

brilliant definitions

A **reference** is a confidential statement about you that is sent direct from your referee to the employer.

A **testimonial** is an open document given to you, usually at the end of a period of employment, which you can use to support job applications, but which will not be accepted instead of a reference.

You may already have testimonials from previous employers; these are open, written statements about you which are given to you for you to use as you wish. Many people keep them in a portfolio along with exam certificates and, while they have value in offering evidence about you, they are not references and will not be accepted as such.

Employers use references for two purposes: to verify information supplied by the candidate; or to obtain information about the candidate's performance to date. Practice varies on how references are used in the selection process; in some cases they are not read until all other parts of the selection process are complete. Most employers seek specific information, either with a tick-box form or a set of structured questions; occasionally the referee is asked to write an unstructured statement.

If you are applying for a graduate job, you should ideally have two referees: an academic referee who knows about your performance on your degree course; and someone who can speak about your performance as an employee. Whether or not you include referees' details on your CV, you will certainly be asked for them on an application form.

Many universities have clear protocols about who can write your academic reference, usually your personal tutor or your dissertation tutor. It isn't just a matter of asking the tutor whom you like the best. So find out who will write your reference and be proactive – make sure that they know what they need to know about you, your ambitions and your interests, so that they can support your application. Academic referees are particularly helpful if you have had any difficulties, such as illness, that have adversely affected your grades. In these circumstances they can offer evidence of your true potential.

For your employer reference, a work placement or voluntary work supervisor is a good choice especially if your placement relates to your chosen career. Alternatively, an employer for whom you have worked over an extended period will be able to comment on your skills in the workplace. At this stage in your life you should no longer need to ask sixth form tutors or your parents' friends, but should be able to call on people who have current or recent knowledge of you.

brilliant example

The aspect that employers seem to be most impressed with was the quality and variety of references I was able to provide. Despite being only 24, I was able to offer references from previous employers including headteachers, university professors and church leaders.

Kim, BA (Hons) Christian Youth Work

A final comment about referees. Once you have their permission (and you should always ask), you don't need to ask again each time you complete an application or send off your CV. But it is useful to keep your referees posted about your applications so that they can respond to requests quickly, or make arrangements to do so if they are going to be away at a critical period.

brilliant timesaver

Keep your referees up to date with your jobsearch progress, so that they can be sure to respond quickly when asked for a reference.

If you follow our guidelines you should be able to produce a good, standard CV that you can take with you to careers fairs, and that you can adapt for particular jobs as needed, by rewriting your personal profile or by emphasising particular skills and achievements.

Before you use your CV, get it checked by a careers adviser or friendly employer and take notice of their feedback. Remember to keep your CV up to date, and to target it to the job you are aiming for.

 recap

- Remember that your CV is a marketing tool.

- Pay attention to presentation, structure and content.

- Have it checked by an expert.

- Choose and brief your referees so that they can give a full account of you.

- Keep your CV up to date.

- Target your CV to each job you apply for.

Your LinkedIn profile

Employers routinely look at the online presence of applicants and we covered some of the options (in Chapter 1), together with a cautionary note about what you would be happy for a prospective employer to see. An important option is LinkedIn – employers now expect final-year students and graduates entering the job market to have a LinkedIn profile. While it is still necessary to have a CV for the reasons we have discussed, a LinkedIn profile has certain advantages – you can add a photo (choose it carefully to present a professional image), you are not limited by length except in your summary, and, as well as being targeted by recruiters, you can connect with professionals (including alumni) and groups to get more information and find out about job opportunities. A good plan is to include the URL for your LinkedIn profile in your CV.

Completing your LinkedIn profile is reasonably straightforward, as you are guided through the process on-screen – again, having your CV to hand will help you with dates, qualifications and previous employment. Keep your profile up to date as you develop your skills through your course and through paid and unpaid work. Your University Careers Service website should have some useful tips about using LinkedIn, and there is some great advice on The University of Manchester careers website, including a sample profile (**www.careers.manchester.ac.uk**).

 tip

Create a LinkedIn profile and keep it up to date – it's a great way for employers to find out about you.

Gathering information about the company and the job

Application forms and covering letters are always targeted to a particular job so, before we can consider these, we need to look at how to gather together everything you can discover about the job, starting with the company itself. This will be vital background for your application, and companies will in any case look for evidence that you have done your homework.

The company

Think about the different ways you can find out about a company or public sector organisation. Then have a look at our ideas below:

- company website;
- newspaper articles on the business pages;
- friends, tutors, careers advisers;
- information in the advert or in the application pack you may have been sent;

- for schools, Ofsted reports and prospectuses;
- respond to an invitation to phone a named employee for an informal discussion;
- visit if there is public access, e.g. a retail company, a gallery or museum.

brilliant dos and don'ts

Do

✔ prepare in good time – at the application stage, not the day before the interview;

✔ ask yourself some questions that may come up at interview or even in the application stage. What is the 'company image'? Who are the key competitors? What are their successes? What is distinctive about them? Why are you attracted to working for them?

✔ plan your questions in advance if you are phoning for an informal discussion.

Don't

✘ rely on what someone else has said – find out for yourself;

✘ leave this research till the last minute.

The job

Once you feel confident that you know something about the company, turn your attention to the job itself.

There are two key pieces of information about any job:

- the job description, which lists the tasks the post holder will undertake; and
- the person specification, which lists the characteristics the employer wants the postholder to have, or criteria they must meet.

In some organisations these will be written statements made available to you before you complete your application; in others, all you might have to go on will be the wording in the job advertisement. While the job description is important and you will need to feel confident about it and interested in what it tells you, the person specification is essential if you are to make a good job of your application.

The person specification

Usually, criteria are divided into areas such as qualifications, experience, skills and aptitudes, and personal qualities, and each criterion is categorised as *essential* or *desirable*.

 brilliant definitions

Essential criteria are those that candidates *must* meet in order to be considered for interview.

Desirable criteria are optional extras that employers would like candidates to have, but are not a requirement of the job.

For example, while it may be essential to have a degree, it may be desirable to have a degree in specific subjects. While competence in Microsoft Office might be essential, ability to use specialist software may be desirable. Relevant employment experience may be either essential or desirable. Usually, desirable criteria are those that the candidate could achieve once in the job.

As a general rule, the words essential and desirable in this context mean just what they say and it is good, fair recruitment practice to apply them rigorously, so it would not be worth applying for a job if you do not meet the essential requirements. If, however, you are close, you might take a chance with an appropriately worded covering letter, for example:

Although I note that you require two years' experience, I have successfully completed eighteen months in my current post which is a two-year contract and I would be very glad if you would consider me.

Desirable criteria are just that – the ideal candidate would meet these in addition to the essential criteria. So can you indicate that you could meet these criteria in due course? For example:

My German is not yet fluent but I can hold a basic conversation and would be keen to carry out intensive training to increase my proficiency with technical and business language.

It's really important that you demonstrate in your application that you have read the person specification and that you offer evidence to show how you meet the criteria.

 tip

Show in your application that you fit the criteria set by the employer and that you are willing to work towards the desirable criteria where possible.

Application forms

An application form is a proforma used by an organisation as the first stage of the selection process. Information required on application forms falls into two categories: factual, for which your CV will provide an excellent quick reference; and job-related, which may take the form of open questions or an unstructured personal statement.

Some organisations have a general application form and therefore some parts might be difficult to complete in certain circumstances, for example, if you are still in your final year as a student and are asked for details of your current employment. Usually common sense will guide you, but do ask for help from your careers service or from a tutor if you are not sure.

Three formats

Employers may offer their application forms in one of three formats:

- **online** – you locate the form on a website, complete and submit it electronically;

- **downloadable from a website** – to be completed and posted or emailed. You will be able to type into your downloaded and saved copy of the form;

- **paper** – this is now extremely unusual but we have found some current examples, so you do need to be prepared for this format. You will need to ask for a form to be sent to you, and you post it after completion. You will need to hand write most of the form, but may be able to attach a typed personal statement.

Completing your form

We'll talk about the content of your form shortly but first, here are some pointers to help you.

Whether your form is paper, downloadable or online, you need to set time and space aside to complete it, preferably well ahead of the deadline so that you have time to revisit what you have written and get someone to look over it for accuracy and clarity. Where possible make a draft copy and only when you are happy with it complete the final version. Take great care with presentation – forms do need to be free from spelling mistakes and crossings-out. If you are posting a paper copy, keep it clean and free from stains, marks and creases.

While each application *must* be tailored to the job for which you are applying, there will be some repetition, so it's good practice to keep a paper or electronic folder of completed applications so that you can remind yourself of how you answered a similar question on a previous occasion.

brilliant tips

- Set time and space aside to complete your form, well ahead of the deadline.

- Where possible, make a draft copy of your form and complete this first.

- Aim for excellent presentation and accuracy.

- Keep a copy for future reference.

Online applications

While online applications are becoming more common, the principles of completion are the same as for the other two formats. However, there are some key differences with online forms. In particular:

- the word limit for more open questions might be rigidly applied;

- the opportunity for someone else to check what you have written may be more limited (though sometimes you can download the form to prepare a draft);

- you may be automatically deselected for something that you believe not to be relevant, e.g. insufficient UCAS points;

- you may not easily be able to keep a copy for reference.

 There are ways around some of the obstacles that people put in your way. There are lots of employers who are not looking for the 2:1, so seek them out.

Carl Gilleard, Chief Executive, Association of Graduate Recruiters

Factual information

Your CV will provide an excellent quick reference for the factual information sought on application forms, which is usually about education, qualifications and employment experience, but read the instructions carefully. You may, for instance, be asked for information in chronological order rather than most recent first. Also, you may be asked to list all the examinations you have taken, whether passed or failed. This part of a form can be tedious to do but, once you have done it for the first time, you have it to hand for the future.

Open questions

We mentioned at the beginning of this section on application forms that job-related information is obtained in two ways: open questions and personal statements. We'll start with open questions.

Here is a set of questions based on a real application form. For each question there is a limit of 300 words.

What are your skills, experiences and personality characteristics that make you suitable for a job in this organisation?

Why do you want to work in the retail sector and in this organisation?

Which of this organisation's current initiatives/projects most interest you and why?

Have a look at these questions and note down:

1 what you think the employer is looking for;

2 what you think you need in order to answer the questions.

Although this may look like a daunting task, it should help you to see that the groundwork done for this application could well help you with others.

Now have a look at our ideas.

Question	What employer is looking for	What you need
What are your skills, experiences and personality characteristics that make you suitable for a job in this organisation?	Your awareness of the person specification for the job and the extent to which you can demonstrate that you are a good fit.	Good, honest self-awareness. A range of evidence to support your statements about yourself. Job and company knowledge.
Why do you want to work in the retail sector and in this organisation?	Your motivation – why retail, why this company? An answer that shows your understanding of the sector and of the distinctiveness of the organisation.	Good knowledge and understanding of the sector and some clear reasons for your choice. Knowledge of the company and how it differs from its key competitors.
Which of this organisation's current initiatives/projects most interest you and why?	Your ability to research and to critically analyse. An indication of your own preferred career direction.	Time to do your homework. An understanding of the techniques of critical analysis. A sense of how your career might develop with this organisation.

Here is another, quite common, example of a set of questions for an application form. This time the format is different: you are asked to use evidence from your previous experience to demonstrate the skills in question.

In each of the following five boxes tell us about an incident that demonstrates your use of the skill named at the beginning of the box. You have 250 words for each box.

Communication

Teamwork

Problem solving

Overcoming a setback

Ability to work under pressure

To answer these questions well it helps to follow a structure. The one we recommend is STAR, which stands for:

Situation

Task

Action

Result

So you outline the situation, describe the task, say what action you took, and state the result. Here is an example of overcoming a setback, using the STAR framework. We have put the headings in to help you, but you would not include them on your application form.

---

brilliant example

(*Situation*) In my second year I successfully applied to complete a work placement in a small but expanding marketing company. I was delighted to secure such a competitive placement. With just two weeks to go, the placement was cancelled due to illness.

(*Task*) I needed to find another placement, or I would have to wait until the summer vacation, which would mean deferring my assessment. The work placement office could offer me an alternative but not in marketing, which is my career aim.

(*Action*) So I thought about departments in the university that might benefit from a marketing project. I approached the careers service because I knew that students who used the service found it really good, but that there were many students who didn't know about it. I offered to design and carry out a survey of student perceptions and to make some proposals about marketing and publicity arising from the findings of the survey. I worked closely with careers service staff and got some advice from my tutor about designing the survey and analysing the results.

(*Result*) I presented the findings to the careers team and in the last two weeks of my placement began to work on a promotional campaign for the new academic year. I was offered the opportunity to continue to work in the careers service on a voluntary basis during my final year, so I have assisted in the implementation of the campaign and regularly speak to groups of students to promote the careers service. After the initial disappointment at losing my placement, my action in securing an alternative has meant that I have seen my project through to implementation and had the chance to do some really useful voluntary work. (*287 words*)

In the examples we have given there is a clear word limit. In online applications you will be cut off once the word limit has been reached, even if you are in mid-sentence, so it's essential that you draft your answers, check the word count and spelling, then cut and paste into the form. One of the workplace skills you need to develop is the ability to be concise, so the practice you get with your application forms will be put to good use in your working life.

 tip

Where you have open-ended questions with word limits, draft then cut and paste into your form.

Personal statements and covering letters

Similarities

Both personal statements and covering letters are opportunities to 'make your case' as an applicant. It should be clear from the employer's instructions which you are being asked to supply. Usually, a personal statement is a section of an application form, while a covering letter is sent to accompany a CV. Here are some dos and don'ts that apply to both.

 dos and don'ts

Do

✔ write in the first person;

✔ tell the employer why you are suitable for the job, and why you want to work for this particular employer;

✔ draw attention to your CV in the content of your covering letter, rather than simply attaching it. Say something like, 'You will see from my application form/CV that I have the qualifications required for this post.'

Don't

✘ begin every sentence with 'I';

✘ duplicate information you have already provided on your application form or CV.

Differences

So, although the purpose and content is much the same, how are personal statements and covering letters different from each other? It's mainly a matter of layout.

A personal statement is part of, or attached to, an application form, and written in prose with your name at the top of each sheet. There may be a word limit or more commonly a size limit – 'not more than two sides of A4' is a common example and also a useful guideline.

A covering letter is set out like a letter, with your address at the top right, the employer's name and address a little lower down on the left, followed by the date and any reference number you have been asked to quote.

Personal statements

Sometimes personal statements are unstructured, for example 'Use this space to supply additional information in support of your application' or 'Please use 150 words or less to tell us why we should take you on. When we say 150 words, we mean it!' Or you may be given a structure – something like:

Use the space below and up to one additional sheet to tell us:

1 why you are suitable for this job and what you will bring to the organisation;

2 why you want to work for this organisation;

3 what your personal strengths and weaknesses are;

4 where you see yourself in 10 years' time.

Usually it helps to have a structure – but note that these questions, which are fairly typical, contain two traps for the unwary. For question 3, rather than listing your weaknesses, write instead about aspects that you would like to develop. For example, 'I have limited experience of writing bids for funding, but this is an area that I am keen to develop and look forward to gaining the necessary knowledge and skill.' The second trap is question 4, the 10 years' time question. A safe and acceptable answer is that you are keen to gain experience and then to identify areas of particular interest in which you might specialise – you may need to vary this according to the sector for which you are applying.

Covering letters

Though you may occasionally be asked for a covering letter with an application form, it is more commonly paired with a CV. You will see references in job adverts to 'apply by CV and covering letter'.

Try to find out the name of the person to whom you are applying, so that you can write Dear Mr Jones or Dear Ms Begum. Even if you are sending your covering letter by email it is good form to set it out like a letter, though you could omit your address and theirs from the top.

Although some people recommend a one-page covering letter, this can be difficult to achieve if you are demonstrating that you fit a fairly detailed person specification, so we would say a maximum of two pages – certainly no more. Where a 'letter of application' rather than a covering letter is asked for – common in teaching posts – this certainly means a two-page response, which clearly demonstrates how you meet the person specification.

Creating a structure

Whether it's a personal statement or a covering letter, your starting point is a rather frightening blank screen in front of you. So, just as with other pieces of writing, you need to think about introduction, middle and conclusion.

Introduction

Say what you are applying for in the first sentence. For example, for a covering letter:

> I write in response to your advertisement on the Graduate Prospects website for a trainee sales negotiator in your Bristol office, reference number xxxxx.

To start a personal statement for the same job, you could say:

> I offer the following information in support of my application for the post of trainee sales negotiator in your Bristol office.

Middle

Firstly, you need to make clear why you are suitable for the job, using the person specification or information from the job advert if no person specification is available. You need to offer evidence in support of your claims; here are some examples to help you.

> As a member of the university IT helpdesk, I have developed excellent communication skills, especially listening, questioning and clarifying, so that faults can be recorded accurately and responded to promptly.

> In my role as a shift leader in the student bar, I motivate and encourage bar staff to achieve high levels of customer service, especially when we are all working under pressure.

> I can work to high levels of accuracy in the laboratory following experience gained in my work placement and in research for my final-year dissertation.

Next, you need to say why you want this job, with this employer, without sounding cheesy. So you need to construct a sentence about your career plan, followed by a sentence or two about what attracts you to this employer. For example:

> Having researched the career options open to an English graduate, I soon focused on publishing, a choice that became even more certain during a successful work placement during my last summer vacation. Your company has an excellent record of publishing first novels, an area of interest of mine and, having spoken to members of your team at a recent graduate fair, I know that you offer good training and prospects to graduate entrants. I would be excited to be part of your organisation.

Conclusion

Finish with a courteous ending that reinforces your motivation for applying for this post. Never write 'do not hesitate to contact me'. This is a negative ('do not') and over-used statement attempting to invite a positive action, and a waste of words. 'Please contact me' is much better. In the case of the covering letter, it's worth repeating your contact details.

Finish a covering letter like this:

> Thank you for reading my letter. Please contact me at any time on 07654 321098, or by email at **jsmith@hotmail.co.uk**. I would welcome the opportunity of an interview and look forward to hearing from you.

> Yours sincerely
> (or Yours faithfully if you don't have a name and have written to 'Dear Sir or Madam')

(if posting a hard copy, sign legibly here).

Finish a personal statement like this:

> I hope that this information has persuaded you to consider me for interview. I am very keen to be part of your organisation and look forward to hearing from you.

Speculative applications and recruitment agencies

In this section we will cover applying to particular organisations without knowing if a job exists, and using recruitment agencies to access vacancies in a specific field.

Sometimes you may want to approach an employer without knowing if a job exists, but because you are attracted to the organisation. This strategy sometimes pays off, especially with smaller organisations. Advertising is costly and if your letter arrives just as someone hands in their notice, or just as expansion plans are being discussed, then you may get a response.

Your wording needs to be a little different from the covering letters we have already discussed, as you are not responding to an advertisement. You need a strong opening paragraph that encourages the reader to carry on. You need to state:

- why you are writing to this company in particular;
- what role you are looking for;
- what you are offering.

For example:

> I am relocating to Anytown and note from your website that you are expanding your company. I am a graduate seeking a first post in technical sales and, as part of my degree, I successfully completed a year-long placement with a major medical equipment supplier.

In the body of the letter you can expand on your suitability and experience, but remember that you are attaching your CV so don't just duplicate its contents. Conclude as in our cover letter example above, with clearly stated contact details to make life easier for the employer. If you have a contact email address you can send the letter and CV as an email – otherwise post them.

brilliant tip

Your signature on a covering letter should be clear and should include your first and last name. An illegible scrawl just looks arrogant.

Recruitment agencies can be very helpful if you are exploring a specific career area, as many of them specialise in, for example, law, social work, public sector jobs, or teaching. You need to register with them first, usually with your CV, so that they can inform you about suitable jobs and let employers know about you. Be aware, though, that you may not have any face-to-face contact with the agencies so ask them what you can expect from them and, if you want them to market you, a strong CV and professional telephone manner is vital. Have a look at Jane, our brilliant example, for her experience of using agencies.

brilliant example

I had worked as a solicitor before having a career break, and on returning to work I wanted to move into housing law. However, I realised after some initial enquiries and spec applications that first I would need to develop my knowledge in a different role. I got my first two jobs, both in the private sector, through networking. I then decided that I would benefit from a move to the public or voluntary sector and discovered that almost all recruitment was through employment agencies. Only one of them asked me for a face-to-face meeting. I had to market myself to all the others with my CV, emails and phone calls. This was an unexpected challenge. Deadlines for applications were often very tight, so I had to make them a priority. However, I am pleased to say that through an agency I learned about a job as a housing adviser in a charity – exactly what I was looking for – and my application was successful.

Jane, LLB (Hons), LPC

Getting feedback and getting help

It can be hugely disheartening to send off dozens of applications and hear nothing back. Many job adverts state that only successful candidates will be contacted. Some say that if an applicant hasn't heard by a given date then they have not been shortlisted, but often it's a guessing game. While it's quite reasonable to contact the employer and ask if they have shortlisted yet, you would be very unlikely to get feedback on an application form alone, as this would be massively time consuming for most employers.

While it's possible that you have just been unlucky, if you have sent large numbers of applications for jobs for which you are suitable, and have not been invited for interview, then there may be a problem with your applications.

So get some expert help – go to a careers adviser, a tutor or someone you know who recruits graduates, and show them some of your recent applications. They may well spot a possible reason, most commonly that the applications are not sufficiently targeted to the employer and the job. Get the same person to look over your next application before you send it to check that you are not making the same mistakes again.

 tip

If your applications don't lead to interviews, get someone to look at them and give you feedback.

Imagine you are the employer

Finally, put yourself in the employer's shoes. Imagine that you run a small enterprise and you have advertised a graduate post, inviting applicants to use downloadable application forms. Over 100 applications for a graduate trainee post in your growing company have arrived and are on your desk. You have to draw up a shortlist, and fast.

You have beside you the details of the job that the candidates received, which include a person specification you spent ages drawing up. This specification was clear about the kind of person and even subdivided the criteria into essential and desirable.

You will probably do a rough sort first, perhaps into three piles of yes, maybe and no. What would make you likely to put an application form into the 'no' pile? Think about this, perhaps make some notes, then look at the list below.

Common reasons for rejecting an application

- No evidence of meeting essential requirements (usually qualifications and/or experience).
- Scruffy form, e.g. creases, food marks, crossings out.
- Poor spelling and punctuation.
- Periods of time unaccounted for by education, work, travel, career break.
- No reference to the company/job.
- No attempt to demonstrate how/why the applicant is suitable for the job.

The more applicants there are, the more rigorously these sorting criteria will be applied, because the employer needs to arrive at a manageable number for interview. Some employers even set a limit for the number of applications they will process, even if further applications are received before the closing date. This would normally be stated in the information for applicants, and means that you must submit your application in good time to be considered.

The image of the employer with a huge pile of forms to sift through is one to hold on to as you are preparing and checking your application. In addition to matching the person specification, most employers are looking for the same things at this stage – good written communication, motivation, and that indefinable 'something extra'.

tip

Visualise the employer reading your application. Will it go into the 'Yes' pile?

And finally, make sure that you check everything that you send to an employer. Use your spellchecker, your university careers service, your tutors and trusted friends.

To get an interview you need a good application. To get the job, you need a good interview, so have a look at Chapter 12 when you are ready.

What to do next

- Prepare your CV and your LinkedIn profile and have them checked.

- Think about who your referees might be and talk to them about your plans.

- Create a folder for application forms, personal statements and covering letters.

CHAPTER 12

Succeeding in selection

W e are now going on to the next stage of the selection process. If you have been called for interview, then you can assume that you have made a good start with your application form or CV. Hold this thought in your mind, and you will approach the next stage with confidence.

There are several good printed and online sources of help with all of the areas we are going to consider in this chapter and we will direct you to some of these but first, let's think about what employers are seeking to achieve.

The employer's perspective

Employers need to choose candidates who have the potential to be successful in the job – not an easy task, when applicants may not have had the opportunity to carry out similar work and may not, therefore, be in a position to offer evidence of success. While the interview is the most popular method of selection – and a strong predictor of success in the job – it is usual for other selection methods to be used alongside, in order to explore applicants' skills, knowledge, personality and motivation.

- In order to assess your *skills*, employers will usually break down the role into smaller components, for example managing a project, or working in a team, which they can find a way to assess.

- Employers may also want to find out if you have the specific *knowledge* needed for the job. They will make some assumptions based on your degree content, but may also test you through exercises, scenarios and case studies.

- An important question for employers is whether or not you will fit in, so they may look at aspects of your *behaviour* and *personality,* including your motivation – *why* do you want the job?

From your point of view (as the candidate), a range of selection methods is helpful because it gives you more chances to succeed and you can offset poor performance in one area by showing your strengths in another. For example, some people are not comfortable contributing to an unstructured group discussion, but can show excellent leadership in a group task.

 tip

Employers use the selection process to look for skills, knowledge and motivation.

Next, we'll look at tests, interviews and assessment centres in turn, outlining what to expect and giving some pointers for good preparation.

Tests

We talked about psychometric tests in Chapter 8 as aids to help you to know more about yourself. They are also used by employers to measure candidates' performance against either:

- the performance of an identified group in the population (graduates, adults, Year 11 pupils, a group in the same profession), known as norm referencing; or

- the standards or criteria determined by the employer, known as criterion referencing.

Psychometric tests must be objective, valid and reliable. In other words, they must be designed to: treat everyone who completes them in the same way so that scores can be compared; be relevant for the purpose and measure what they set out to measure; be consistent in the scores they produce, both over time and across similar groups of candidates. A quiz in a magazine, though interesting to do, is not objective, valid and reliable in comparison to a well-established personality test.

Kinds of tests

Most tests fall into one of two categories:

- **Ability/aptitude:** e.g. verbal, numerical and abstract reasoning tests, examine your ability to think logically and to problem solve, using words, numbers, diagrams, shapes or pictures. These tests consist of questions with right and wrong answers, and they should not depend too heavily on what you have learned at university, unless they are for a job-specific aptitude, e.g. in computing. Questions are often multiple choice, which should enable you to work more quickly. You will find lots of sample questions in books on how to succeed in psychometric tests – some titles are included in our useful reading list at the end of this book.

- **Personality:** e.g. measures of leadership, teamwork and creativity are usually questionnaires; the questions often ask what you would prefer in a choice of situations, or how you would behave in a given set of circumstances. Employers may not see how you have answered individual questions, but will have a profile or summary that tells them about how you typically respond. While these tests don't usually have right and wrong answers (and shouldn't really be called tests), employers will often have a preference for what kind of person they are looking for. They may be looking for evidence of your ability to act decisively, or exploring your preference for working in a team or alone.

tip

In a timed test, do as much as you can – don't waste time on a difficult question.

Most tests are time-limited, and are administered either online or in conditions that will remind you of taking an exam. An online test is often used as a first stage in selection, with successful candidates invited to the next stage.

Exam conditions are not meant to add stress, but are to ensure that candidates' results can be meaningfully compared with others, as all will have carried out the test in the same conditions.

How to prepare

 dos and don'ts

Do

✔ practise – use 'how to' books and online practice sites, and ask your careers service if they run practice sessions;

✔ try to do it in 'test conditions' when you practise – no interruptions or distractions, working to a time limit;

✔ find out as much as you can about what to expect – look at the employers' information online or in print;

✔ read letters and emails carefully: check what the employer is looking for and get the basics right, such as when and where the tests will take place;

✔ be aware that some online tests are lengthy and you may not have much notice. Be prepared to rearrange your schedule to clear a time and space to work on it without interruptions or distractions.

Don't

✘ linger over a difficult question. Move on to the next – a good strategy in a timed test is to answer as many questions as you can;

✘ guess at random in a timed test as you may be penalised for wrong answers;

✘ leave it to the last minute: it won't help your performance;

✘ try to get out of it or offer excuses for lack of time.

Interviews

A job interview should not be a contest between two opponents – both you and the employer want the job to be filled. The vacancy is a problem to be solved, and both of you are on the same side of the problem. Employers want to get it right – it is costly to advertise, interview and appoint and they don't want to have to do it again – and you want to be a successful candidate. Be aware that employers are increasingly using telephone and video interviews, usually at an early stage in the selection process. We will talk about the particular demands of these interviews later in this section.

brilliant example

'I was a bit unsure as to how to approach finding jobs in the area of nutrition. I approached the university careers service and they gave me guidance, helped me prepare for interviews and informed me about the type of conditions to expect in an interview.'

Adam, MSc Public Nutrition

In the book *Brilliant Answers to Tough Interview Questions* the author, Susan Hodgson, provides an excellent summary of the purpose of interviews. She says:

Interviewers are seeking the answers to three fundamental questions: Can you do the job? Will you do the job? Will you fit in?

Break the interview down

Like all challenging tasks, tackle this one by breaking it down into three stages:

- general preparation before the interview;
- during the interview;
- after the interview.

General preparation before the interview

- **Research the organisation and the job.** You will have done this already for your application form – do it again, go deeper this time, talk to people who work there or are in similar work. Who are their main competitors? Where does the revenue come from? What are the developments and trends in the sector? How are new entrants trained and supported?

- **Check your invitation to interview.** This may sound obvious, but make sure you know where you are going, how you will get there and how long it takes. If you are driving, where will you park? Arriving in good time isn't just good manners, it will help you to feel calmer and more confident.

- **Decide what to wear and take.** No matter how informal the dress code is for the people who already work there, there is usually an expectation that interview candidates will dress fairly formally and conventionally. This doesn't mean an expensive suit that you will never wear again, but it does usually mean a smart suit or jacket and trousers, and a shirt and tie for males, and a smart suit or jacket and skirt/trousers with a shirt, blouse or top for women. If you are worried about your student budget, tour the charity shops for great bargains. Above all, make sure that your outfit – including footwear – is clean and well fitting, and that you can be comfortable without even thinking about what you are wearing. Check your personal grooming, and keep make-up, jewellery and perfume understated. Take with you as little as possible, in a neat bag or briefcase. If the interview requires you to take some documents (proof of identity, qualifications, sample lesson plans for a teaching post), put them in a tidy folder.

- **Just before the interview.** Your final preparation means checking that your phone is switched off, staying calm and quiet, being pleasant to other candidates if they are present, and to any staff you meet – but focusing on yourself with a few deep breaths until you are called in.

 tip

Look and feel smart, ditch the clutter, and you will be able to focus totally on the interview.

Question preparation

Remember those three questions we looked at earlier – Can you do the job? Will you do the job? Will you fit in? – and think about how you will demonstrate that the answer is yes to all three. Employers increasingly want evidence to back up candidates' answers, so think of examples that will illustrate your ability to solve a problem, work in a team, manage your time under pressure, meet targets, follow instructions, lead others and so on. This might seem impossible – but think about not just your academic work but your part-time and vacation jobs, voluntary work and activities in student societies and sports teams.

What evidence can you offer to support the following skills? Make a note of your answers.

Skill	Evidence
Solving problems	
Working in a team	
Managing your time under pressure	
Meeting targets	
Following instructions	

The question 'Will you do the job?' is a tricky one and it's about motivation. So an employer will ask you why you have applied and how you see your career progressing. No one expects you to have had a lifelong ambition to work for a specific organisation, and employers will realise that you might have several applications under way at the same time. What they are looking for are signs of planning and of choosing their organisation because it offers the opportunity for you to do what you want to do.

There are some great examples of interview questions and answers in our companion publication *Brilliant Answers to Tough Interview Questions* – more details in the 'Further reading' section at the end of the book. While it would be a mistake to learn an answer by heart, the examples given will be a big help in your preparation.

Graduates need to ask where they fit into the critical path within the business process. What do I look for in an employee? The attributes that are important to any business: honesty, integrity, loyalty and reliability. Why reliability? It's pretty obvious: because we're a business. It winds us up terribly if somebody doesn't turn up and doesn't have the decency to phone and explain. Or walks in late, not saying anything to the manager. Nothing winds us up more.

Julian Radley, Director, Evotel Holdings

During the interview

First impressions count!

A smile will help you to relax as well as giving a good impression. Experienced interviewers know that candidates are nervous and will do their best to settle you down. Wait to be invited to sit and shown which is your chair. If there is more than one interviewer (which is usual), make eye contact with them all – often those who did not ask the question are listening most intently to the answer.

Open and closed questions

Most interview questions will be 'open' – tell me about . . . describe a situation when you . . . how difficult did you find . . . If you get the occasional 'closed' question, such as 'Did you enjoy your degree course?', then give a full answer – they want more than yes or no.

 tip

Smile at the start of your interview, wait to be invited to sit, and make eye contact with all the interviewers. Breathe out, gently but purposefully.

Your turn

Be prepared for your turn – when you can ask the panel your questions. It's tactful to avoid questions about pay and holidays at this stage – all that can be discussed when an offer is made. So, focus on topics like training and development, opportunities to specialise, future plans for the organisation and the role. Try not to take too long – the candidate who gets out a list of questions fills the interview panel with dread. If you came prepared with questions, but in the course of your visit they have been answered, for example during a pre-interview talk or tour, then it's fine to say, 'Thank you, I did have some questions but they have all been covered.'

brilliant tip

Being interviewed is a skill. As with any skill, you will get better with preparation, practice and feedback.

After the interview

If you are successful in your interview, your feedback will be that you are offered the job.

If you are not successful, you might want just to put it behind you and move on. However, if you do the two things we suggest here, your next interview will be better.

- **Firstly, reflect on your own performance.** While the interview is fresh in your mind, make a note of the questions you felt you struggled with, so that next time you can do a bit more preparation. Think too about the questions you felt you handled well and where the panel seemed to respond well – sounds like you have the right idea with those questions.

- **Secondly, seek feedback from the employer.** They are not obliged to give you feedback but, if you ask in the right way, i.e. that you want to learn from the experience for next time, not that you want to challenge the decision, then you may get something really useful. A helpful employer might say something like, 'In the interview, you didn't convince us that you would be an effective team member. You talked generally about teams you had been in without identifying your own role in the teams.' So make a list of the teams and groups you have been, or are, in and the role you play(ed). Next time around, then, you might be able to talk about your own part in a final-year group project – keeping the group to deadlines, or being the one with the creative ideas.

 Even if you go for an interview, and you don't get it, you have moved forward because you'll learn from it. And if you get feedback, do listen to it.

Carl Gilleard, Chief Executive, Association of Graduate Recruiters

A word about telephone and video/Skype interviews

These are becoming increasingly common, especially early in the selection process, unsurprisingly as they are more time- and cost-efficient for both the employer and the applicant. They might also be a possibility if you are unable to attend a face-to-face interview – it's always worth asking.

Much of what we have already said about interviews still applies, especially with respect to anticipating and preparing for questions. There are, however, some important additional considerations.

Unlike a face-to-face interview, you are using a form of communication that you already use extensively to speak to friends and family, so it's important to make a conscious effort to be more formal and businesslike. We have mentioned inappropriate email addresses elsewhere – you should also ensure that your Skype profile username and image are fit for jobseeking.

For both telephone and video interviews, choose your setting carefully to be free from extraneous noise, interruption and distraction, and warn anyone who might 'barge in' that you are not to be disturbed. Make sure that your phone/laptop is charged and that any sound alerts are muted. Sit at a desk or table with your CV and any notes you might need to hand, and for video interviews make sure that the background behind you is clean and simple so that the interviewer focuses on you.

We recommend that for a video interview you dress as you would for a face-to-face interview – this is your first chance to make a visual impression – and always look into the camera to make eye contact with the interviewer. Even for a telephone interview you are likely to perform better if you feel alert and as if you are in interview mode – hangovers and pyjamas are inadvisable!

A particular challenge of telephone interviews is that you have no visual cues to help you and you need to concentrate even harder on both what is being said and the impression you are giving through your answers. Pauses are particularly difficult on the phone compared with face to face or even video. Take care not to interrupt as this is easily done with the slight delay over the Internet. Don't be afraid to ask for a question to be repeated if you didn't hear it or if you are not clear what it meant.

Once the interview has come to an end, send a short email thanking the recruiter.

 example

'I applied online to a big company near Paris. I sent in my CV and a covering letter (in French). They did a telephone interview which was fact finding really. That was terrifying because I wasn't used to speaking French on the phone, but it went OK. They invited me to Paris for the second interview . . . there were the usual questions: strengths and weaknesses, experience of team work, that kind of thing. At the end of the interview she offered me a job on the spot.'

Hannah (Undergraduate), Economics and Politics with International Studies

Assessment centres

For our final section in this chapter, we'll take a look at assessment centres – what they are, how to prepare and how to find out more. While not all employers use the term 'assessment centre', most will include other activities, in addition to an interview, in the final selection process.

definition

An **assessment centre** is a collection of activities that are designed to test candidates' suitability for a job.

Some of the activities are simulations of workplace tasks or activities, as many employers believe that such tasks give candidates a better chance to show their suitability for the job than a straightforward interview. They do not replace interviews though – typically an assessment centre might include short interviews, and then the most successful candidates are invited for a final, long interview.

Assessment centres can last for one day or more, and may even include cocktail parties and formal dinners.

There are usually several assessors, who may be assigned to individuals or to activities. The assessors will mark performance on each task according to predetermined scoring criteria. After all the tasks are completed and scored they will reach a collective view about candidates' suitability.

What they include

A typical assessment centre may include:

- **Psychometric tests:** as discussed earlier in this chapter.
- **Group discussions:** these could be on a work-related topic such as, 'How can this company increase its market share of 18–25-year-olds?' Or a current affairs topic like, 'To what extent should economic migration to the UK be controlled?' The purpose is to assess candidates' ability to speak and listen, to persuade, to seek agreement, to contribute without dominating. If the topic is job-related, candidates' contributions could be assessed for the extent to which they demonstrate business awareness and understanding of the organisation.

- **Group tasks:** again, this might involve a job-related task, such as, 'Devise a marketing strategy to reach 18–25-year-olds', or an apparently irrelevant task like constructing a bridge from Lego. Candidates are assessed for the extent to which they contribute to the successful completion of the task, and the role they play in the group.

- **Presentations:** these assess the ability to communicate in a clear, structured and persuasive manner. An additional challenge might be to prepare the presentation in a very short time, say 20 minutes.

- **Simulations:** these are tasks that resemble activities which occur in the job. A popular simulation is the 'in-tray exercise' where candidates are asked to indicate how, and in what order, they would tackle a collection of messages and requests they might find on their desk on arrival at work.

- **Job-related tests:** these are activities that assess specific skills and knowledge required in the job and that candidates would have been expected to develop in their previous work or study. For example, preparing a budget based on information supplied, or demonstrating competence in specialist software.

- **Case studies and scenarios:** candidates, either individually or in groups, are presented with a job-related situation and asked to answer specific questions or to make recommendations on how the situation could be addressed.

- **Social events:** these can range from a 'cocktail party' setting to a formal dinner. Candidates are assessed for their ability to identify and interact with key people in the room, to engage in social interaction, and even for their table manners where formal dining might be part of the job role. Assessors are looking particularly for candidates' ability to remain professional in an apparently off-duty setting where there may be generous supplies of alcohol and food.

An employer with a group of applicants may programme the day as a 'carousel', so that, while some candidates are carrying out psychometric tests, others may be tackling a group task.

tip

In an assessment centre, remember that you are under observation at all times, including meals and social time, so stay professional.

How to prepare

You may already be hoping that you will never be invited to an assessment centre – but it need not be daunting, especially if you think about two things:

● the organisation and its position in the sector;

● what you have already done that will prepare you for the assessment centre.

You know what the employer is looking for from the person specification for the job – and by putting yourself in the employer's shoes. Good interpersonal skills, showing initiative without being pushy, the ability to complete a task accurately and under pressure, sensitivity to and awareness of others – these are all fairly obvious requirements of most jobs. However, remember that the employer is looking for evidence, and the assessment centre is an ideal source of first-hand evidence as it provides it in a number of ways.

In terms of what you have already done that will help to prepare you, look back at the list of likely activities we have just mentioned. You have a lot to draw on – presentations in seminars, group projects, organising your work as a deadline approaches – and we have already talked earlier in this chapter about preparation for psychometric tests.

So, to prepare for an assessment centre:

● think about what the employer wants;

● identify what you have already done that might make you feel more familiar with, and therefore less intimidated by, the tasks you are asked to do;

- check with your university careers service to see if they do practice assessment centres;

- use some of the excellent books on the subject – see our 'Further reading' section at the end of this book.

 brilliant recap

- To succeed in selection, make sure you know what the employer is looking for.

- Focus in particular on the person specification for the job.

- Employers use tests, interviews and assessment centres to select staff; make sure that you understand and are prepared for all these methods.

CHAPTER 13

My decision, my context, my life: why all this matters

This might seem like a very heavy title. Put more simply, the purpose of our final chapter is to help you to recognise and take into account the factors about you and your circumstances that may influence your career choices. Some circumstances might be outside your control, for example a shortage of jobs due to the economic climate but, even if you can't change these circumstances, you can adapt to them so that you gain in the longer term.

 example

'When I started at university I never thought for a second that I would be a teacher. It shows that what you learn along the way is so important to your ultimate career destination, and how much the path changes each day.'

Becky, BA (Hons) French and Tourism, now a primary school teacher

Decisions in context

Firstly, it's important to remember that none of us makes decisions in isolation. You might have a dream holiday destination – but the decision about where you actually go is influenced by cost, your availability, the availability of the holiday, your companions' wishes, and so on.

Who would you rather be?

Because you are positive and proactive, in planning your holiday you work with each of the factors we have just mentioned, deciding if you can do anything to give you more choice – do some extra hours at work to increase your budget, be more flexible with dates or destinations. Unless things go very wrong, you should still end up somewhere you want to be and be able to look back on an enjoyable experience.

Your friend, however, takes the passive, negative approach. She goes with the flow even if it's not what she wants, because she can't be bothered to get involved, or she opts out because her choice isn't on offer. She ends up spending the whole time resenting the fact that it isn't her choice, or worse, grumbling at home because she isn't going on holiday. Who would you rather be?

 tip

Don't opt out, opt in. Be positive and proactive in your approach to career decisions.

Factors that affect career decisions

If we extend the example of the holiday decision in the last section to career decisions, we can identify aspects of your personal circumstances and preferences that could be relevant to your choice of career. We can call these personal factors.

In Chapter 2 we talked about supply and demand in the graduate labour market; the demand for the kind of job you have in mind is very much influenced by external factors, which are outside your own control, but which have a key impact on your choices.

Here are some examples of these two kinds of factors, and how they might impact on your career plans.

Personal factors and their impact on career plans

- **Family circumstances:** is anyone relying on your income? Are you a carer for a child, a younger sibling, a sick or elderly relative? Do you have a partner who is committed to a course or job in a particular area? *Impact:* you may need to look for work in a particular location; your available hours for work may be determined by your responsibilities for others; you may feel under pressure to take any job in order to bring money in; or you may have to delay your entry to the labour market.

- **Finances:** apart from servicing your student debt (which applies to most graduates) do you have any significant debts? Do you have savings, or access to financial support?

  Impact: you may feel that you have to take any job to start to pay off debt; alternatively, if you have savings and/or financial support, this could give you freedom to undertake further study or voluntary work.

- **Location:** do you need to stay in or return to a particular area, for example because of family circumstances? Do you have preferences about location and how important are they? Are you willing to move for work? Can you drive?

  Impact: opportunities may be more limited if your location is restricted, and conversely more wide ranging if you are willing to move. Housing/living costs in a new location may be relevant.

- **Family influence:** is there an expectation that you will enter an occupation held by your parents, or that you will join a family business? Will your choice of career be a family decision, or one made by you alone?

  Impact: it could be helpful to enter an occupation that you know intimately, including understanding the benefits and drawbacks for your way of life. A family business might provide a good start, especially if opportunities are otherwise limited. In either case you can work towards a specialist area based on your interests and preferences.

- **Further study and training:** are you willing and able to commit to further study? If full-time, how will you support yourself financially? *Impact:* some jobs require further study so, if this really isn't an option, you may have to re-plan or defer entry.

- **An existing job:** could you work full-time for the employer you have worked for during university? Are you under pressure from the employer to do so? What's in it for you if you do?
  Impact: this route could leave you wondering why you went to university; alternatively, it could give you the prospect of a graduate-level job by another route.

- **A grand plan:** do you have a longer-term aim that is influencing what you do after university?
  Impact: sticking rigidly to a set plan can be dangerous if it just leaves you marking time; it can be good if you use the time constructively.

- **Health:** is there anything about your health that might have implications for your choice of job?
  Impact: there may be some jobs from which you are excluded (e.g. people with epilepsy cannot usually work with machinery), or some that you need to seek out, for example a job where you are mainly sitting down. Be aware that, if you have a disability, you have certain entitlements by law; if you meet the selection criteria for a job you must be offered an interview; and once you are in employment, your employer is expected to make reasonable adjustments to your workplace and equipment to enable you to carry out your work.

Reasons, not excuses

 definitions

A **reason** is an attempt to explain.

An **excuse** is an attempt to avoid.

It might help to assess where you stand in respect of each of these personal factors, both now and in the future, and to consider what is negotiable and what isn't. You might not like working at weekends because it interferes with your social life, but is it a reason? On the other hand, you might coach a junior football team on Sundays and just now there isn't anyone else, it's a tough part of town, and you won't let them down.

Once you have identified honestly what is non-negotiable, be positive, not apologetic, both with employers and with yourself – it's a reason, not an excuse; and review regularly – circumstances change, a new coach comes along, your partner finishes their course so you can relocate – and you can reassess your situation.

 tip

Review your personal circumstances regularly – a change of situation may enable you to broaden your job search.

External factors

There is really just one, big external factor affecting graduate jobs and that is the economic climate. More localised events that impact on jobs, such as the opening or closing of finance houses, production plants and distribution centres, are all the result of changes in the economic landscape.

The good news is that the graduate jobs market has improved significantly in the last two years – more graduates have found work than ever before and almost 70% of those going into work are getting jobs for which a degree, though not necessarily in a specific subject, is a requirement. The most recent information (in *What Do Graduates Do?*, October 2015 and published annually) tells us that graduate unemployment is down by 2.5 percentage points compared with two years previously.

A few years ago, at the start of the recession, graduate unemployment had its biggest increase for some years. Even though the picture is much better now, be aware that there are still some negative headlines about, especially stories about graduates doing jobs for which they don't need a degree. However, these graduates are likely to move into a graduate-level job in due course – they are wisely getting some experience of work and some income in the meantime. Later in this chapter you will meet four successful graduates, in graduate jobs, three of whom had an interim job between graduating and their present role.

So do get accurate data, especially about your own subject area and your own university. Have another look at Chapter 3 for an analysis of what graduates do, and talk to your university careers service for information about recent graduates from your university.

 example

'Within two months of leaving university, in a very tough economic climate, I had secured a great job, providing consultancy to some large firms. I had delivered workshops, presentations and pitches to both sole traders and national companies. I believe my time at university equipped me with the creative problem-solving skills and self-awareness I needed to excel within my industry.'

Alex, BA (Hons) Graphic Design

As the economy recovers there are reports of shortages of graduate entrants in some occupational areas. Recent studies by the Bank of England and by the UK Commission for Employment and Skills refer to unfilled jobs in a number of areas including IT and web design, most branches of engineering and, in some parts of the country, marketing and retail management. However, despite the upturn, patterns of recruitment do still mean that there may be a delay between graduating and moving into a graduate job, so be prepared to be flexible:

- it may take longer to get to where you want to be;
- you might go by an unexpected route.

If you do find yourself in the very unfortunate position of not having a job, not having anything to do and there's nothing in the pipeline, you must do something to get yourself out of that rut. Any job is better than no job. If it's not a job, if it's voluntary work or a training course . . . there's a whole range of things you could be doing.

Carl Gilleard, Chief Executive, Association of Graduate Recruiters

Being a supermarket assistant is not my dream job; however, neither is it beneath me.

Kim, BA (Hons) Christian Youth Work

If at first you don't succeed

Mind your language

If you have identified factors in your own context that will influence your career planning, then you need to work with these factors, rather than regarding them as barriers to a graduate job. Even small statements can signal this kind of positive approach. Compare these two:

> I can't drive so I'm limited to jobs in this town.

or

> I'm looking for work that is accessible by public transport and I'm willing to travel for up to 90 minutes each way.

The first contains two negatives – 'can't' and 'limited'; the second, two active positives – 'looking' and 'willing'.

Now these two:

> I can't work in school holidays because of my children, so I probably won't be able to get a job until they are old enough to leave.

or

> I'm exploring all the organisations that might offer term-time-only work – not just schools, but colleges, the local university, and the local authority Children's Services Department. My friend works in Governor Services and has a really interesting job supporting school governing bodies – and it's term-time only.'

Again we can see 'can't' and 'won't', compared with 'exploring'.

There is very clear evidence from psychological research, which shows us that a change in attitude can lead to a change in behaviour. So look again at the second example in each pair. The positive statements are a clear indication of jobsearch behaviour. So, if you can adopt a more positive attitude, this will have an impact on your behaviour.

Can you turn the following statements round to demonstrate a more positive approach?

- 'I want to keep on living here after university because all my housemates are staying, but I don't know if there are any jobs.'
- 'I might as well stay on at the supermarket after I graduate – they've offered me a job and the papers say there aren't any graduate jobs.'
- 'I need to clear my debts so I have to stay on in the bar where I've been working.'
- 'There's no point in doing any voluntary work because I'd only have to give it up if I get a job.'
- 'No one from this university ever gets into a blue chip company so there's no point in applying.'
- 'If only I had a 2:1 instead of a 2:2, it would make all the difference.'
- 'Yes, but what about all the other people who'll apply for that job?'

So, reflect on the language you use – not just in applications and careers interviews, but in informal conversations with your family and friends and, if you hear lots of negatives, try to turn your language around to signal a positive, constructive approach.

 You've got to remain positive. I'll give you one guarantee: if you give up, you'll never get a job. And it's easier to get a job when you're in employment than when you're unemployed. Any job is better than no job. That's the starting point.

Carl Gilleard, Chief Executive, Association of Graduate Recruiters

Enhance your skills and learning

Increasing the range of opportunities open to you calls for creative approaches. The best counterbalance to an unfulfilling job is to get involved in learning something new. Not only will you maintain the momentum of study you built up during your degree, but you will send a good signal about yourself to prospective employers – and you will ward off boredom. Here are some of the ways you can continue to study:

- Do a short course at your local further education or community college – IT, a language, or a project management course could all be useful in a future job. Get a prospectus online or enquire at your local library.

- Look at postgraduate study. If you can't afford to do a full-time course, you can study part-time or through distance or blended learning – we looked at these in detail in Chapter 7. Many universities offer single modules if you don't want to commit to a complete course.

- Maximise your chances of learning from your job. Look at training offered in the workplace – first aid, supervisory skills – or create your own learning – ask if you can assist with a special project or promotion. Look at this brilliant example.

brilliant example

'One night the barman seemed to be on holiday, so they put me behind the bar on a busy night. I had done the dispensing bar, which was pretty straightforward, so when it was quiet I asked the bar supervisor to show me the cocktails. But it was like – what the hell am I doing? How can they expect me to do this when I've never done it in my life? I looked like a complete muppet . . . but I'll give anything a go once, and they figured out I could do it and I wasn't that bad, so they put me on the bar a lot more. And it's good because I can show that I've got more all-round experience and I'm happy to learn, and I'm flexible, so I will be able to negotiate a higher rate of pay when I go back next time.'

Hannah (Undergraduate), Economics and Politics with International Studies

- Look out for special programmes for graduate jobseekers offered by your university – we gave you an example in Chapter 9.

- Create a portfolio of experience. For example, a psychology graduate interested in working in an advisory role with young people could take a counselling skills course in the evenings, do some voluntary work in an advice centre and support himself with a part-time job in retail or hospitality, both of which are excellent settings for developing skills with people. This three-part package will be far more use in developing his employment prospects than the job on its own.

Be flexible

It's becoming more common, even for recent graduates, to slot together fulfilling part-time jobs in order to make progress and earn a living. In our next brilliant example, Kim's chosen career of youth work can often be pursued only in part-time or sessional roles. So she paired her youth work post first with a supermarket job, then with a part-time position as a student welfare officer.

brilliant example

'Due to the nature of my career, I often have at least two part-time jobs on the go to "make ends meet". Alongside, I attend job-related training as often as possible and keep up to date with the changes in the sector. I have learned a number of things through this process. To get where I am today, I had to persevere through applying for countless jobs and being rejected for all but one of them. Doing unrelated work allowed me to support myself financially while I searched for more suitable work. Working two high-pressure jobs, being contracted 50 hours a week and often working overtime is not easy. But I love what I do and the long days are worth it. Deciding to pursue a career in an area that I love was the key to my professional success.'

Kim, BA (Hons), Christian Youth Work

Don't be afraid to change your plan

We have talked about the benefit of having a plan, from a longer-term career plan to a short-term weekly jobsearch plan. And we still think this is important. But sometimes the right decision is to change your plan. One reason might be that your initial idea just isn't working out – you've given it a decent and realistic length of time but the signs aren't good and you need to rethink. This might happen if you are in a highly competitive area, such as Forensic Science or Bar Professional Training, where there are far more graduates than jobs. There may be a point when you decide to widen your search or even rethink completely.

Perhaps an even more compelling reason to change your plan is when you realise that your chosen route just isn't right for you. This is hard to face – you have invested time and probably money and it's tempting to feel some pressure to keep going. But have a look at our brilliant example, Steph, who not only changed her plan but believes that she has gained from the roundabout route she took.

brilliant example

'For my first degree I studied English Language. I had a couple of wobbles and nearly dropped out twice but kept going and did well. I had been thinking of teaching but because of the wobbles felt I wasn't good enough to teach . . . after doing some research I applied for the Graduate Diploma in Law (GDL) and the PGCE – I got three offers for the GDL and none for the PGCE, so that convinced me I had made the right choice.

I had it in my head that practising law would allow me to talk to people and help them like I'd always wanted to do; but it became more and more apparent that getting a job in law was harder than drawing blood from a stone, unless you were all singing and all dancing. I started to feel like I was trying to be something I wasn't towards the end of the course; I'm very driven, but the course had driven all the drive out of me. I knew in my heart that it was absolutely not for me.

I undertook some work experience at a local secondary school and absolutely knew that teaching was, after all, what I wanted to do, so I reapplied for my PGCE and was accepted. Half-way through the year I had my first job interview at a really good school – and got it! I don't think I'd be who I am or have had the confidence to apply for it again without having done the GDL, and plus it's always another string to the bow!

My advice to anyone in my position would be to do what they think is right. I know education doesn't come cheap, but I truly believe that you need to fall flat on your face before things start working out for you. Try everything and grab every opportunity that comes your way. Life has a funny way of working things out for you: you just have to work your hardest at it and even when it gets tough, you've got to keep going.'

Steph, BA (Hons) English Language

Be in charge of yourself

In Chapter 1 we introduced you to the job fairy. It will sometimes seem as if other people get the benefit of this friendly little person, while you miss out; and it's certainly the case that some jobs come out of happy accidents and chance meetings. However, it's also the case that the people this happens to have their ears and eyes open, and respond positively to the opportunity presenting itself. So it's not entirely accidental after all. By all means get help from others – but recognise that you have the control, and no one else. You might have other people to think about, and other people's expertise to draw on, but you are still the person in charge of your future.

 tip

When it comes to your career plan, you are responsible for yourself and nobody else; and nobody else is responsible for you.

Your first graduate job

 You move from school and home to experience the freedom and independence of university; then suddenly you are thrust back into an environment where you must abide by much stricter codes of conduct and adhere to an unwritten rulebook of new behavioural expectations that are often difficult to interpret.

Rose, BSc (Hons) Biology

Focusing on your final year and on getting a job can mean that you start work as a graduate without thinking too much about what it will feel like to be a graduate employee, and how your life will change. For example, in many graduate jobs there is no flexibility to your working day – good timekeeping is critical and lunch breaks and time off are fixed. This might seem like a small detail, but it's a big contrast to your student life and one that many new graduates struggle with and find unexpectedly tiring. And you will almost certainly be working at a different level of responsibility from the jobs you have done as a student, as in this brilliant example.

brilliant example

'Working for an engineering consultancy means you're taking responsibility for expensive, high-profile designs and you're working alongside high-achieving professionals who have spent their careers reaching where they are. It's the complete opposite end of the spectrum from working with other students on a bar at a festival, where your manager is a similar age and on a temporary contract.'

Ed, MEng (Hons) Civil Engineering

There are additional pressures if you have had to relocate for your graduate job, and even making sure that you have suitable, clean work clothes each day adds another new demand. So, imagining yourself in your new job and anticipating some of the challenges might help you to make this crucial transition more smoothly. To help you to do this we have spoken to some recent graduates about their experiences and asked them for their best advice.

The good news is that it really does feel different, and better, to be a graduate employee.

---

brilliant example

'Being a graduate employee (a formulation scientist in a large multinational company), compared with being a student, I felt more grown up and it felt like I had finally joined the real world. I could now start building a career and earning my own money, which I could use or save for whatever I wanted. Compared to the stopgap job I had after graduating – which was useful for earning money and gaining work experience – I felt happier as I was now doing a job relevant to the career I wanted to build.

Sally, MChem

For many employers, too, graduate trainees are good news, and ambition is rewarded with support for professional development. In our next brilliant example, Rob talks about the high expectations his employer (a large insurance company) has of graduate trainees.

---

brilliant example

'I am currently a team leader (of nine people in customer service). The expectations, especially with an ambitious graduate scheme like mine, are that you will take responsibility and that you will work and drive your career – which, while it opens up huge opportunities, is also very testing . . . my employer will give me every tool to succeed and I am currently studying for my qualification in insurance, paid for by my employer.'

Rob, MSc International Business and Management

When you are applying for jobs and going through the selection process you will hear a lot about the induction programmes employers require new entrants to follow. These can be quite informal, especially in SMEs, or highly structured and lasting several weeks. But what about the unwritten rules? All organisations have these, from coffee routines to protocols for communicating internally and externally, and they can be hard to grasp. Judging how much to use your initiative is a tricky one, especially in the first few weeks, which might feel a bit slow while you are learning the background to your work – yet you are working alongside very busy people, and you may be unsure about speaking up. Our graduates are very clear about the best approach – get to know people and how they work and don't be afraid to ask for help.

The sooner you build confidence to offer help, be proactive and offer solutions and ideas, the better.

Rose, BSc Biology

Everyone works in different ways and is motivated by different things . . . you have to key into this and it's important not to rub people up the wrong way.

Rob, MSc International Business and Management

One thing I have learnt is that you can never ask too many questions, for example don't just do something because you have been asked to do it, ask why and how and try to understand the background . . . always try and do as much as you can; this shows you are willing to learn new things and improve.

Sally, MChem

Don't be afraid to pick up the phone. Our generation is used to instant messaging – but people place a lot of value on speaking to humans and it gets problems solved much faster, especially where there is urgency or scope for confusion.

Ed, MEng Civil Engineering

We mentioned earlier in this chapter that three of our four graduates had intermediate jobs, ranging from restaurant work to unpaid internship, so, if you don't have a job straight after graduating, keep applying and build up your work experience and your skills. Here's our graduates' advice to final-year students:

brilliant tips

- Start early in your job search.

- Look for companies you admire, in the field you are interested in.

- Go for something that will give you training and progression opportunities.

- Make the most of any training and courses you are offered, whether you have a temporary or permanent position in the company.

- Go out of your comfort zone – otherwise you will limit what you learn and the experience you gain.

- Working with people at the top of their game means you have to elevate yours and you can learn a lot, fast, to broaden your skillset for the future.

Moving on

Your second graduate job

This might seem an odd topic to introduce when you are probably still looking for your first one, but by the time this happens to you – two, three or four years down the line – you may feel cut adrift from the sources of help you have been able to use at university, so here are some thoughts for you to keep in the back of your mind till you need them.

✖ brilliant dos and don'ts

Do

✔ use the skills of reflection we discussed in Chapter 8 to assess how your first job is going;

✔ record your key achievements along the way – they will be invaluable in updating your CV and in completing future applications;

✔ seek out professional help – some university careers services will help graduates with subsequent job moves for a fixed period of time after graduation. Others offer a fee-charging service to graduates from any university.

Don't

✖ move without giving your first job a chance. Discuss with your manager what you need to develop your experience and interest, and how your job will develop in the future, before you decide to move on.

In this example, Victoria, whom you met in Chapter 5, describes moving from her second to her third graduate job, so she is at a point of leverage rather than a point of entry.

brilliant example

'(In my second consultancy) I worked hard to get integrated and continue to pursue retail projects. However, I didn't feel there was much retail opportunity available so, after a year, I decided to leave and then find a new job. It's really hard to find a new job when you are working long days at your existing one!

I put my CV on Internet job boards and used my network of contacts from the two previous companies to find introductions at retail companies and also recruitment agencies.

I began by considering any job opportunity both consulting and "industry" (i.e. for actual retailers) but, as my search progressed, I realised I actually only wanted to work in "industry". I ended up with three offers on the table.'

Victoria, MA Geography

Notice that she was in a much stronger position than when she had first graduated, because she had her own network of contacts. Note too that the actual process of jobsearch helped her to identify her preferred focus.

In our next example, Estee left university seeking a job which made direct use of her psychology degree, but was unsuccessful. However, she made the connections in the job that she did get, so that the next time around she was a much stronger candidate and succeeded in her goal.

brilliant example

'I worked as a university employability assistant for approximately 18 months. In this time I believe I learnt more than when I was a student! I had the opportunity to work on a wide variety of projects, make decisions, and go on courses to improve my skills. I particularly enjoyed giving personalised feedback to students on application forms.

I still had my goal set on a career related to psychology at this point and decided to apply for a trainee psychological wellbeing practitioner role with a local mental health charity. I applied for one of these roles when I first graduated but found that the competition is fierce and candidates straight from university were rarely employed. Therefore alongside my job I volunteered for a mental health charity to be a computerised cognitive behavioural therapy support worker. This voluntary experience coupled with my expertise from my employment allowed me to have the skills needed to carry out the role. I believe my understanding of the role and the ability to reflect on my experience went in my favour at the interview. I really wanted the role so I researched a lot about the project beforehand. In doing this I was also able to ask some questions at the end of the interview that surprised the panel. I started my new role three months ago now and once again I am on a steep learning curve.'

Estee, BSC (Hons) Psychology

Your life and why all this matters

As a current graduate, you will be affected by two of the biggest changes to working life in recent years.

Firstly, you will be working for longer than your parents did (but you will benefit from flexible working patterns, including homeworking).

Secondly, you will probably have several jobs and many careers during this time. It helps that relationships between health and well-being and job satisfaction are well established, and there is much more recognition of the need for a good balance between working life and life outside work. Some organisations even make provision for staff to have 'career breaks' of a few months' unpaid leave, to go on that trip of a lifetime.

So it's worth investing some time and effort on your career plan, not just now, but at key decision points as they come up. For example, it's never too late to start postgraduate study, and it's often even more rewarding and interesting when you have some experience behind you.

It's impossible to predict now what your working life will look like over the next 40 or so years. It will help if you are open to changes of direction and new opportunities and it's important to recognise that your own interests, skills and values will change over time and that good career progression need not necessarily be upwards.

 Most of those who are graduating now will have two or three careers – not jobs, careers. Be confident enough to step off the career ladder in order to be the best at what you do.

Carl Gilleard, Chief Executive, Association of Graduate Recruiters

We wish you the very best of luck for your future and we hope that our book is there for you along the way – and remember, you are the one in control of your brilliant graduate career.

Online resources

www.bbc.co.uk/labuk/experiments/employability

Offers lots of support for your jobsearch, contains a range of online psychometrics including Transferable Employability Skills Scale (TESS), which measures your transferable skills.

www.centreforentrepreneurs.org

For research, news and updating.

www.contractoruk.com

For information about being a self-employed contractor.

www.eu-student.eu

Comprehensive guide to the Erasmus programme for study and internships within the EU (internships minimum one month).

www.fco.gov.uk/en/travel-and-living-abroad

For worldwide advice on travelling, working and living abroad.

www.graduate-jobs.com

Web-based job listing for graduates.

www.graduatetalentpool.direct.gov.uk

Information about, and details of, internships.

www.gttr.ac.uk

The Graduate Teacher Training Registry: official website where you can research postgraduate programmes and apply online.

www.hesa.ac.uk

Higher Education Statistics Agency: range of publications including *Destinations of Leavers from Higher Education (DLHE)*.

www.jobs.nhs.uk

Comprehensive guide to all NHS vacancies. This includes healthcare professions, but also a range of technical and management jobs.

jobsearch.direct.gov.uk

Official government site: job vacancies searchable by region, industry or company.

www.mastersportal.eu

Lists postgraduate programmes across the EU, covers master's and doctoral level; useful search engine.

www.milkround.com

A member of the News International Group, this website lists graduate jobs and internships.

www.monster.co.uk

Online job vacancy site, searchable by occupational or geographical area, or by skills.

www.ncee.org.uk

National Council for Entrepreneurship Education: information about how universities can support students and graduates who are interested in self-employment as an option.

www.prospects.ac.uk

Comprehensive online information, advice and guidance for students in higher education.

www.roberthalf.co.uk

UK-wide vacancies in the financial services sector. This includes accounting, finance and related management, extending to specialist technical services.

www.shell-livewire.org

For online support and access to funding for 16–30-year-olds.

www.startuploans.co.uk

Information about the current government scheme to lend up to £2,500 to start-up businesses.

www.startups.co.uk

General information about business start-ups.

www.statistics.gov.uk

The gateway to UK national statistics, including reports on the labour market in general.

www.thegraduate.co.uk

Web-based job listing for graduates; includes placement, undergraduate and postgraduate-level opportunities, along with useful salary comparison feature.

www.ukces.org.uk

UK Commission for Employment and Skills: up-to-date articles on skills demand and sector changes.

Further reading

Association of Graduate Recruiters (AGR) (2015). *AGR Annual Survey: Gender diversity a challenge in a growing graduate market.* Available at: **http://www.agr.org.uk/News/agr-annual-survey-gender-diversity-a-challenge-in-a-growing-graduate-market/117484\#.VqdCJDZGjlI**

BIS (2012) *Business Population Estimates for the UK and Regions.* Sheffield: Department for Business, Innovation and Skills (BIS).

Blundel, R. and Lockett, N. (2011) *Exploring Entrepreneurship.* Oxford: OUP.

Bright, J. and Earl, J. (2014) *Brilliant Graduate CV.* Harlow: Pearson.

Byron, M. (2011) *The Graduate Psychometric Test Workbook.* London: Kogan Page.

CBI (2011) *Building for growth: business priorities for education and skills.* London Confederation of British Industry.

CBI/NUS (2011) *Working towards your future: making the most of your time in HE.* London Confederation of British Industry.

CBI/Pearson Education and Skills Survey 2014. [pdf] Available at: **http://www.cbi.org.uk/media/2809181/embargo_00.01_4_july_cbi_pearson_education_and_skills_survey_2014.pdf**

CIHE (2011) *Global graduates into global leaders.* Council for Industry and Higher Education.

Cole, D. and Tibby, M. (2013) *Defining and developing your approach to employability: A framework for higher education institutions.* Higher Education Academy. Available at: **https://www.heacademy.ac.uk/resource/defining-and-developing-your-approach-employability-framework-higher-education-institutions**

Hind, D. and Moss, S. (2011) *Employability Skills.* Sunderland: Business Education Publishers.

Hodgson, S. (2010) *Brilliant Answers to Tough Interview Questions.* 2nd edn. Harlow: Prentice Hall.

Hodgson, S. (2008) *Brilliant Tactics to Pass Aptitude Tests.* 2nd edn. Harlow: Prentice Hall.

Knight, P.T. and Yorke, M. (2004) *Learning, Curriculum and Employability in Higher Education.* London: Routledge Falmer.

Mulvey, R. (2015) *Brilliant Passing Psychometric Tests.* Harlow: Pearson Education.

Parkinson, M. (2010) *How to Master Psychometric Tests.* London: Kogan Page.

Taylor, D. (2010) *Now You've Been Shortlisted.* Petersfield: Harriman.

Universities UK (2007). *Research report: the economic benefit of a degree.* London: Universities UK.

Welsted, S. and Whiteling, I. (2011) *Start Your Own Business 2012*: Richmond: Crimson Publishing.

Index